PRINCE FELIX ZU
SCHWARZENBERG

PRINCE FELIX ZU

SCHWARZENBERG

Prime Minister of Austria

1848 - 1852

by Adolph Schwarzenberg

NEW YORK · COLUMBIA UNIVERSITY PRESS

COPYRIGHT 1946
COLUMBIA UNIVERSITY PRESS, NEW YORK

First printing 1946
Second printing 1947

Published in Great Britain and India by Geoffrey Cumberlege,
Oxford University Press, London and Bombay

MANUFACTURED IN THE UNITED STATES OF AMERICA

TO

Mrs. Nicholas Murray Butler

PREFACE

I T IS with a sense of deep responsibility that I have attempted the task of making Felix Prince zu Schwarzenberg better known to the English-speaking world. It is obviously not easy to write about one's own great-grand-uncle without offering more than one grain of propitiatory incense to his shade. But a monumental commemoration of a great statesman is not the aim of this study. Since in a portrait only the scenes and objects against which the human figure is thrown give the likeness meaning and substance, the important and relevant facts of the era under survey are recorded and interpreted. The drama of an Austrian sociopolitical transformation, with its concurrent by-play of international problems confronting the Empire, will be presented with that impartiality which human nature, challenged by a ready and understandable sympathy, permits. Constitutional questions within the narrow frame of this work will receive special attention. My approach to them is the American method as taught in departments of government, not the European purely juristic way followed by law schools of the European continent. At the same time, the specific content of this work remains Felix Schwarzenberg's human and political personality.

It is a curious fact that Austria's history in general, and notably the era chiefly discussed in the text—1848–1852—has not been too frequently the object of scholarly investigation. Among the relatively few good German works on the subject must be mentioned in the first place Heinrich Friedjung's *Österreich von 1848 bis 1860*, because it is the work dealing most comprehensively with the events and the procession of striking personalities of those times. Friedjung, the Pan-German, championed a unified Germany which should comprise all the hereditary lands of the Austrian Monarchy. Naturally, from his standpoint he disapproved of Felix Schwarzenberg's German policy. Joseph Redlich, a liberal, in *Das österreichische Staats-und Reichsproblem* and in his other works, centers his criticism on Felix Schwarzenberg's internal policy. Ritter von Srbik finds fault with Schwarzenberg because he did not recognize the importance of emerging nationalities. The National Socialist Victor Bibl, a journalist rather than a historian, in his *Der Zerfall Österreichs* censures almost everything undertaken by the chief character of this book. Later researches by Colonel Heller, embodied in his monograph *Fürst Felix Schwarzenberg*, have persuasively rectified some of Friedjung's statements and have been duly taken into consideration. The other monograph, that of Adolph Franz Berger, written by a family historiographer, and sketches of Felix Schwarzenberg's life found in biographical editions are so indiscriminately laudatory that these memorial writings call for careful scrutiny.

Unfortunately Prince Schwarzenberg has left no memoirs. His sister, Princess Mathilde, who kept house for the bachelor Prime Minister, ordered most of his letters burned after his death. The Schwarzenberg archives at Krumlov, Bohemia, seized from me by the German government, hold only a few pieces referring to Felix Schwarzenberg; they are letters written before 1848 and are, therefore, unconnected with the main story of this work. State archives could not be consulted, since this book was written during the war. The archives of Vienna have been exhaustively examined by Professor Friedjung and Colonel Heller, and it may be fairly assumed that they will not yield substantial material shedding further light on the era of Felix Schwarzenberg's activities. Other state archives have been pillaged and destroyed, for instance, those of Naples, according to Professor Benedetto Croce's letter to me under date of February 27, 1945. I had to rely on the libraries in the United States, and their excellence has enabled me to gather the factual bases of this book. For these reasons this study is one of interpretation, not of sensational disclosures. It attempts to present material not found gathered in any one book or not available in English.

I wish to express my deep gratitude to Professor Lindsay Rogers, of Columbia University, under whose guidance and supervision this work was undertaken and completed. Professors Charles W. Cole and John H. Wuorinen, and Dr. Antonín Basch have read the manuscript and have offered many valuable criticisms which I have incorporated in the work. Drs. Paul H. Beik and W. R. Dittmar, also of Columbia University, have been of considerable assistance in preparing the manuscript for publication. To the latter I am also indebted for his guidance to the location of pertinent literature in various American libraries and other places. Last, but not least, I mention with great pleasure the charming lady who repeatedly encouraged me to undertake this study and to whom I have been permitted to dedicate the following pages.

ADOLPH SCHWARZENBERG, JUDr., PH.D.

New York
August, 1945

CONTENTS

ILLUSTRATIONS

CHRONOLOGY

1848

Nov. 21   Appointed Austrian Prime Minister; Austrian Diet meets at Kremsier.

Dec. 2   The Emperor Ferdinand I abdicates in favor of his nephew Francis Joseph.

Dec. 10   Prince Louis Napoleon elected president of the French Republic.

1849

Feb. 26   Victory of Austrians over Hungarians at Kapolna.

Mar. 4   New Constitution proclaimed in Austria.

Mar. 23   Battle of Novara; abdication of Charles Albert, King of Sardina, in favor of his son Victor Emanuel.

Mar. 28   The German National Assembly elects the King of Prussia "Hereditary Emperor of Germany."

Apr. 5   King Frederick William IV declines the Imperial Crown.

1849

Apr. 12   The German National Assembly recognizes the provisional government of the Duchies of Schleswig-Holstein.

Apr. 14   Kossuth, in the rump of the Hungarian Diet, declares the forfeiture of the Habsburg succession to the throne; Windisch-Graetz relieved of his command.

May 1   Francis Joseph asks the Czar for aid against the Hungarians.

May 26   Formation of the League of the Three Kingdoms.

July 28   Anton Ritter von Schmerling appointed Minister of Justice; Count Leo Thun, the First Austrian Minister for Education and Ecclesiastical Affairs.

Aug. 13   Hungarian Capitulation at Világos.

Aug. 15   Alexander Bach appointed Minister of the Interior.

Sept. 30   Compact of the "Interim": a Treaty between Prussia and Austria for the formation of a new central authority in Germany for a limited time.

Oct. 10   Schwarzenberg made Honorary Chief of the Infantry
             Regiment No. 21.

1850
Feb. 23   Appointment of Hassenpflug as Minister in Hesse-
             Cassel.
Feb. 27   Federation of the Four Kingdoms.
Mar. &
  Apr.   Union Parliament meets at Erfurt.
May 8   Meeting of Princes in Berlin.
May 10   Confederate Congress, summoned by Austria, meets
             at Frankfurt.
July 2   Separate Peace between Denmark and Prussia.

1850
Aug. 2   Protocol signed in London by the Great Powers, pro-
             claiming the integrity of Denmark.
Sept. 2   Restoration of the Confederate Diet at Frankfort;
             Prussia and her associate States refuse to join it.
Oct. 12   The Bregenz League formed against Prussia by Austria,
             Bavaria, and Württemberg.
Oct. 26-29   Conferences between Schwarzenberg and Branden-
             burg, Prussian Prime Minister, at Warsaw.
Nov. 8   Skirmish at Bronzell.
Nov. 9   Schwarzenberg demands the abolition of the Prussian
             Union.
Nov. 29   Convention at Olmütz.
Dec. 23   Conferences at Dresden on German affairs, continuing
             to May 15, 1851.
Dec. 24   Schwarzenberg visits the Prussian King.

1851
Jan. 24   Schmerling resigns as Minister of Justice; Karl von
             Krauss appointed in his place.
May 23-25   Bruck resigns as Minister of Commerce; Andreas
             Baumgartner appointed in his place.

May 30	The re-established Confederate Diet assembles with its former membership.
May 31	Meeting of the Emperor of Austria, the King of Prussia, and the Czar at Warsaw.
Sept. 7	Commercial Treaty signed between Prussia and Hanover.
Dec. 26	Finance Minister Philip Krauss resigns; Minister of Commerce Baumgartner takes over his portfolio.
Dec. 31	Revocation of the Constitution of March 4, 1849, by the Emperor Francis Joseph.

1852

Apr. 5	Death of Prince Felix Schwarzenberg.

PRINCE FELIX ZU
SCHWARZENBERG

❧ I ❧

FAMILY AND
EARLY YEARS

PRINCE FELIX LUDWIG JOHANN VON NEPOMUK FRIEDRICH ZU SCHWARZENBERG was born in Krumlov nad Vltavou (Krumlov or Krummau on the Moldau), in the Bohemian Forest, southern Bohemia, on October 2, 1800. He was the second son of Prince Joseph, head of the older Schwarzenberg line, and his wife Pauline, née Duchess of Arenberg. Thus, he bore an illustrious family name. As in the case of all prominent noble families of Central Europe, the history of the Schwarzenbergs is closely connected with the history of the Holy Roman Empire of the German Nation and of the Austrian Monarchy.

The original name of the family [1] was Seinsheim, also spelled Sovvensheim, Sounsheim, Sauensheim, and in other similar ways. One branch later adopted the name Schwarzenberg, another Seinsheim. The castle and the estate of Schwarzenberg were successively in the hands of the family for about six hundred years, until it was confiscated from the present owner, the author of these lines, by the German government in 1940.

[1] On the history of the house of Schwarzenberg see *Allgemeine Deutsche Biographie,* Vol. XXXIII; Berger, "Das Fürstenhaus Schwarzenberg," *Österreichische Revue,* Heft 11 (1866), pp. 1–215; Haimb, *Schwartzenberga gloriosa sive epitome historica;* Hübner, *Genealogische Tabellen,* Vol. III, Tables 936 *et sqq.;* Mareš, "Nové příspěvky k pam. roku 1848," in *Český Časopis Historický* (the gazette published by the Bohemian Museum); Mörath, *Das Schloss Schwarzenberg in Franken;* "Die Schwarzenberge," *Neue Freie Presse,* No. 2742 (April 13, 1872); Schmidt, *Das Kaiserthum Österreich,* Parts IX–X, especially pp. 177–79; Ritter von Schönfeld, *Adels-Schematismus des österreichischen Kaiserstaates,* 1824, pp. 34–38, 1825, pp. 167–71; "Das Fürstenhaus Schwarzenberg," *Transylvania* (Beiblatt zum *Siebenbürger Boten*), No. 3, 1856, p. 12; von Wurzbach, *Biographisches Lexicon des Kaiserthums Österreich,* Part 33.

The Seinsheims belonged to one of the oldest clans in Franconia, comprising the western, southern, and northern parts of Bavaria.[2] Many historians claim the ability to trace the family back to the times of Charlemagne; others, more reserved, start the genealogy at a later date. It is sufficient to quote the familiar saying about the quaintness of some families in this region: "The Einheims are the haughtiest, the Grumbachs the mightiest, the Seckendorfs the most prolific, and the Seinsheims the oldest." A hoary saga has it that one Seinsheim, Erkinger, assisted by his brother Berthold, aimed at acquiring the title of duke in the early tenth century. They engaged in feuds not only with the Bishop of Constance but even with King Conrad I, with dismal results—they were executed. According to another legend Erkinger's widow contrived to find refuge in the Steigerwald, where her son subsequently built a castle, calling it *Sein Newes Heim*, from which term the name Seinsheim was constructed.[3] Erkinger von Seinsheim, from whom Felix descended, became the first Freiherr zu Schwarzenberg, in the fifteenth century. From then on, the Seinsheims formed a separate branch, which died out recently.

The members of the Schwarzenberg family distinguished themselves in different fields, serving their emperors or local princes as administrators or soldiers. Others were in the clergy or managed their properties, which in the course of centuries attained a very considerable size and value; some members gained fame as writers and others as scholars. Among the latter may be mentioned a Johann and a Friedrich Schwarzenberg. A few words about Friedrich, a cousin of the principal character of this book, will be said later. Johann, also known under the name John the Strong, lived at the beginning of the sixteenth century. His chief works were *Consolation in Grief* (*Kummertrost*) and the well-known *Bambergensis*, a penal code and a code of criminal procedure.[4] A good many members of the family met death on the field of honor, offering their lives as a su-

---

[2] A good description of this part of Bavaria is given by Götz in *Frankenland*.

[3] For details of the early history of the Schwarzenberg family see Berger, "Das Fürstenhaus Schwarzenberg," *Österreichische Revue*, Heft 11 (1866), pp. 1–215.

[4] See Malbank, *Geschichte der peinlichen Halsgerichtsordnung Kaiser Karl V. von ihrer Entstehung und ihren weiteren Schicksalen bis auf unsere Zeit;* also Balfanz, *Beiträge*

preme sacrifice to emperor and fatherland. At the close of the six-teenth century one Adolph distinguished himself under Emperor Rudolph II in the battle of Raab (Györ) against the invading Turks, where the enemy was completely defeated. The promotion from baron to count and the embellishment of the escutcheon by a Turk's head, whose eyes are picked by a raven, were the rewards for valiant deeds.

Count Adam (1584–1641) engaged in the services of the Elector of Brandenburg Georg Wilhelm during the Thirty Years' War. A Roman Catholic in a Protestant country, he had a difficult position, but was able to establish excellent relations between the Emperor and Brandenburg. Honors upon honors were heaped on him. The family gained in wealth and prestige. At the close of the seventeenth century the title was raised from count to prince. Sovereignty was exercised until 1806 over some parts in Franconia (Bavaria) and the landgraviate of Kleggau (Baden).

Count Adam's son, Johann Adolph, acquired the property called Mšec (Kornhaus in German), not far from the Žatec (Saaz) re-gion in Bohemia, where the world's best hops cover the red, fertile soil. Mšec was the first Bohemian property owned by the family, and it laid the foundation for what was later called the "Schwarzenberg Kingdom" in Bohemia. The Schwarzenberg estates were among the largest landed properties in Central Europe until they were struck by three momentous events: the Czechoslovakian land reform cut down their size; in 1940, the German Secret Police seized them with-out advancing a reason; and the Czechoslovak Republic today, con-sidering large estates to be incongruous, has refused to restore these lands to their owner. Even now the titles to large landed properties seem not to be guaranteed as safe, and the Schwarzenberg properties are being confiscated according to a special law. Every square inch of the Schwarzenberg properties was inherited, purchased, exchanged or otherwise legally acquired; no parcel was derived from formerly confiscated property. Felix Schwarzenberg's father must have

zur staatsmännischen Wirksamkeit des Freiherrn Johann von Schwarzenberg; Herrmann, *Johann Freiherr zu Schwarzenberg;* Johann, Freiherr von Schwarzenberg, *Trostspruch um abgestorbene Freunde (Kummertrost)*, ed. by Willy Scheel.

owned about 495,000 acres, the major portion lying in Bohemia, the minor in Styria, in addition to the ancestral castle of Schwarzenberg in Franconia, near Scheinfeld, Bavaria. Most of the family's property consisted of forests, but farmland was also abundant. Coal and graphite mines, breweries and other industrial establishments supplied numerous undertakings and a large income. Many castles were scattered over the various demesnes; magnificent palaces in various cities, harboring exquisite treasures of art, pictures, china, tapestries, and rugs, were part of the holdings. Castle Krumlov, where Felix was born, is one of the most beautiful and interesting manors in Bohemia. The castle is situated on dominating rocks and overlooks the lovely River Vltava (Moldau) amidst marvelous forests, the family's understandable pride for generations; buildings were added to the main structure by successive generations, so that the designs range from Gothic to baroque. It houses the family archives; archives of a general nature are at Třeboň (Wittingau in German). Here Palacký did part of his research while writing his history of Bohemia.

Perhaps the most outstanding member of the Schwarzenberg family, and the best known in history, is Felix's uncle, Field Marshal Charles Philip,[5] who was ambassador to the great Napoleon in Paris and then defeated him at Leipzig in 1813. He was the founder of a younger branch, which also owns large estates in southern Bohemia. In addition to the two lines, there exists a third one, Barons Schwarzenberg and Hohenlandsberg in Frisia, Holland. It is curious that in the seventeenth century the city of Zurich conferred citizenship on the members of the Schwarzenberg family. Felix was there-

[5] A selected bibliography on the Field Marshal is Anders, *Schwarzenbergs Disposition für den 14. Oktober 1813*; Berger, "Zum Ehrengedächtnisse des k.k. Feldmarschalls Karl Fürsten zu Schwarzenberg," *Wiener Zeitung* (the official gazette), No. 250 (1867), p. 246; "Fürst Karl Schwarzenberg," *Illustrierte Zeitung*, No. 1040 (1863); Kerchnawe und Veltzé, *Fürst Karl zu Schwarzenberg, der Führer der Verbündeten in den Befreiungskriegen; Memoir of the Operations of the Allied Armies under Prince Schwarzenberg and Marchal* [sic] *Blücher during the Latter End of 1813 and the Year 1814*, by the author of "The Duke of Wellington in Portugal and Spain"; *Militär Schematismus*, pp. 761, 829; Prokesch von Osten, *Denkwürdigkeiten aus dem Leben des Feldmarschalls Fürsten K. von Schwarzenberg*; Friedrich Fürst Schwarzenberg, *Karl Fürst Schwarzenberg* (a biography by his son).

fore a *sujet mixte*—an Austrian and, by the whim of history, a Swiss.

A tragic fate willed that Princess Pauline, Felix's mother, could guide her son for only ten years. While on a visit to Paris with her husband, Prince Joseph, she attended a state entertainment given by her brother-in-law, Field Marshal Charles Philip Schwarzenberg, as Austrian ambassador, in honor of Marie Louise, Napoleon's bride. To hold the many guests a temporary wooden pavilion had been annexed to the Austrian embassy. Suddenly a fire broke out in the annex. The princess reached safety, but she returned to the burning structure to search for one of her daughters who, unknown to her, had already been removed from the flaming building. The ceiling of the flimsy structure gave way; mother love incarnate lay dead under its planks.[6] Her body was recognized by a collar of diamonds marked with a rare brownish hue by the blaze. This was a guarded and precious heirloom until it was seized under the Hitler regime.

Prince Joseph, Felix's father, devoted his whole life to the administration and development of the vast estates of proud parentage. Out of virgin forests he cleared and cultivated thousands of acres of fertile farmland. Under his direction the watershed between the North Sea and the South Sea was pierced, by the construction of the Schwarzenberg Canal in the Bohemian Forest, which connects the rivers Danube and Vltava. Thus, lumber could be floated to Prague and to Hamburg, as well as to Vienna, from the Bohemian forests. A Maecenas, he supported the fine arts and sciences according to family tradition. Numerous charitable institutions and benevolent organizations owed their existence and continuance to his generosity. At his death the *Augsburger Allgemeine Zeitung* wrote: "So he stood—the embodiment of the old times, the very model of a system to which, after its destruction, our grandchildren will look back, with good reason, but in vain, as an era of happiness and peace." These words were prophetic; indeed, the author of this book can testify to their bitter truth.

[6] For a detailed description of the fire see Ebersberg, "Das Fest des österreichischen Botschafters am 1. Juli 1810 in Paris," *Feierstunden,* Nos. 50–52 (1833); "Eine Feuersbrunst in Paris," *Temesvarer Zeitung,* No. 127 (1860).

Felix was the fourth child and the second son of an ideal marriage.[7] His parents had in their happy and harmonious matrimonial life, extending over sixteen years, nine children. Marie Eleanore, the eldest, wife of Field Marshal Prince Alfred Windisch-Graetz, was accidentally killed by a bullet during the Prague revolution of 1848. Next was Marie Pauline, wife of Prince Heinrich Eduard Schönburg-Waldenburg. After her came Johann Adolph, my great-grandfather (1799–1889), who married Eleanore Princess Liechtenstein. His next brother was Felix. His chief Christian name was probably chosen to signify the luck which befell the family by the birth of a second son, since now the continuance of the family name received another guarantee. The name Johann Nepomuk was added because this saint is Bohemia's patron and is regarded as the family's special protector. Felix was followed by Aloisia, who married the above-mentioned Prince Schönburg after her sister's early death. Next in line was Mathilde, for years Felix's "housekeeper" and confidante. His other junior sisters were Caroline, wife of Prince Ferdinand Bretzenheim, and Bertha, wife of Prince August Longin Lobkowicz. The youngest child was Friedrich, Doctor Theologiae, Cardinal-Archbishop of Salzburg and then of Prague, to whom a few references will be made later.

According to family custom, the birth and baptism of Felix were occasions of general merrymaking, in which the members of the family, the household, the employees of the estates, and the population in general took part. Since many families had served the Schwarzenbergs for generations in the capacity of administrative officials and employees, jubilant events of this sort always strengthened the loyalty of the estates' staff to the immediate family. Among the poems and aphorisms presented on this occasion, one is significant and sounds like a prophecy: "CresCe Deo et hoMInI VIVeqVe FeLIX, tV Vera spes fVtVrI." [8]

---

[7] On Felix Schwarzenberg's youth and early years see especially Berger, *Felix Fürst zu Schwarzenberg;* Wurzbach, "Felix Schwarzenberg," in *Biographisches Lexicon des Kaiserthums Österreich;* Zeissberg, "Fürst Felix Schwarzenberg," in *Allgemeine Deutsche Biographie,* XXXIII, 266 et sqq.

[8] Berger, *Felix Fürst zu Schwarzenberg,* p. 162.

The boy's first ten years were happy under the protective guidance of his mother's love and care; he was sheltered against the intrusion of unharmonious influences within an ideal family life. To lose a mother at the age of ten must leave a certain vacuum even in the vagrant mind of a child. The mourning widower's youngest sister, Eleanore, a truly good and warm-hearted woman of high culture, dedicated her life to the welfare and education of her brother's children and undertook with admirable devotion to replace a seemingly irreplaceable mother. In the Schwarzenberg archives numerous letters can be found which prove with what minute exactness and "motherly love" she looked after the physical well-being and mental development of her nephews and nieces.

The two older boys, John Adolph and Felix, separated in age by one year, were brought up together. John Adolph became later, in 1833, the head of the family, succeeding his father to the entailed estates and family titles. Like many of his forefathers, he devoted the best part of his life to the administration of his properties. A man of progressive ideas, he introduced modern forest management on his estates and industrial methods to exploit them.

The education of the young princes was of the broad general character in harmony with the upbringing of great nobles of their time. They had a tutor to direct their studies and a *gouverneur* to initiate them into the social graces. This was the last generation that enjoyed the instructions by a *praeceptor elegantiarum,* a man of the lower nobility who gave the training formerly acquired by serving as a page at foreign courts. The two boys had been excellent linguists since their childhood. With their first words in German, they learned French from their mother. The native language in the flatlands being Czech, they acquired a working knowledge of the Bohemian idiom from the people around them. Latin was Felix's avocation. At the age of ten he tried his hand at a translation from Flavius Eutropius; the pages have been preserved in the family archives. *On revient toujours à ses premiers amours,* and so he read when a mature man, while traveling or during leisure hours, his favorite Roman authors in the original. The mental capacities of

the pupil were high. His grasp of a matter at first sight, combined
with thoughtfulness for the subject in hand, made all learning easy.
The free open-air life led by Felix at Castle Krumlov was especially
favorable to his development. The romantic landscape could not
fail to quicken to life in a nature so finely chiseled the appreciation
of the beautiful. This feeling for the graceful and the exquisite was
an asset to him for the rest of his life. When the time arrived to send
Felix Schwarzenberg out into the world, his aunt, Princess Eleanore,
could be proud of having made of him a fine-looking and well-
mannered young man who was clearly marked out to become the
worthy scion of distinguished lineage.

It was customary for second sons of noble families to join the
army. In Felix's case an excellent physique, mental alertness, personal inclination, and the impressive example of his uncle, the
laurel-covered victor of Leipzig, made the following of the traditional career a matter of course. He became a cadet in the famous
Eighth Cuirassiers, which bore the name of the Russian Grand Duke
Constantin; its colonel-commander was Felix's brother-in-law,
Prince Windisch-Graetz, the husband of his eldest sister, Marie
Eleanore. A soldier at heart Felix Schwarzenberg remained all his
life. Even when prime minister and foreign minister he wore a military uniform. Of all the orders and decorations he acquired, none
was prized higher by him than the Maria Theresa Order conferred
upon him for valor displayed in Italy.

Windisch-Graetz enjoyed the reputation of a competent officer.
Perhaps his abilities were overrated, as his campaign in Hungary in
1849 seemed to prove, but he undoubtedly was an ideal type of superior officer to initiate a young warrior into the traditions of the
military forces of his fatherland and into the art of war as it was
understood at that time. But these advantages were offset by disad-
vantages. Now for the first time Felix Schwarzenberg, in the capacity of a subaltern, came in contact with Alfred Windisch-Graetz
in the capacity of regimental commander and his superior in the
military hierarchy. The colonel was a man of uncompromising views
and rigorous convictions as to military discipline; the young officer

CASTLE KRUMLOV

was a stormy youth, anxious to plunge into the social whirlpool. Strict discipline might have been gracefully accepted from a stranger; it was irksome to endure it from a relative. Here were sown the first germs of friction that led to more serious conflicts when in subsequent years the Field Marshal, as the leader of the conservative Fronde, was arrayed against the Prime Minister, as the reforming head of the state. Felix Schwarzenberg was made out of steel a few degrees harder than his brother-in-law, as later pages will confirm.

The life of an Austrian subaltern cavalry officer was usually confined to a small place in the country where he could occasionally get leave to visit a near-by town. Felix Schwarzenberg's most faithful companions—books—broke the monotony of a barracks' life for him. When near his birthplace on furlough, he would get in touch with the teachers of the Agricultural Institute, an organization founded and endowed by his father, and the large family library readily supplied reading material on various subjects. At one time he became interested in anatomy and physiology and attended lectures on these subjects. He was not an omnivorous, systematic reader, but it is a shallow appraisal of the future statesman to state, as Eugene Bagger did, that he acquired "his education in a regiment of dragoons [!]" and to charge him with a total lack of book knowledge.[9] No one realized better than he himself that there were gaps in his education. A dramatic example is his exclamation on the day of his death. He had attended a cabinet meeting, during which his finance minister, Baumgartner, reviewed in masterful fashion the questions in hand. The Prime Minister was so struck by his minister's fecundity of thought and felicity of expression that he suddenly cried out: "Yes, one ought to have learned more, earlier!" Probably he had in mind the luxurious times spent in various capitals at a later period of his life rather than the curiously unremitting activities of his early years. Accompanying his love for reading was a love for music, in which his sister Mathilde supported him. Brother and sister occasionally arranged for a *missa solemnis* in one of the

[9] *Francis Joseph*, p. 194.

village churches belonging to their ancestral holdings. Felix had a good voice, and being fond of religious chants, he frequently sang in the choir. In a country in which game is abundant and hunting is the time-honored pastime of his class, it would be natural to expect him to engage in the sports of the field and the forest. But strangely enough, he was never keen on shooting. Instead, he preferred to enjoy the loneliness of the Bohemian woods or to fish for trout in the brooks in the vicinity of Krumlov.

With the exception of a short, rather conventional attachment to the Emperor Franz Hussars, he stayed with his original regiment until December 1, 1822, quickly advancing to captain. With this rank he was transferred to the Second Uhlans, the "Schwarzenberg Uhlans," named in honor of his uncle, the victor of Leipzig.

The year 1824 opened a new chapter in Felix Schwarzenberg's life. He had several times met Prince Metternich, and the potential diplomatic talents of the Uhlan captain had not escaped the chancellor's sharp eyes. Schwarzenberg was easily persuaded to enter the diplomatic service, because he was not compelled to give up the profession he liked best—soldiering. Henceforth Felix Schwarzenberg had two careers, a diplomatic career and a military one. In both he rose concurrently, until he reached the first place in the government, the premiership; with the exception of the period of the Italian campaign in 1848, he did not again exchange the pen for the sword.

The first assignment of the new attaché was to the legation at St. Petersburg, presided over by Baron Lebzeltern. The captain-diplomat traveled via Dresden and Berlin to the capital of His Imperial Majesty, the Czar of all the Russias, Alexander I.[10] For entertainment during a tedious journey he relied upon the books he had taken with him; whatever he did not enjoy he pitched out of the window.

In St. Petersburg the Austrian attaché was cordially received. The Czar, a great friend and admirer of Field Marshal Charles

[10] For a description of Russia at that time see Waliszewski, *La Russie il y a cent ans, le règne d'Alexandre Ier*.

Schwarzenberg since the Napoleonic wars, openly extended his patronage to the nephew; once he even visited him graciously in his apartment—an extraordinary act of imperial favor. The century-old bond of affection between the two houses was renewed.

Felix Schwarzenberg was introduced to Russian society during the army maneuvers at Krasnoie Selo. The tall and slim attaché, with a handsome face and the smart bearing of an Austrian cavalry officer, made an excellent impression, and from that time on the best salons were open to him. On his side, he was fascinated by the gorgeous display of oriental taste, the almost "barbaric pomp" of Russian living in the grand style. Frequent journeys in this vast country, almost a continent by itself, widened his horizon. He went to Astrakhan and to the famous fair at Nijni Novgorod. He attended the coronation of Czar Nicholas at Moscow after the death of his benefactor Alexander I. Subsequently Felix Schwarzenberg became innocently involved in the Dekabrist revolt.[11] Among the leaders of this movement, who, imbued with Western ideas, disputed the Czar's autocratic reign, was a Prince Serge Trubetzkoi, colonel of the Preobrashenski guards. Trubetzkoi, the brother-in-law of the Austrian envoy, Lebzeltern, had become one of Schwarzenberg's friends, and through him the Austrian attaché had made the acquaintance of other noblemen implicated in the plot. When the conspiracy was discovered and quelled, with dire results for the participants, Felix Schwarzenberg found himself in an embarrassing position. While his innocence was acknowledged by the Russian government, nevertheless he was no longer the *persona grata* of former years. A transfer to another diplomatic post seemed advisable, and therefore Metternich assigned the young diplomat to a special mission. Before his departure from St. Petersburg, the Czar bestowed on him the Order of Vladimir.

Traveling at the end of 1826 via Paris, he joined, in London, Baron Neumann, who was charged to present Dom Miguel's claims

[11] On the Dekabrist revolt and on Nicholas see, for instance, Hermes, *Geschichte der letzten fünfundzwanzig Jahre*, II, 138 *et sqq.*; Schiemann, *Geschichte Russlands unter Kaiser Nikolaus I.*

to the regency of Portugal in Rio de Janeiro.[12] Baron Neumann and
his suite left Portsmouth on November 21 and arrived on the British
frigate "Forte" in Rio on February 7, 1827. Since Dom Pedro I was
married to a daughter of the Austrian Emperor Francis I, the Austrian diplomats received a cordial reception. They stayed only ten
days in Rio—the Empress had died shortly before their arrival in
Brazil—and Schwarzenberg returned via London and Brussels to
Vienna and his family estates in Bohemia. After a few months' rest,
he was sent to Lisbon to prepare for the arrival of Dom Miguel, who
was Metternich's choice for the Portuguese throne.[13] While in Lisbon he once had to undergo a rather rare experience for a diplomat
and representative of a great power—he was pelted with stones—
but it cannot be stated with certainty whether the adherents of
Dom Miguel (the absolutists) or the partisans of Dom Pedro (the
constitutionalists) perpetrated the breach in international etiquette.
The incident was overlooked and had no diplomatic repercussions.
Dom Miguel arrived in Lisbon on February 22, 1828, and after he
had sworn to uphold the constitution (February 26) as regent for
his niece Maria da Gloria, Dom Pedro's daughter, Schwarzenberg's
mission to Portugal came to an end.[14]

   After his Portuguese assignment he was attached to the Austrian
legation at the Court of St. James and arrived in London in the
spring of 1828, just in time to see the downfall of the celebrated
Tory Cabinet of Wellington and Peel. In England he had his first

   [12] See *The Diary of Philipp von Neumann, 1819–1850*, trans. by E. Beresford Chancellor, I, 142 *et sqq.*
   [13] For details see Beirão, *El-Rey Dom Miguel I. e a sua descendência;* Freire de Carvalho,
Ensaio politico as causas que preparão a usurpação do infante Dom Miguel; Castro, *Portugal
em Roma;* Herchen, *Dom Miguel I., König von Portugal. Sein Leben und seine Regierung;*
Siebertz, *Freimaurer im Kampf um die Macht;* Lima, *Dom Pedro e Dom Miguel,* pp. 171 *et
sqq.*
   [14] In this connection the British statesman Canning uttered these prophetic words: "Of
all the wars which we had seen, and which had brought desolation in their train, the wars
of opinion had been decidedly the most fatal; and a single spark . . . might light up a
conflagration on the Continent, which no after exertions could extinguish—might lead to
a contest of opinions and principles, which would divide all the nations of Europe, and
only terminate, probably, with the total destruction of one of the contending factions."
Canning, *The Speeches of the Right Honourable George Canning,* comp. by R. Therry,
V, 172 (address on the King's Speech, February 3, 1824).

great love affair, which affected him deeply. Soon after his arrival in England he met one of the most famous beauties of English society, Lady Jane Ellenborough, the wife of a Lord Privy Seal and Admiral Digby's daughter.[15] It was love at first sight, in true Byronic style, between the Austrian nobleman and the English noblewoman. Their reckless behavior led to a parliamentary divorce.[16] A divorce bill was rarely introduced into the House of Commons unsupported by a first preliminary, a decree in the ecclesiastical courts, and a second preliminary, a verdict in one of the courts of common law.[17] Lord Ellenborough was granted a divorce, but only after the unpopular, middle-aged Lord had been handled rather roughly by members in both Houses.

The social scandal forced Felix Schwarzenberg to leave England rather precipitately. Metternich condoned his conduct and transferred him to the Austrian legation at Paris, where Jane Ellenborough followed him. The bright gold of their romance was soon tarnished by disappointment: both lovers discovered that neither one was constituted to be faithful to the other.[18] The offspring of this illicit love affair, a daughter, who was later married to an Austrian official, became the pampered child of a loving father.

A year after his arrival in Paris, in 1830, Felix Schwarzenberg witnessed the revolution which deposed Charles X and put Louis

[15] On the life of Lady Ellenborough, a lovable, foolishly loving, and greatly loved woman, see Oddie, *Portrait of Ianthe;* also Corti, *König Ludwig I. von Bayern.* (Ianthe is Bavarian Greek for Jane).

[16] Hansard's *Parliamentary Debates,* Commons, Vol. XXIII, cols. 1116, 1128, 1214, 1340.

[17] Sir C. Wetherall explained the procedure to the House on April 1, 1830 (*ibid.,* col. 1134): "On the subject of divorce, I beg leave to add, that every man has a right, when an act of adultery is proved against his wife, to obtain a sentence of divorce in the Ecclesiastical courts; not so, however, with respect to a parliamentary divorce. That rests not on the mere proof of an act of adultery: other and scarcely less important matters, are required to be satisfactorily proved by the individual who applies for it, and one most indispensable ingredient is, the total absence of all neglect, misconduct, connivance or collusion on the part of the husband, who complained of his wife's adultery."

[18] Jane Digby Ellenborough left for Bavaria. From King Louis I of Bavaria she went to a German baron, who married her, and after another marriage with a Greek count she passed into the harem of a Bedouin sheik. She died in Damascus in 1881. Jane has been the subject of several portrayals by novelists; for instance, by Balzac, as Lady Arabelle Dudley in *Le Lys dans la Vallée.*

Philippe on the throne. Here he gained valuable experience, because he could study the technique employed by Metternich in handling the change in regime. It was an experience which stood him in good stead when he had to deal in his capacity as prime minister with a similar situation, the *coup d'état* of Napoleon III on December 2, 1851.

In 1831 he returned to his native country. He needed a rest; he was in poor health and low spirits. The Ellenborough affair and the perpetual whirl of activity and excitement had left their mark. The sojourn with his family and the quiet life in the Bohemian forests restored his physical and psychic well-being. The consequences of the unfortunate crisis with regard to his psyche were, however, remarkable. Concomitant with a certain frivolous and flirtatious tendency, he had an inclination to piety. It may seem surprising that the man who was so fond of the fair sex should instruct his valet always to pack in his luggage at least one Latin classic and the *Imitatio Christi* by Thomas à Kempis. "Les extrêmes se touchent."

On September 9, 1831, Felix Schwarzenberg was promoted to major in the Emperor Francis Uhlans and to councillor of legation, an extraordinary advancement for a man of thirty-one years of age. In 1832 he was transferred to the legation at Berlin, where he remained for the comparatively long period of six years. In Berlin he witnessed the creation of the Customs Union, and here he came to understand that not all German-speaking people were alike, but that among them great differences existed. In 1835 my great-grandfather, John Adolph, the head of the family, was charged with the mission to announce to the Prussian Court the ascension of Emperor Ferdinand to the Austrian throne. Since Felix had not taken a leave of absence from his post in the preceding years, the two brothers celebrated a happy reunion in Berlin.

In August, 1835, Felix Schwarzenberg was promoted to colonel in the Uhlan Regiment No. 1, bearing the name of the Duke Saxe-Coburg-Gotha. As the imperial document declared, the promotion was granted "in grateful recognition of the services rendered to the Imperial House, and in expectation of further good services, as well as proof of the highest confidence." Two journeys were undertaken in this period. The first was in line of duty, to Münchengrätz, in Bohemia, where the Austrian Emperor met Czar Nicholas I. His attendance at the imperial meeting is evidence of the fact that the Trubetzkoi incident had been forgotten by the Russian Court. The second was a trip to Rome, where he visited his youngest sister Mathilde and studied the immortal monuments of art. The Berlin assignment ended one phase of Felix Schwarzenberg's life, because it terminated his role as a subordinate diplomat. Before his departure from Berlin he received the usual Prussian decoration.

Henceforth, until his appointment as prime minister in 1848, he functioned as minister at two Italian courts and as commander on Italian battlefields. Felix Schwarzenberg was appointed envoy extraordinary and minister plenipotentiary to the courts of Turin and Parma in 1839. Only his mission to Turin was important. In those days an Austrian envoy's position at an Italian court was at best a difficult one, and it was especially delicate at Turin. The relations between the courts of Vienna and Turin were strained to the breaking point. Even the marriage of the Duke of Savoy, later King Victor Emanuel II, to an Austrian archduchess did not relieve the tense atmosphere. A few years later the conflicts between the two countries were to flare into war.

King Charles Albert's [19] aspirations to liberate the Italian lands from the "Austrian yoke" were well known to the new Austrian envoy. He handled a perplexing situation more tactfully than his predecessor, Count Brunetti, but he was by no means popular at the court of Turin. His sarcastic smile was feared by the King, and his biting remarks were not relished by the minister of foreign affairs of Piedmont, Count Solaro della Margarita. Illustrative of the lack of diplomatic amenities prevailing between the Austrian legation and the Piedmontese foreign office is the beginning of a note sent by Felix Schwarzenberg to Count Margarita concerning the importa-

[19] On King Charles Albert see, for instance, Capelletti, *Storia di Carlo Alberto e del suo regno;* Carutti, *Bibliografia Carlo-Albertina;* Vidal, *Charles Albert et le Risorgimento italien.*

tion of salt: "*Je vous adresse une note sur l'affaire des sels et vous trouverez qu'elle est bien salée.*" [20] No wonder Felix Schwarzenberg was not exactly popular at Turin.

Felix Schwarzenberg kept "open house" in Turin and thus met everyone of importance. He became the friend of Marchese Alfonso Lamarmora, then merely a captain in the horse artillery and the military teacher of the Duke of Genoa, whom he was destined to meet again as peace negotiator between Austria and Piedmont in 1848. On account of the friction between the two countries, it was intimated to the Marchese that he should abandon his frequent visits to the Austrian legation.[21] Well aware of the frigid and stuffy atmosphere at Turin, the Austrian envoy sought refuge at Milan, where the intellectual life was more stimulating and liaisons with the fair sex could be discreetly maneuvered. In 1844 Schwarzenberg, who meanwhile had been promoted to major general and privy councillor, was transferred from dull, cloistered Turin to gay, expansive Naples, taking along the Piedmontese Grand Cross of the Order of St. Mauritius and Lazarus.[22]

The first years of his envoyship, which Felix Schwarzenberg passed at Naples, belonged to one of the happiest periods in his life. "See Naples and then die!" is a well-known Italian saying. The sweetness and beauty of the landscape so lavishly displayed, the manifold monuments of art, vestiges of Roman and Greek splendor, and the high regard for amenity in human intercourse on the part of the inhabitants made a deep and lasting impression on him. In the beginning of 1852, when his health began to fail, he longed for one place—Naples—but duty and work kept him in Vienna until a premature death frustrated his plans.

At court he was *persona gratissima*. Ferdinand II, King of the Two Sicilies, also called King of Naples,[23] a Bourbon, was married

---

[20] Austria's reprisal was an increase in import duties on Piedmontese wines. Much light is thrown on Austro-Piedmontese relations of this period by Solaro della Marghuerita's *Memorandum storico-politico.*

[21] Zeissberg, "Felix Fürst Schwarzenberg," in *Allgemeine Deutsche Biographie,* XXXIII, 268.   [22] *Ibid.*

[23] On Ferdinand II of Naples see, for instance, Amante, *Di Ferdinando II, re delle due*

PRINCE FELIX ZU SCHWARZENBERG

to an Austrian archduchess, a daughter of Field Marshal Archduke Charles, the victor over Napoleon at Aspern. Thus, the friendly feelings of the reigning Italian families of this era towards the Habsburg dynasty were especially understandable. But the Bourbons at Naples, as well as "the Savoys," ultimately yielded to the frenzy of their subjects. Incited by propaganda and the "irredenta" movement, popular hatred was bound to lead to bloodshed. In 1845 Felix Schwarzenberg met Nicholas I of Russia, whose wife was sojourning at Naples to restore her health in the balmy air of that country. When the Czar's attention was called to rumors that the Austrian envoy at Naples was slated to be transferred to St. Petersburg, the Czar remarked, "Contre le Prince Schwarzenberg de Naples je n'ai aucune objection." This is evidence that the unfortunate Trubetzkoi affair was finally condoned.

In 1846 Schwarzenberg was still able to negotiate a commercial and navigation treaty between Austria and Naples favorable to his country,[24] but by the fall of that year the signs of the impending national and popular uprisings in Italy had become so unmistakable that he thought it advisable to talk matters over with his chief, Metternich. Therefore, he traveled to Vienna.[25] No records of the conversations between chancellor and envoy are extant. On his way back to Naples, in January, 1847, he contracted typhus fever at Trieste. For weeks he hovered between life and death, but eventually he recovered, outwardly as well as ever save that his hair had grayed. Yet it seems that his sickness was the predisposing cause of some later ailments (nervous irritability, myopia, cardiac thrombosis), which prematurely ended his life in 1852.

When Schwarzenberg returned to Naples, he found that the diplomatic relations between his country and Naples had decidedly deteriorated. Dealings with the Naples foreign minister, Prince

Sicilie; Ayala, *Vita del re di Napoli;* Croce, *Storia del regno di Napoli;* Nisco, *Ferdinando II e il suo regno.*
[24] Berger, "Das Fürstenhaus Schwarzenberg," *Österreichische Revue,* Heft 11 (1866), pp. 348–49.
[25] Zeissberg, "Felix Fürst zu Schwarzenberg," in *Allgemeine Deutsche Biographie,* XXXIII, 268, 271.

Scilla, became so unpleasant that he asked the King to be allowed
either to communicate with him directly or to negotiate through
another intermediary.[26] Shortly afterwards the revolutionary movement of the year 1848 spread to Naples. Contrary to actual facts,
Schwarzenberg was considered by the population the most influential of the foreign advisers who prevented the King from granting
desired concessions.[27] On March 25, 1848, a riotous mob gathered
before the Austrian legation, tore down the Austrian double-eagle—
the century-honored escutcheon of a proud monarchy—and burned
it on the Largo Santa Caterina without interference by the police.[28]
The directing spirit of this pagan use of violence was the Lombard
Princess Belgioioso,[29] in whose salon the revolutionaries staged an
auto-da-fé for the cremation of the eagles' heads.

Schwarzenberg was not the man to remain idle when his fatherland's honor and his monarch's prestige were at stake. The affair
that had occurred two decades earlier at Lisbon, when stones were
thrown at him, could be regarded as a private matter, but at Naples
a public offense had been committed. He lost no time in filing a
strong protest with the Naples foreign office, and when he received
an evasive answer,[30] he decided that the moment had come to fire
powerful diplomatic ammunition. He now demanded the restoration of the Austrian emblem in the presence of a Naples function-
ary and a statement in the official gazette that the government disapproved the incident. The climax came when he learned that the
Naples government had sanctioned the formation of a corps of
volunteers for the war in northern Italy. He called for an explanation within twenty-four hours, and when this explanation was not
forthcoming, he took matters into his own hands by wiring to

[26] Wurzbach, "Felix Schwarzenberg," in *Biographisches Lexicon des Kaiserthums Österreich,* p. 48.
[27] Berger, "Das Fürstenhaus Schwarzenberg," *Österreichische Revue,* Heft 11 (1866),
p. 359n.
[28] Helfert, *Geschichte der österreichischen Revolution im Zusammenhange mit der mitteleuropäischen Bewegung der Jahre 1848–1849,* p. 368.
[29] See Barbiera, *La Principessa Belgioioso;* Remm-Whitehouse, *Une Princesse Révolutionnaire.*
[30] Wurzbach, "Felix Schwarzenberg," in *Biographisches Lexicon des Kaiserthums Österreich,* p. 49.

Vienna that he would "leave the very same day a country where his
official relations had been interrupted by a gross violation of international law and where his further residence not only would be use-
less but also would compromise the honor and dignity of the imperial court." [31] Subsequently the Vienna cabinet endorsed the step
taken by its Naples envoy.[32] Therewith Felix Schwarzenberg's activities in the diplomatic service proper came to an end.

Goethe said that a curse rests upon one fixed in one place; if this
is true, Felix Schwarzenberg must have belonged to the least cursed
among men. For the next few months he was constantly on the
move. On March 28, 1848, he boarded the Austrian battleship "Vul-
cano," hearing the outcries of the populace *Italia farà da sè*, words
which the unperturbed exenvoy wittily translated into *L'Italie se
perdra d'elle-même*. After a five-day voyage, during which he had
to assert his authority as a general to suppress a mutiny among the
crew, chiefly composed of Italian sailors, he landed at Trieste.[33]

The stirring military events in northern Italy drew Schwarzenberg with inexorable force back to the army. He stayed a few days
in Vienna, but as early as April 17, he crossed the Isonzo River as
brigadier under General von Nugent. At the beginning of the
Italian campaign the military situation for the Austrian army was
by no means favorable.[34] But the brilliant strategy of old Field
Marshal Count Radetzky—his soldiers called him simply the *Feld-
herr*—soon turned a precarious military position into glorious victory. On April 17 Schwarzenberg's brigade threw back General
Zuchi's sortie from Palmanuova.[35] At Bisnadello Schwarzenberg
effected a junction with an imperial reserve army in which two of

[31] Berger, "Das Fürstenhaus Schwarzenberg," *Österreichische Revue*, Heft 11 (1866),
p. 363, and Wurzbach, *op. cit.*, who quotes a notice that appeared in the official *Wiener
Zeitung.*

[32] Before the break of diplomatic relations, Schwarzenberg had received from the King
the Order of St. Januarius, one of the highest decorations of Naples, and on the occasion
of negotiating the treaty of commerce and navigation, he had received the Grand Cross
of the Leopold Order from the Austrian Emperor.

[33] Helfert, see note 28, above.

[34] *Kriegsbegebenheiten bei der kaiserlich österreichischen Armee in Italien*, vom 18. März
bis 6. Mai 1848, Section I, pp. 74 *et sqq.*

[35] *Ibid.*, Sections I–III.

his cousins, sons of the late Field Marshal Charles Philip, Prince zu
Schwarzenberg, the victor over Napoleon in the battle of Leipzig,
served as generals. On May 20 he directed the bombardment of
Vicenza; on May 29, having been promoted to the rank of a division general, he took part in the storming of Curtatone. On May 30,
during the battle of Goito, while fighting as usual in the front lines,
he was wounded in the left arm. For gallantry displayed in the
battles he received the Maria Theresa Cross, the equivalent of the
Congressional Medal or the Victoria Cross. The regular army officers
were wont to look down on "diplomatic generals," but Schwarzenberg's courage and understanding of military matters gained their
respect. In their eyes he had now become their equal. Guided by
noblesse oblige, he was popular with his soldiers, just as he had been
in his younger days when a lieutenant and a captain.[36] A few weeks
were required for the healing of his wound, but as soon as he reported for duty to Marshal Radetzky, the commander-in-chief had
a mission of the greatest significance for "the diplomat of his army."
In spite of Radetzky's victories, the Vienna cabinet took a gloomy
view of the Monarchy's position. Fearing a rupture with France, it
had practically decided to surrender Lombardy to Savoy. The marshal, furious at the exhibition of such weakness, sent Schwarzenberg to Innsbruck, where the Court had sought refuge, to convince the cabinet of the absurdity of the plan and to propose to it to
send him reinforcements of 25,000 men. Overcoming the objections of the minister of foreign affairs, Baron Wessenberg, he succeeded in persuading the cabinet to grant Radetzky's request and,
instead of concluding an ignominious armistice, to trust in the for-
tunes of war. It was a signal triumph of daring and vision that was
bound to mark Schwarzenberg as the coming leader of the Monarchy's destinies.

Felix Schwarzenberg took a leave of absence and went to Bohemia
to seek full recovery from his wound. Utilizing his time, he became
a candidate for a seat in the first constituent Reichstag, but the

[36] Zeissberg, "Felix Fürst Schwarzenberg," in *Allgemeine Deutsche Biographie*, XXXIII,
272.

agitated peasants preferred one of their own to the "aristocrat"—
he failed of election. The defeated Reichstag candidate, now promoted to lieutenant field marshal, hurried back to Italy, where
Radetzky had routed King Charles Albert's army at Custozza on
July 25. Ensuing armistice negotiations were fruitless. It was the
irony of fate that among the negotiations two friends were on
opposite sides, Schwarzenberg on the Austrian, and Colonel Lamarmora, daily his guest when he was envoy at Turin,[37] on the Italian.
The war continued. On August 5 Radetzky occupied Milan and
appointed Felix Schwarzenberg its military governor.

Radetzky had such confidence in Schwarzenberg's political
acumen and diplomatic skill that he decided to send him to Vienna
as soon as the peace preliminaries with Savoy had been cleared away.
There he was to render assistance to the dictator Field Marshal
Windisch-Graetz in suppressing the revolution and in restoring
tranquillity in the country. Meanwhile, Schwarzenberg had also
won the sympathetic recognition of his brother-in-law, with whom
he had formerly been on bad terms.[38] The marshal offered him a
cabinet post through his aide-de-camp Baron Langenau; [39] however,
Schwarzenberg declined to join the moribund Wessenberg ministry. In Vienna, Schwarzenberg displayed the same energy he had
shown in Italy in organizing military resistance to the revolting
students and workers. But his efforts were frustrated by the incapacity of Vienna's commander, General Count Auersperg. Now
the great moment in his life had come. Windisch-Graetz, "the embodiment of resolute will, of all that was still strong and capable
in the Austrian noble class," [40] was determined on firm action.
With him, Schwarzenberg was to lead the country through the
dark valley of indecision to the bright summit of certainty in its
own purpose. Before the marshal moved from Bohemia against
Vienna, he summoned his brother-in-law to Olmütz, where the

[37] See *supra*, p. 16. See also Lamarmora, *Alcuni episodi della guerra nel Veneto*.
[38] See *supra*, p. 9.
[39] Zeissberg, "Felix Fürst Schwarzenberg," in *Allgemeine Deutsche Biographie*, XXXIII,
274.
[40] Redlich, *Emperor Francis Joseph of Austria*, p. 25.

Court had moved from the capital, and recommended him to the imperial family as prime minister in a new government. By the Emperor's unpublished holograph letter of October 19, 1848,[41] Felix Schwarzenberg was entrusted with the formation of a new cabinet.[42]

[41] Zeissberg, "Felix Fürst Schwarzenberg," in *Allgemeine Deutsche Biographie*, XXXIII, 276.

[42] On Felix Schwarzenberg's activities in Vienna at this time and the negotiations leading to his appointment as Prime Minister see the reminiscences of his assistant, the later Austrian ambassador in Paris, Josef Alexander Graf von Hübner, *Ein Jahr meines Lebens, 1848–49*.

2

INTERNAL POLICY

WHEN THE MILITARY DICTATOR, Prince Alfred
Windisch-Graetz, selected his brother-in-law, Felix
Prince zu Schwarzenberg, to save the Austrian Empire
from disintegration, an iron will and energizing, virile resiliency
replaced torpor and vacillating feebleness. The irresistible dash and
indomitable daring of the cavalryman, characteristic of this particular branch of the Austrian army, was now imported into the
palace at the Ballhausplatz. Schwarzenberg seemed to the powers
behind the throne the man sent by Providence to perform the primary business of government, that is, "to govern." They were not to
be disappointed.

A brief survey of preceding events will enable the reader to grasp
the scope and sweep of the multitude of weighty tasks confronting
the new Prime Minister. "Good" Emperor Francis had died on
March 2, 1835. The "era of good feeling," the *Biedermeier* epoch,
lingered in Austria for thirteen years under the nominal rule of the
weak Emperor Ferdinand, but under the actual direction of a
triumvirate, the so-called State Conference, consisting of Archduke
Ludwig, Prince Metternich for foreign affairs, and Count Kolowrat
for domestic affairs. Society had been long in peace and comfort,
when suddenly, in 1848, the revolutionary lightnings were carried
from Rome to Naples, from Naples to Paris, and from Paris to the
capitals of the Germanic Confederation. In Vienna, on the thir-
teenth of March, the minister who had guided Austria's destiny
for thirty-eight years was swept from office "amidst threats of
vengeance and shouts of triumph." "Yet," so continues his enthu-

siastic biographer, Algernon Cecil,[1] "there were those like Disraeli
who saw that a stately column had been broken; that a beacon light
had been quenched in smoke; that, for all the noise of brazen
trumpets, a silver voice had ceased; that a watchman, grown old in
the safeguarding of peace, kept vigil no more in the high place of
Vienna." The succeeding Liberal cabinet, composed of civil servants
and headed by the weak Baron Pillersdorf, fulfilled the fancy felt
everywhere for constitutions and published a fundamental law on
the Belgian pattern on April 25, 1848. In spite of this placating
measure, the democratic storm was blowing to a stronger gale. On
May 15 a second insurrection took place in Vienna.[2] A new ministry
of Liberals or Constitutional Monarchists, with the seventy-five-
year-old exdiplomat, Baron Wessenberg, as prime minister, was compelled to consent to the convocation of a constituent diet. A committee of public safety, made up of students and workers, controlled
Vienna after May 26. In June a Slavonic Congress was called to
Prague by the Czechs to unite the opposition of the Slavic people of
Austria against the growth of German influence and culture. Hungary was in an uproar; she demanded and received a separate ministry in April. The opposition of the Slav population and the ap-
panages of the Crown of St. Stephen (Croatia and Transylvania) to
the supremacy of the Magyars, stealthily supported by Vienna, led
to open warfare. When on October 6 an Austrian battalion was to

---

[1] *Metternich, 1773–1859; a Study of His Period and Personality*, p. 301.

[2] The liberal nobility, the bourgeoisie, and the peasants were satisfied with the restraint
of the absolute monarch within the limits of a constitution, a free press, and the promised
liberation of peasants' lands from feudal dues. Opposed to these "Constitutional Monarchists" were the "Democrats," made up chiefly of the nonpossessing classes, who demanded
a unicameral system, with no fixed census for voters, and the drafting of a "truly democratic constitution." For the workers political institutions were to be the means for gaining economic ends. "Elements which now appeared for the first time on the scene of public
life . . . sought in confused, disordered, and purely sentimental ideological conceptions,
not seldom in unrealizable dogmatic exaggerations, the way of solution." Socialist ideas
were, however, unknown in the Austria of these days. "The street, the pressure of the
violent demogogic agitation, the politicians of the petty bourgeois coffee houses . . .
feasted now in street demonstrations and hootings and howlings as they formerly revelled
in roast chickens and the waltzes." Jászi, *The Dissolution of the Habsburg Monarchy*,
pp. 87–88; by courtesy of the publishers, The University of Chicago Press.

be despatched from Vienna to Hungary to reinforce the imperial transleithan troops, Viennese students and workers, as well as the national guard, prevented its departure, and the revolution flared up again. It was the army which re-established the Habsburg power in the German-Slav hereditary lands. First Cracow, then Prague (June 12–17) and Milan, after the defeat of Charles Albert, King of Sardinia, at Custozza (July 25) by Radetzky, and finally Vienna (October 26–31) were subdued.

The questions to which the new Prime Minister had to find the answers were immeasurably more difficult than those which confronted Metternich at the Congress of Vienna. At that time, a decision by force of arms had already been made; a powerful Austria supported the plans of the "Coachman of Europe." Schwarzenberg was faced with a congeries of problems, for none of which had yet been found a definite solution: the contemplated abdication of Emperor Ferdinand, the Austrian diet, the German National Assembly at Frankfurt, the revolution in Hungary, and the war in Italy. His views regarding the revolution and the task placed before him are revealed in a letter addressed to Field Marshal Count Radetzky, dated Olmütz, October 22, 1848.[3]

The European revolutionary party has, for a considerable length of time, had its eye on Austria and, especially, Vienna. A decisive coup was to be attempted. No place in Europe seemed to be more suitable for such a scheme than a city whose population, easily agitated, politically quite unripe, and partly morally corrupted, had for months been worked upon and had gradually been accustomed to a state of anarchy. The government and the diet assembled there strengthened this undertaking, partly intentionally, partly unconsciously.

The government lacked leadership, unity, and energy of action. Instead of being itself at the helm of the state, instead of taking the initiative vis-à-vis the utterly unco-operative parliament, it fitfully wavered between opposing poles—a symbol of incapacity, a plaything for passions, a tool of the revolutionary party, neglecting its primary and most important duty of opposing that party.

[3] Redlich, *Das österreichische Staats- und Reichsproblem*, Vol. I, Annex pp. 80–82.

The diet showed a fatal resemblance to this government. Born of an immature population, elected . . . in circumstances which excluded from its membership practically all prominent persons of property, intelligence, experience or knowledge of affairs, it could not be expected to seize the reins that had slipped from the hands of the government and to direct the stream of the movement into well-regulated channels. The necessary prerequisites were missing: knowledge, understanding, political courage. Nevertheless, the desire for tranquillity, order, and legality made itself felt even within this very assembly, and although incapable of leading, it did not negate the hope of being led. Your Excellency will understand that under these conditions the coup, primed by far-reaching propaganda and prepared with great dexterity and sizable amounts of money, was not without chances for success. On October 6 the coup was carried out. It was fully successful in the City. Poor military arrangements allowed the completion of the undertaking. The garrison left the City; within a few hours, Vienna was under the iron yoke of revolutionary terror. Conditions were less favorable for the anarchists in the flat country and in the provinces. Not that the minds there had been left uncorrupted, but jealousy of the metropolis, the lesser mobility of the masses, and sounder judgment barred the way to the machinations of the agitators. Especially the peasantry, since its liberation from feudal services, showed itself averse to revolution and, on the whole, displayed loyalty. This had been the reason why the insurrection, despite all attempts to incite the broad mass of the people to revolt, did not transgress the confines of Vienna; on the contrary, the execrable spectacle of the metropolis handed over to the horrors of anarchy and terrorism has had a deterring effect on the provinces and has raised the lowered spirits of the well-meaning.

. . . Suppression of the revolt everywhere and at any price, preservation of the privileges of the dynasty over against all usurpations of the revolution, recognition of the liberty granted by the Emperor to all his peoples, regulation of this liberty in the interior, and maintenance of the totality of the Monarchy towards the outside world will be the program of the new Ministry of which His Majesty has commissioned me to be a member . . . Resolved to uphold the undiminished integrity of the Empire, we shall endeavor also to place Hungary in a relation to the Monarchy consonant with these principles. Prince Windisch-Graetz, after having established order in Vienna, will eventually take the necessary measures with the army under his command.

In Italian affairs, His Majesty puts full and exclusive confidence in Your Excellency and the gallant Italian army . . .

THE SCHWARZENBERG CABINET [4]

Nature had created the new Prime Minister a born ruler. High ambition and tremendous will power conquered a weakened body when Prince Schwarzenberg became the dictator of an Empire. From the moment his aspirations were given free rein he, formerly an aristocratic Epicurean, displayed an extraordinary capacity for work. Just as by reckless abandon in the face of danger and complete disdain for personal safety he had been a stimulating source of encouragement to the soldiers leaving the capital before the revolting population upon orders of their incompetent commander, Count Auersperg, so he faced with complete unconcern and icy calm his new, crushingly heavy duties of rebuilding the shattered Monarchy. Despite his passionate confidence in himself, his intellectual gifts made him a master who knew his limitations. Generally he had the talent for judging men correctly, selecting able collaborators and putting mental strength in place of tangible utility. The impact of the Prime Minister's will was indelibly stamped everywhere. He was more than *inter stellas luna minores;* in his ministry he was the sun around which planets revolved. But, if one of Lord Roseberry's phrases may be borrowed, "he was not the senior partner in every department." Knowing, as Voltaire did, that *le détail est comme une vermine qui ronge les grandes choses,* he kept only the initiative concerning and the guidance of broad outlines of policy. As a superior, he was hard-driving and hard-hitting, but not impervious to reason; cogent counterarguments, if presented with perspicacity and lucidity, were always received with good grace.[5]

[4] A selected bibliography is Bibl, *Der Zerfall Österreichs,* II, 161 *et sqq.;* Helfert, *Geschichte Österreichs vom Ausgange des Wiener October-Aufstandes 1848,* Vols. III–IV; Josef Alexander Graf von Hübner, *Ein Jahr meines Lebens,* 1848–49; Redlich, *Das österreichische Staats- und Reichsproblem,* Vol. I, Section iv, with literature in Annex, pp. 78–79. In Czech literature see Hrnčíř, *Dějepis národa československého;* Karas, *Stručná kronika československá;* Kotrč and Kotalík, *Stručné dějiny československé literatury:* Mareš *"Nové příspěvky k pam. roku 1848,"* in *Český Časopis Historický;* Traub, *Naše politické dějiny v 19. století.*

[5] See Joseph Alexander Graf von Hübner, *Ein Jahr meines Lebens, passim,* and *Neun Jahre der Erinnerungen eines österreichischen Botschafters in Paris unter dem zweiten Kaiserreich 1851–1859.*

As Schwarzenberg was primarily a diplomat and an officer, he stood in special need of a capable minister of the interior. Count Franz Stadion,[6] considered the best mind in the higher bureaucracy, was selected for this post upon Prince Windisch-Graetz's recommendation. Temporarily, he also took over the department of education. Born in Vienna on July 27, 1806, the third son of Count Johann Stadion, who had been minister of foreign affairs in 1805–1809 and finance minister in 1815–1824, he represented a type of Austrian aristocrat different from that of Schwarzenberg and his brother-in-law. Solid theoretical studies and extensive practical experience as governor of Trieste and Galicia had made of this liberal a first-rate administrator. Recognizing the flagrant defects in the administrative machinery and constitutional setup of the Monarchy, he was ready to step forward with a reform program. The mental ailment that manifested itself in April, 1849, and removed him forever from the political scene cut short the question whether two divergent philosophies, one held by the Prime Minister and one by the minister of interior, could exist side by side for any length of time.

Dr. Alexander Bach (Freiherr von after 1854),[7] whose motto must have been "to improve is to change, to be perfect is to change often," was made minister of justice. Indeed, not many political careers include as many contradictions and shifts of attitude as does his. Born on January 4, 1813, he was the son of a well-to-do Viennese lawyer and cofounder of the Juridic-politic Reading Society, the center of liberal opposition to the pre-March regime. After the death of his father, in 1843, he took over his practice, and as a gifted and eloquent member of the bar and a shrewd and practical businessman, he quickly forged ahead. In the spring of 1848 he was the driving force behind the liberal-bourgeois movement against the Metternich system. As minister of justice, he was the spokesman for the Wessenberg-Doblhoff ministry; by craft and resource he tried

---

[6] See his biography by Hirsch, *Franz Graf Stadion.*

[7] See *Allgemeine Deutsche Biographie,* XLVI, 158 *et sqq.;* Kotrč and Kotalík, *Stručné dějiny československé literatury.*

to hold the floodgates of revolution. When the people no longer offered any gifts to his consuming ambition, he broke with his past and, after some tergiversations, finally moved to the Right. By the time of Schwarzenberg's death, Bach, "once the vestal virgin of liberalism" (if Lloyd George's pun about Winston Churchill may be drawn upon) "had by impeccable behavior" as a good reactionary "succeeded in living down his past." As the initiator of the "Bach police system," the former leader of the revolution surpassed Metternich's system in arbitrary rule. He ended as the obedient servant of clericalism. An able organizer, an excellent administrator, this political chameleon was thoroughly hated by the people and contemptuously looked down upon by the aristocracy as a parvenu. General detestation smothered the little that stood to the credit of this supple, unscrupulous lawyer-politician, who did not die until November 12, 1893. Schwarzenberg, whose knowledge of human nature perceived quickly that the bourgeois upstart would more readily adjust himself to his views than his compeer Stadion, would have preferred to make him minister of the interior, but the "minister of the barricades" was unacceptable to Windisch-Graetz, at that time the omnipotent dictator, and the Prime Minister had to bow to his brother-in-law's veto.

The minister of commerce, Karl Bruck [8] (Freiherr von after 1849), born in Elberfeld on October 8, 1798, the son of a bookbinder, represented the type of self-made man. Not finding passage to Greece at Trieste to take part in the war of liberation, he settled in the latter port. His prepossessing physique gained him the hand of the daughter of the rich merchant Buschek; a Protestant, he rapidly climbed the social ladder in a Catholic country. Because of his energy and vision, he became one of the city's leaders and the founder of the Austrian Lloyd. While Bach was cool, calculating, and cunning, Bruck was fiery, enthusiastic, and idealistic. His schemes, both those as a merchant and as a statesman, showed aspects of the plunger. This trait explains why he accomplished more as

[8] See *Allgemeine Deutsche Biographie*, III, 376 et sqq.; Charmatz, *Minister Freiherr von Bruck: Der Vorkämpfer Mitteleuropas.*

minister of commerce in the Schwarzenberg ministry (until May 23, 1851) than later (1855–1860) as finance minister. He died on April 23, 1860.

Stadion, Bach, and Bruck, all were outstanding persons—celebrities of prime ministerial timber. Less influential and capable was the finance minister, Baron Philip Krauss (1792–1861), but he was an honorable and efficient civil servant, attached to duty and his church. During the revolution the short man with a little *embonpoint* was at once a joker and a joke. To safeguard the state's funds this watchdog of the treasury invented a technique that might arouse the envy of a South American politico: in consideration of moneys paid out of the treasury to the revolutionary students (part of which they promptly invested in alcoholic beverages), he exacted from them the promise to leave the national bank unharmed. And unharmed it remained. Edler von Thinnfeld, a member of the liberal Styrian circle of Archduke John, the Imperial Administrator residing at Frankfurt, took the ministry of agriculture, and Major General Baron Cordon, the popular commander of Vienna, the ministry of war. The cabinet appointments were officially announced on November 21, 1848. A little later Baron Kulmer, a Croat, was admitted to the cabinet as minister without portfolio, in recognition of the loyalty manifested to the Habsburgs by the South Slavs.

The reconstitution of the Austrian Empire in the shape of a unitary Monarchy under the scepter of the Habsburgs, entailing the re-establishment of the dominant position of that dynasty in Europe, was the aim of Schwarzenberg's policy. In contrast to his brother-in-law, he thought it expedient, however, to follow the current of liberal opinion and to appear, at least temporarily, in the garb of a constitutional minister. It was a time when the traditional mode of thinking was dislocated and the hard crust of usage broken. Schwarzenberg had to figure on the democratic temper in the rest of Germany; the Austrian radicals could easily poke the embers of the revolution into another conflagration, and the Hungarian revolutionaries were far from being subjugated. These were all factors that seemed to call for restraint rather than for violent action.

The ministerial declaration read to the diet on November 27,
1848, was framed accordingly. "Sincerely and without reserve" the
cabinet pledged itself to a constitutional monarchy. "The parity of
all nationalities, the equality of all citizens before the law, the free
commune as the basis of the free state"—these were the fundamental engagements undertaken. A few references were made to the
most difficult problem of the Monarchy, the question whether the
Monarchy was to be constituted on a federalistic or a unitary basis.
The issue was straddled by promising the federalists a free development of all the parts of the Monarchy in internal affairs and the
centralists a strong pivotal power. The dismal strife of the nationalities [9] was touched upon in a few words. With regard to the
Lombardo-Venetian kingdom, the declaration affirmed that after
the conclusion of peace it would find a trustworthy guarantee for
the maintenance of its national character in the organic connection
with constitutional Austria. Hungary, it was stated, had violated
this first right of nations, because the peoples in revolt in Hungary
desired "maintenance of the Monarchy as a whole, a closer connection with Austria, recognition and guarantee of their nationalities."

[9] The sharpness of national strife as early as 1848, as well as the existence of two factions among the Bohemian nobles, one championing the German cause, the other taking a
more sympathetic view of Czech aspirations, is shown by a letter written in that year by
Prince Edmund Clary to Felix Schwarzenberg's brother, Johann Adolph Prince zu Schwarzenberg (Schwarzenberg archives, Krumlov): "A few days ago I voiced the apprehension
of many that the separation of Bohemia from Austria may be expected in the near future,
if the Czech element gains the upper hand in actual affairs just as it is now exercising a
moral terrorism. . . . Some of these political parties are solely guided by personal ambition, because they hope to have a better chance in playing a role in an independent Bohemia
than in the fatherland as a whole—a ministry of their own is very attractive for those who
have talent and energy. Others have outright communistic and republican intentions. . . .
Finally there is a secret Russian party which has entered into contact with Slavic emissa-
ries from Carinthia. . . . The Czechs do not desire an imperial diet. They do not want
a consolidation with Germany, that is, they want to quit the German Federation, Austria,
as well as Hungary. The German-Bohemian Association, of which I am a member, tries to
counteract these tendencies. It would be highly advisable if some Bohemian estate owners
joined the Association, especially such as possess Bohemian and German estates, and of
those again especially you, my dear Prince, who own the twelfth part of Bohemia, and, if
you so desired, could exercise an enormous influence."
See Molisch, *Briefe zur deutschen Politik Österreichs von 1848 bis 1918*, pp. 1–2.
According to Felix Schwarzenberg's later scheme of a unitary state, the Empire should
be the balancing and deciding force, showing itself stronger than the nationalities, thus
forestalling internal dissensions.

Hope was expressed that "with the consent of the different peoples, a new union would be formed, comprising all the regions and the races of the Monarchy in a single great state body." [10] "The government will not lag behind the aspirations for free and popular institutions," the Prime Minister announced finally; "on the contrary, it deems it its duty to place itself at the head of this movement."

"Who offers much brings something unto many. . . . Give them more . . . even more than they ask," says the theater manager in Goethe's *Faust*. The ministerial declaration of the Schwarzenberg cabinet filled these prescriptions. None of the 275-odd deputies [11] had expected that aristocrats like Schwarzenberg and Stadion would come forth as fervent protagonists of liberalism, constitutionalism, and popular institutions. The Czechs rejoiced, because they saw rising before their eyes a state of their own, in harmony with the announced "free development of the different parts of the Monarchy." Even the Democratic Left, through its chairman, Franz Schuselka, expressed its thanks to the ministry. Thus, the acclaim of the deputies assembled at Kremsier, in the summer residence of the archbishop of Olmütz, was loud and general.[12] It was a chastened

[10] The passage of the ministerial declaration dealing with Germany is referred to in Chapter III. For a fairly full text in English see Coxe, *History of the House of Austria,* Vol. IV, p. C.

[11] In December the Kremsier diet had 342 members, with some elections still outstanding, while the Vienna diet had 368 deputies. Helfert, *Geschichte Österreichs vom Ausgange des Wiener October-Aufstandes 1848,* III, 417n. In November, 1848, the party grouping was as follows as far as it can be estimated: The Slavic Party (Czechs, South Slavs, inclusive of Ruthenians, about 120 members) was the largest group; the Germans were split into a Central Club, or "ministerial" Germans, about 60 members (standing for the equality of all nationalities like the Slavs and advocating an independent position towards Frankfurt) and the German Austrians, about 40 members (stressing their German nationality more than did the Central Club, but also condemning a Frankfurt supremacy); the Democratic Leftists, the Radicals, formed the smallest group; others were Poles and Independents. Schwarzenberg had so little interested himself in party politics before he headed the ministry that his secretary, Hübner, had to enlighten him on their intricacies.

[12] Vienna, too, was favorably impressed: an address, bearing the signature of 15,000 citizens, expressed confidence in the new ministry. Before the new Prime Minister could deliver his speech, an interesting constitutional point was raised by the president of the diet, Smolka. Schwarzenberg's appointment as prime minister had not been countersigned, and therefore Smolka refused to officiate unless he were confronted by a minister in good constitutional standing. Angered, Schwarzenberg hurriedly secured the counter-signature of his predecessor in office, Wessenberg. Now Smolka could open the session of the diet with

chamber that the Prime Minister faced. By imperial rescript the diet
had been "exiled" from Vienna, where the gallery and the street
could be too conveniently drawn upon to echo democracy's vocif-
erous claims, to this quiet Moravian place. At the beginning of the
delivery of his inaugural speech, Schwarzenberg showed signs of
uneasiness—he twisted his manuscript nervously—but soon he regained his composure and addressed the assembly with his habitual
icy calm. The deputies quickly realized that there was standing
before them a man of tougher caliber than that of his predecessors
Pillersdorf and Wessenberg. But only his few confidants read his
inner thoughts: *odi profanum vulgus et arceo.*

THE ACCESSION OF FRANCIS JOSEPH TO THE THRONE

A few days later, on December 2, 1848, a memorable event, the
final act of the counter-revolution, as it were, took place: the abdication of the Emperor Ferdinand and the Archduke Francis Charles,
and the accession of Francis Joseph to the throne. The men who
had rallied around the Court since the March days, with Prince
Windisch-Graetz at the head, considered it imperative, if the dynasty was to be saved, to forge all the peoples and lands of the Empire into a composite whole and bend them again to the imperial
will. The very kind Emperor, weak in mind and understanding,
was not the sovereign under whom the imperial authority could be
auspiciously restored. Nor was his brother, next in line of succession
to the throne, endowed with sufficient qualifications for coping
with the problems presented by democracy. The new times called
for active men, for the strong hands of youth, unfettered by ties
either Austrian or Hungarian. Schwarzenberg and Count Stadion
had made the abdication of the princes a condition of their acceptance of the posts of prime minister and minister of the interior,
respectively. Abdication did not, therefore, brook delay. Neither
the Emperor nor his brother, Archduke Francis Charles, however,
consented to the renunciation of the throne as readily as had been

serenity; he had repaired the defect in constitutional law. K. Ostaszewski-Barański, *Rok
Złudzeń,* p. 451.

expected by their consorts. The Emperor tenaciously clung to his
shadowy power, just as his learned ancestor Rudolph II (1576–
1612), although he had considered governing an unpleasant inter-
ruption of his studies in art and science, had made supreme efforts to
regain his throne after his forced abdication. It took all the persuasive power of his pious and devoted wife, Empress Maria Anna, the
daughter of King Victor Emanuel I of Sardinia, to induce the Emperor to yield to the inevitable.[13] Even the Archduchess Sophia,
Francis Joseph's beloved mother, the strong-willed and highly
gifted, but more temperamental than discerning, Bavarian princess,
grimly determined upon sacrificing the rights of her husband and
relinquishing her own imperial ambitions in favor of her son, almost
failed in her role as Egeria.

The preparations for the change in sovereigns required the solution of troublesome constitutional questions; numerous manifestos,
statements, and declarations had to be framed. One difficulty was,
for instance, that the various Austrian lands had different laws cov-
ering the coming of age of the sovereign. But the wealth of ex-
pedients at the disposal of the inventive and mobile mind of the
minister of justice, Dr. Bach—qualifications which ingratiated him
with his Prime Minister—never failed to disentangle the most intricate legal situations. Immediately before the solemn act of abdication, the Emperor, upon ministerial advice, declared Archduke
Francis of age.

At eight in the morning, on December 2, 1848, the imperial
family, Field Marshals Windisch-Graetz and Jellačić, and the highest ranking state officials assembled in the archbishop's palace at
Olmütz. The purpose of the ceremonial gathering was known to
only a few—not even the future Emperor's brothers had been acquainted with the historic act in preparation. The scene that followed was short, gripping, and for the uninitated breath-taking.
"It has been the motto of Our Government to be a protector of the

[13] In the last moment, just before he was supposed to enter the room where the abdication ceremony was to take place, the Emperor had a fit of stubbornness. The Landgravine
Fürstenberg, the Empress' lady-in-waiting, had to do a lot of cajoling and a bit of pushing
before His Majesty was in the room.

law," so spoke the Emperor to his peoples for the last time; "it has been its aim to promote the welfare of its peoples. But the impact of events, the unmistakable and conclusive desire for a far-reaching and comprehensive modification of constitutional forms, which we have endeavored to initiate in March of this year, have, however, convinced us that younger shoulders are needed to foster the lofty work and to bring it to fruitful completion." [14] Then Prince Schwarzenberg, in a loud but trembling voice, read the documents of abdication to which the main persons involved in the mournful drama affixed their signatures. When the new sovereign sank on one knee before his uncle, the Emperor Ferdinand, in a scarcely audible tone, uttered these extemporaneous, simple, and touching words: "God bless you. Bear yourself bravely. God will protect you. It is done gladly." A few hours later Archduke Francis, who wisely assumed the name of Francis Joseph, in memory of Emperor Joseph II, rode beside the coach that drove the departing Emperor and Empress to the railroad station where they entrained for Prague. Here, in the *Hradčany,* the palace of the Bohemian kings, the Emperor died in 1875, at the age of eighty-two.

In the afternoon Prince Schwarzenberg read the manifesto of the new Emperor to the hastily convoked diet at Kremsier. It began with these ingratiating words:

Convinced of the need and value of the institutions expressive of the spirit of the age, we enter with due confidence on the path leading to a salutary transformation and rejuvenation of the monarchy as a whole. On the basis of genuine liberty, on the basis of equality of all the nations of the realm and of the equality before the law of all its citizens, and of participation of those citizens in legislation, our Fatherland may enjoy a resurrection to its old greatness and a new force. Determined to maintain the splendor of the Crown undimmed and the Monarchy as a whole undiminished, but ready to share our rights with the representatives of our peoples, we count on succeeding, with the blessing of God and in understanding with our peoples, in uniting all the regions and races of the monarchy in one great state.[15]

[14] Helfert, *Geschichte Österreichs vom Ausgange des Wiener October–Aufstandes 1848,* III, 333.

[15] Redlich, *Emperor Francis Joseph of Austria,* pp. 32–33.

The diet's president, Smolka, enthusiastically greeted the address in the name of the profoundly impressed deputies with the words, "Long live the Constitutional Emperor Francis Joseph." In the country, as may be expected, the abdication created a sensation. As the official reason for the change in sovereigns, the Emperor's ill health was given, contrary to the Empress' understanding with Prince Windisch-Graetz that the proclamation should assign as motive the condemnation of the revolution. Stadion and Bach, however, recommended for Francis Joseph's first proclamation a document that abandoned patriarchal absolutism and in modern terms promised the reign of a constitutional monarch. The Prime Minister deemed it prudent to follow the course suggested by his colleagues, since democracy paraded too plainly in the land to be treated harshly from the beginning. A protagonist of the state's authority, he was not interested in constitutional forms, but his great intelligence and sharp political acumen counseled him not to rely on bayonets at once, although, no doubt, he secretly sided with the old school. It is fallacious to assume that at this period he planned to restore absolutism and thus cunningly prompted his young Emperor to start his rule with a lie on his lips. Assuredly, he was firmly resolved to oppose the tenets of European revolution and of Western democracy. But as a Tudor or Stuart king ruled with parliament if he could and in spite of parliament if he must, so Schwarzenberg would have governed with a parliament if he could, and only in spite of a parliament or without a parliament if he thought the interests of the dynasty or the state so demanded. It is only due to circumstances—chiefly, the radicalism of the Kremsier diet, the autocracy created for the Emperor by Baron Kübeck, and Schwarzenberg's early death in 1852—that he ultimately did not come to terms with a parliament, as Napoleon III and Bismarck did, influenced by ideas akin to his.

The Emperor accompanied his elevation to the throne with the remark, "Goodby, youth!" and, indeed, it was a life of "endless toil and never-ending woe" that fate had in store for him. His Prime

Minister, in furtherance of the proclamation of December 2, had now to give part of his attention to the framing of a constitution.

THE KREMSIER CONSTITUTION AND THE DICTATED CONSTITUTION OF MARCH 4, 1849

Deliberations concerning the Future Austrian Constitution

It was a bizarre situation that simultaneously at Olmütz and at Kremsier, by the government and by the representatives of the people, a constitution was being drafted for Austrian lands. It seems more grotesque yet that at a third place, Frankfurt, constitution makers were drawing Austria into the field of their activities. The reason for the independent action of the government was the acceptance of fundamental rights by the diet, especially of paragraph one: "All political rights emanate from the people." The very enunciation of a doctrine expressive of the revolutionary origin of the popular representatives assembled at Kremsier aroused the ire of Schwarzenberg and Windisch-Graetz. On the plea of Count Stadion, the deputies eliminated the offensive paragraph; they probably recognized that they had formulated a principle in glaring contrast with the facts, since they had set up claims against a Crown whose army had just reconquered Italy and quelled the riots west of the Leitha. Nevertheless, Schwarzenberg's mind was now definitely made up concerning this particular parliament, the "miserable Chamber" and its "dangerous and wretched" members. On January 20, 1849, even before the organizational part of the constitution was discussed by the diet, he acquainted the cabinet with his decision to dissolve the Kremsier parliament.[16]

In view of the clash of philosophies, collaboration between the government and the deputies in drafting the constitution would at best have been difficult, but it might not have been impossible. In deference to the Prime Minister's wishes, however, Stadion and Bach appeared before the diet only sporadically, although the former kept

[16] See the minutes of the ministerial conference of January 20, 1849, reproduced in Redlich, *Das österreichische Staats- und Reichsproblem*, Annex, p. 86.

in touch with some of the leading deputies. The passive resistance of
the ministry to the diet's work became transparent. The Pole
Smolka, the president of the diet, asked ironically, "Why expend
any efforts? Do you really think that our proposed constitution will
be accepted and executed?" In the same vein the well-known German author, Gustav Freytag, spoke of the "sad comedy" that was
played to a finish at Kremsier.[17] The reaction of the deputies to the
ministry's attitude was mirrored in their increasingly radical temper and the insertion of constitutional provisions curtailing the
powers of their masters. Yet on one aspect of the matter the two
hostile camps agreed, divergent as their political tenets otherwise
were: the Habsburg lands did not constitute a "state" according to
modern concepts; something entirely new had to be created to take
the place of the shattered dynastic organization that had been Maria
Theresa's. But while the diet was laying a new foundation for the
cisleithan parts of the Habsburg lands only, the ministry's aim was
to establish the unity of the entire realm through a written constitution flowing from the will of the Crown and thus to bring into being
a new Austrian Empire, embracing all its lands.

As to the other basic ideas that should govern the new constitution, no unanimity prevailed in government circles. Prince
Windisch-Graetz, who had received from the old regime the privilege of sanctioning any constitution to be promulgated, yearned for
the restoration of the political rule of the nobles. A stanch aristocrat,
he expected the estate-owning nobility to be recalled to leadership
in the crownlands and their subdivisions. In this order the center of
gravity would have been placed in provincial diets only loosely
united by a severely restricted imperial senate. On the other hand,
Stadion, the father of what was to become the dictated constitution
of March 4, 1849, intended to create a centralized state, governed
by a well-disciplined bureaucracy, but embellished with liberal
trimmings. As the statesman of the middle class and the representative of the credo of the German bourgeoisie, he needed a parliament
made up of members of the propertied and intellectual strata of

[17] Bibl, *Der Zerfall Österreichs*, II, 176.

society. The difference of opinion between these schools of thought was irreconcilable. Minister Bruck was sent to Budapest to persuade the commander-in-chief, then conducting his campaign against the Hungarian insurrectionists, to give his consent to the constitution as projected by the cabinet, but he failed in his effort. Four ministers, those of a liberal hue, Stadion, Bach, Krauss, and Thinnfeld, handed in their resignations, which the Emperor, upon Schwarzenberg's advice, refused. The Prime Minister now had to make a decision in favor of one or the other doctrine. In principle he shared the ideas of his brother-in-law about liberalism. Thus, Windisch-Graetz scorned Stadion's "fabrication" as "utopian and bad"; Schwarzenberg, in the circle of his intimates, derisively spoke of "modish bagatelles," of the "trumpery of modern ideas," and of "the misconstitution or the dirt-constitution." [18] On one important point, however, the views of the two princes varied widely. While Windisch-Graetz wanted to reconstitute Austria on an aristocratic-feudal basis, Schwarzenberg desired unity of thought, purpose, and action throughout the entire Empire. For him the Monarchy should supply a model of corporate union, not merely a composite structure in assorted aristocratic styles. Local singularities were incompatible with this orderly concept of a realm whose civilization was to be poised on the notion of the Throne and whose existence was to depend on bayonets, a bureaucracy recruited from talent, wherever it could be found, and an alliance with the Russian Czar. In this pattern there was no space for the nobility unless it could be utilized for the organic whole. Besides, he held so low an opinion of the capacities of the Austrian aristocracy that he refused to create a chamber of lords. His letter of February 11, 1849, addressed to Windisch-Graetz, expresses this view in a language far from flattering to his compeers. He wrote:

It would be a simple matter to give the new constitution an aristocratic coloring, but I consider it impossible to instill into our aristocracy true life and much needed resiliency, because to this end not only respectable people are required, but also a politically trained, well organized and cou-

18 Redlich, *Emperor Francis Joseph of Austria*, p. 77.

rageous class. This class we lack competely. I do not know of more than
twelve men of our class in the entire Monarchy who could in the present
circumstances serve profitably in an upper chamber. In my opinion, an
institution which does not fulfill its purpose—representation of the conservative principle—could only weaken the government and render its task
more difficult.[19]

The Polish and Hungarian nobles were looked upon with suspicion by Schwarzenberg as potential rebels. Upon his orders, Bach
drew up a memorial designed to show that a composition of the
imperial diet according to the Windisch-Graetz plan would inelucta-
bly lead to the dominant position of separatist and nationalistic elements. This argument was based on solid foundation, as the con-
temporaneous events clearly furnished the evidence. In fact, only
a generation later the Bohemian aristocracy, too, hoisted the banner
of federalism in defense of its own privileges against centralistic
liberalism and its prerogatives. Schwarzenberg now entrusted his
secretary, Hübner, with the mission of submitting to the marshal
Bach's memorial and a redrafted constitution, in which the rights of
parliaments had been somewhat curtailed. By this time Windisch-
Graetz's operations in Hungary had proved unsuccessful, and his
conduct of the campaign was severely criticized in Vienna. Evidently aware of the fact that his position was no longer strong
enough to maintain his veto against a prime minister who, more than
anyone else, had the Emperor's ear, the commander-in-chief withdrew his opposition. The first obstacle to conferring a constitution by
imperial decree was thereby removed.

Divergences of opinion within the ministry were ironed out without difficulty. Usually Bach's great ability to mesh conflicting ideas
into a convenient compromise proved to be an excellent attribute.
Thus Stadion, an admirer of the French administrative system, had
originally planned to divide a unitary state into counties compara-
ble with the French *départements* (although his counties were given
greater autonomy than the French subdivisions), but he was persuaded to respect the historical development of the Monarchy by

[19] Bibl, *Der Zerfall Österreichs*, II, 186.

recognizing individual "crownlands"—a term which the various kingdoms and other Habsburg possessions now received for the first time.[20] With the exception of one important amendment—the emergency paragraph—the elder statesman, Baron Kübeck, who attended the ministerial sittings as a consultant, suggested only minor changes. When a minister ventured into a field in which he was not an expert, Schwarzenberg knew how to check want of wisdom. For instance, when Bruck, a competent economist, but a poor constitutional lawyer, recommended the adoption of the Norwegian constitution for Austria, the Prime Minister shut his snuff box with a click, and that was the end of the project.[21]

"The Stadion constitution" of March 4, 1849, a work of broad sweep, was in part inspired by the Kremsier constitution.[22] As both documents, destined to remain drafts, furnished valuable material to the bureaucracy and the political parties of a later generation, a brief analysis, as well as a comparison between them, is fruitful.

The Kremsier Constitution

These first lines of the poem "Der Reichstag" reflect the judgment of a political commentator of the day, Franz Grillparzer.[23]

> Wohlan! Werft um, reisst ein! macht euch nur laut!
> Verkennt der Gottheit stillgeschäft'gen Finger,
> Und all woran Jahrhunderte gebaut,
> Erklärt es als der Willkür Sklavenzwinger.

One less conservative than the celebrated Austrian poet might accuse the Kremsier deputies of political astigmatism when they wrote their fundamental rights and organizational provisions. They should have realized that the hour of democracy's responsibility had not yet fully struck and that the Crown would never voluntarily consent to relinquish the motive power of the ship of state.

According to the Kremsier draft of the diet's committee, unan-

[20] Redlich, *Das österreichische Staats- und Reichsproblem,* p. 354.
[21] Josef Alexander Graf von Hübner, *Ein Jahr meines Lebens,* p. 341.
[22] The constitutional laws of this period are conveniently found in Bernatzik's compilation, *Die österreichischen Verfassungsgesetze,* 2d ed.
[23] *Gedichte,* ed. by August Sauer, Erster Teil, p. 234.

imously accepted on March 4, 1849, Austria formed a constitutional monarchy.[24] The old societal structure, "built over centuries,"
was torn down. The emperor, the head of the executive power, had
only a suspensive veto of the laws; a bill, twice proposed and twice
vetoed, entailed the automatic dissolution of the house of representatives, but when the new diet accepted the contested bill, the measure
became law. Titles of nobility were abolishd, in utter disregard of
the fact that the aristocracy had played an important part in Austrian history. The Roman Catholic Church lost its character as the
state religion. Each denomination was granted administrative autonomy, but the right to appoint church elders was conferred upon
ecclesiastical districts and synods.

Parliament consisted of two chambers, a house of representatives
directly elected by voters at least twenty-four years of age and
paying a minimum tax rate of five florins. Deputies had to be
twenty-eight years of age and were elected for three years. The
Länderkammer, the second chamber, elected for six years, was made
up of deputies chosen by the provincial diets and one deputy by the
counties (*Kreise*), into which the larger *Länder* were divided according to national differentiations. The proposed composition of
parliament ingeniously came to terms with the problem of nationality. The majority of the house would necessarily have been predominantly Slavic, although the electoral law favored the Germans
in urban districts; on the other hand, the equal representation of the
fourteen *Länder,* maintained in their historic positions, would have
worked out to the benefit of the German population, this advantage
being somewhat lost again through the representation of the counties. The historian is struck by the remarkable phenomenon that
the various nationalities reached a compromise among themselves
on the intricate issue concerning how they wanted to live together,
although, or perhaps because, neither the Crown nor the nobility
nor the clergy acted as mediator. Evidently the people desired to
erect a strong bulwark in the shape of a powerful diet against a

[24] Eisenmann, *Le compromis Austro-Hongrois de 1867,* p. 129.

bureaucratic and epauletted government, which appeared to them more dangerous than a near-by alien nationality.

The Kremsier draft-constitution endowed the *Länder* with a degree of autonomy in matters of agriculture, education, and public welfare, but presumption of competence was in favor of the Empire. Therefore, the constitution showed centralistic features which in a later period would have been totally unacceptable to the non-German nationalities. The governors of the *Länder*, appointed by the emperor, were responsible to the individual diets (in contrast to the constitution of 1867, modeled in a good many other respects on the Kremsier constitution), just as the ministers were responsible to the *Reichstag*. Below, the powers of the individual *Länder* were restricted by those of the counties, and at the base of the pyramid by the autonomous rights of the communes. Thus, with regard to the part of the proposed constitution dealing with the structure of the Empire, the diet exhibited moderation and vision, as evidenced by the arrangements concerning the relationship of the provinces to the state and the nationalities to the Empire.[25]

On March 2, 1849, the committee members, adorned with the new tri-colored (white-red-gold) emblems, proudly entered the diet to announce to the thrilled assembly that the task of drafting the constitution was finished. The deputies had decided to consider the committee's product the be-all and end-all of national organization and to accept it in one sitting, possibly on March 15, the anniversary of Emperor Ferdinand's promise of the grant of a constitution. But this plan was fated to remain the airy fabric of a dream.

[25] On February 8, 1849, Radetzky sent an address to Vienna in which his soldiers declared themselves ready to form a protecting wall between the throne and the diet (Menzel, *Geschichte der Deutschen bis auf die neuesten Tage*, p. 268). Not much importance can be attached to soldiers' addresses. How voluntary are they? One is reminded of the amusing story which Stanislas de Girardin (*Mémoires*, p. 272) tells about a French general haranguing his troops: "Camarades, il est question de nommer Bonaparte consul à vie. Les opinions sont libres; entièrement libres; cependent je dois vous prévenir que le premier d'entre vous qui ne votera pas pour le consulat à vie, je le ferai fusiller à la tête de son régiment. Vive la Liberté!"

The government was, of course, aware of the diet's schemes. In the evening of March 6 the minister of the interior, Count Stadion, accompanied by his under secretary, Alexander Helfert (the author of the monumental work dealing with Austria's history of this period), arrived unexpectedly at Kremsier in order to pronounce the dissolution of the diet. Before he took this drastic step, however, he acquainted the members of the governmental party of the cabinet's design. The deputies were shocked. Their counter-arguments, especially their proposal that the diet constitute a committee for the purpose of coming to an understanding with the government, made such a deep impression upon Stadion that he traveled back to Olmütz the same night in order once more to discuss the constitutional problem with his colleagues and eventually to ward off the contemplated *coup de main*. Already a sick man, no longer master of his nerves, he entered Bach's room, with a candle in his hand, between three and four o'clock in the morning and excitedly reported the gist of his negotiations at Kremsier. The minister of justice, amazed at Stadion's sudden faltering, brusquely replied that the minister of the interior should be the first to realize the immutability of the cabinet's decision. The dissolution of the diet was now ordered by telegraph. On the seventh, grenadiers occupied the diet's session hall; patrols circulated throughout the city to keep order. It was Schwarzenberg's intention to incarcerate those members of the diet who had been the ringleaders of the revolt of students and workers at Vienna, but Stadion forewarned them. The enraged Prime Minister then issued peremptory orders to Major Count Huyn, the commander of the troops charged with the closure of the diet, to apprehend the deputies singled out for their political radicalism, but they had fled. Huyn handled his delicate mission with tact. He managed to remain on cordial terms with the moderate deputies of the diet and invited them to tea.[26] But it might be asked whether acceptance of the *"Sklavenzwingers"* invitation by expelled representatives of the people was not an unwarranted largesse of *Gemütlichkeit*. At any rate, the Kremsier institution, a social

[26] Redlich, *Das österreichische Staats- und Reichsproblem,* Annex, pp. 101–3.

action pattern with its warp of democratic equality and woof of radical human and civic rights, was peaceably, though hastily, removed from the scene. As has been pointed out, there was passion on both sides, and "one passion is never cured by another." No doubt much harm would have been saved the Austrian state if an understanding between the government and the diet of 1849 could have been attained.

The Dictated Constitution of March 4, 1849

At the same time that the Kremsier diet was dissolved, the constitution drafted by Count Stadion was promulgated, accompanied by a hortatory imperial communication in which the deputies were scornfully criticized for their theoretical outpourings "sharply conflicting with the true conditions of the Monarchy" and, "in general, with an orderly, legal state of affairs." Its publication was precipitate, since the handiwork of the Kremsier diet had to be offset by a counteracting document. Therefore, much of the law in this constitution hung loose, to be worked out into more rigidly framed norms as circumstances might dictate. Furthermore, Schwarzenberg's foreign policy would have been jeopardized if his aim of insuring the continued existence and unity of the Habsburg Monarchy had been presented in naked absolutist form. The promulgation of a liberal constitution was the means likely to swing the still dominant liberal tendencies in Germany to Austria's side and to frustrate the plan of the party in favor of the incorporation of the western half of the Habsburg lands into the German Confederation. Evidently Austria could not lag behind a Prussia endowed with a fundamental law if the hands of the little Germans, Prussia's partisans, were not to be strengthened. From a physical standpoint the ministers were severely handicapped in holding consultations; partly they administered their departments in Vienna, partly they attended ministerial conferences under the presidency of the Emperor at Olmütz; in addition, some of them had to maintain contact with the diet at Kremsier and the commander-in-chief, Prince Windisch-Graetz, at Budapest. Schwarzenberg frankly ad-

mitted that pressure of business permitted neither "long deliberations nor deep studies" and that a mere base was laid for the rebuilding of the authority of the Throne. In fact, fundamentally it was
immaterial to him what the detailed provisions of the constitution
were, as long as his constitution creating a unitary state anticipated
the Kremsier draft with its features of decentralization.[27]

The imperial manifesto accompanying the constitution designated the "rejuvenation" of a unitary Austria, symbolized by the
adopted motto *viribus unitis,* as the life's work of the young Emperor. The intention was to draw a line of demarcation between
the era of the old loosely connected Monarchy and that of the newly
proclaimed organic and centralistic Empire. In his constitution
Count Stadion endeavored to accomplish two things: to utilize in
a parliament the fruits of the Kremsier attempt at the unification
of Austria's peoples, not merely for Austria but also for Hungary
and her dependent lands, and then to supervise the whole organization of ostensibly autonomous provinces from Vienna through the
creation of a rigidly conceived system of legislation, administration,
and jurisdiction.

Naturally, different philosophies, as exemplified by the distribu-
tion of governmental powers, guided the Kremsier and Stadion constitutions. While the former stressed democratic principles, the latter made monarchical authority the keystone of the political arch.
The emperor's suspensive veto became an absolute one. Parliament
took part in legislation and the granting of taxes, but was subjected
to stringent restrictions. First of all, the legislative power of the
Crown was maintained until the convocation of the chambers,
although legislative acts so promulgated were to be of only provisional validity until their final examination by the people's representatives. In cases of crisis the Crown kept the prerogative of
enacting laws independently, but the constitution was silent on the
point whether or not emergency acts could be set aside by parliament. The relevant paragraph 87 of the Stadion constitution was
the generative cell of the frequently used, and just as frequently
attacked, paragraph 14 that crept into the revised constitution of

[27] Bibl, *Der Zerfall Österreichs,* II, 187.

1867 in a somewhat emasculated form.[28] It is that well-known emergency provision of which in later years, during extended periods of parliamentary obstruction, the government availed itself for the purpose of keeping the state machinery in operation. A bicameral parliamentary system is also found in the dictated constitution, but the suffrage requirements were made dependent on higher tax payments by the electors than the corresponding stipulations in the Kremsier draft. Voting was open—in conformity with John Stuart Mill's precept, "under the eye and criticism of the public." The legislative period of the lower house was five years; that of the upper house, ten years. The latter, the *Länderkammer*, received two delegates from among the members of the individual diets; the other members were not delegates of the counties, as in the Kremsier constitution, but were chosen by the diets from among well-to-do subjects paying direct taxes of five hundred florins or more. Thus, although stamped with the mark of plutocracy, both houses remained elected chambers; no house of lords was created.[29]

Changes, truly revolutionary considering the times, were introduced in the economic field. A homogeneous entity forming one solid customs union for the whole Empire was set up. All citizens were permitted freely to change their domicile within the imperial borders. Now, for the first time in Austria's history, they could acquire real estate in any part of the Empire and choose their occupation.

If the Reichstag at Vienna suffered a *capitis diminutio* at the hands of the Schwarzenberg cabinet compared with the status under the Kremsier constitution, it is not surprising that the individual diets in Austria's different kingdoms and provinces, built on estates, did not fare any better. The constitutions of the various *Länder* were abrogated, with one exception. The Hungarian constitution was recognized in principle, but it had to be in harmony with the dictated imperial constitution. Consequently, laws of the Empire took precedence over provincial law. Stripped of camouflage, even the prescriptions concerning Hungary spelled the loss

[28] *Ibid.*, p. 188.
[29] Redlich, *Das österreichische Staats- und Reichsproblem*, p. 356.

of her independence. Concessions were granted to the transleithan lands only with regard to civil and penal laws; in these fields the diet of Hungary kept its autonomy, but was obliged to share it with the diets of Croatia and Transylvania. Administrative measures, taken by the individual diets, could be amended or set aside by the imperial government. In this respect, as in the case of paragraph 87, the way was laid wide open to apocalyptic rides of a dictatorial government. In the last paragraph of his political testament Stadion anticipated the wish of its executors to administer Austria's fortune in a way different from the one he had willed: a qualified majority of both houses were empowered to amend his constitution.

To comply with popular demands—*les hommes sont comme les enfants, il leur faut des hochets,* the government thought—fundamental laws guaranteeing civic and human rights according to accepted liberal standards were appended to the imperial constitution. Likewise, a press law, a municipal code, and the very important law freeing the peasantry from socage service were promulgated.[30]

The cabinet's work, designedly rejecting inherited patriarchal law and the former status of the individual *Länder,* showed liberal-nationalistic characteristics. The elements of nationalism, however, outweighed the ingredients of liberalism. In reality, a liberal constitution was the stalking horse behind which the attempt was made to erect a unitary militaristic and bureaucratic autocracy. This gigantic structure, assembled in purely mechanical fashion, did not rest on the free co-operation of the divers *Länder* and nationalities but on the loyalty of all to the dynasty and their submissiveness to the weapons of a police state. The essence of the constitutional policy pursued was succinctly expressed in these significant words of the imperial manifesto: "We confide in the bravery and the honor of Our glory-covered army."

Schwarzenberg, like Palmerston, his great antagonist in the international field, "was a statesman for the moment; he did not lay down in his closet plans to be worked out twenty years hence."[31] If one plan failed, he at once adopted another. But there was no

[30] These laws are referred to *infra,* pp. 84 *et seq.,* 102.
[31] Bagehot, *The Works,* ed. by Forest Morgan, III, 422.

need to alter the course of the ship of state in this case. Not even he could have foreseen that the Austrian lands, especially Vienna, the hotbed of the revolution of 1848, would meekly resign themselves to the "provisional" regime set up by him after Francis Joseph's accession.

SCHWARZENBERG'S HUNGARIAN POLICY

The Military Subjugation of Hungary [32]

When Francis Joseph ascended the throne, he was far from being the undisputed ruler over all his inherited dominions. In Italy the revolution had to be suppressed, and the invading army of Piedmont-Sardinia had to be conquered. In Hungary the insurrectionary movement had vitally changed the social and political system of a country that threatened to break away from the Habsburg Empire.

Briefly, the antecedent events in Transleithania were these. The Hungarian magnates, unable to resist the lower house, voluntarily relinquished a good many of their privileges, especially those relating to feudal servitudes and tithes payable by the peasants. Now the people, with the exception of the conservatives, were closely bound to the national cause under Kossuth's fiery leadership. The Hungarians demanded and received a separate ministry (March 31/April 7, 1848). Magyar nationalism was, however, striving for the ascendancy of its own race only, to the exclusion of the *partes adnexae,* Croatia and Transylvania. As a consequence, five million Serbs and two and a half million Wallachs (Roumans) rose in arms against five million Hungarians. A last attempt was made by the Vienna government to forestall a civil war by appointing General Count Lamberg commander of all transleithan troops, but he was assassinated on his arrival in the Hungarian capital. Emperor Ferdinand dissolved the Hungarian diet on October 3, 1848, and declared a state of siege for the whole country. Tacking unskillfully in the revolutionary storm, caught between the Vienna gale and the bois-

[32] A good description of the invasion of Hungary is given by Coxe, *History of the House of Austria,* IV, civ *et sqq.*

terous Budapest sea, the Wessenberg cabinet sank to the paltriness
of day-to-day maneuvering.

Calamitous uncertainties were dispelled when Prince Schwarzenberg became prime minister. Now the burning issue between the
two halves of the Empire became clear-cut. The Hungarians insisted on the independence of their country, as sanctioned by the
April laws of 1848; they recognized neither the abdication of Ferdinand and Francis Charles nor the accession of Francis Joseph. It
was legitimate for Kossuth to take a hopeful view of the aspirations
of his country, but unfortunately for his country he had just as
much vanity as he wanted understanding. He woefully underestimated his Austrian adversary's mental endowment and dauntless spirit as well as the manifold resources at his disposal. Felix
Schwarzenberg had not become the first minister of his young master in order to preside over the dissolution of the Empire. He was
determined upon the transformation of Hungary into an Austrian
province and the destruction of Hungary's old historic rights, including those of "loyal" Croatia and Transylvania. Thus, there was
no common understanding in fundamentals, no commendable restraint of give and take on either side. The result was storm and
stress, with tragic consequences.

On December 15, 1848, Prince Windisch-Graetz crossed the
Hungarian border to subdue a rebellious people. The nucleus of the
rebel troops, its best combat force, was formed by the Magyar troops
of the imperial army, twenty-one battalions and ten regiments of
hussars. The plight of the officers' corps was pitiable. They were torn
in their loyalty between adherence to Magyar nationalism and
faithfulness to the Emperor. They had taken the oath to the constitutional king of Hungary and were under orders issued by Emperor
Ferdinand's ministers. On the other hand, if they kept their oath to
the king of Hungary, they were now considered traitors in Vienna.
This tragic conflict, the result of the amazingly inept policy of the
Pillersdorf and Wessenberg cabinets, was insoluble. Pricked forward
by the spur of ambition or galvanized by the new credo of liberty,
about seven hundred officers, most of them from the lower ranks,

joined the revolutionary cause. A good many of them made a distinguished career, but in the end death before a firing squad or on the gallows, or long incarceration was their lot. They had followed a mirage luring to disaster.

In the last weeks of the year 1848 Hungary's military situation seemed hopeless. From the west and the north the imperial troops started an invasion; Transylvania was in revolt; in the south the Serbs were attacking the Magyar troops. In these circumstances Windisch-Graetz's expedition promised to be nothing more than an extended maneuver. As a matter of fact, he had occupied the capital on January 5, 1849, but instead of exploiting the confusion in the ranks of the insurrectionists and pouncing upon their still unorganized forces, he injudiciously remained inactive in Budapest and waited until he, the victor, was attacked. In the battle of Kapolna (February 26, 1849) the Pole Dembinski, a distinguished general in Poland's fight against Russia in 1830 and the temporary commander-in-chief of the Magyar forces, was defeated, yet the encounter—in view of the lack of *élan* and the slight casualties on both sides, the name "battle" for this conflict is a hyperbole—remained undecisive. Fortune, however, soon smiled upon the Hungarian arms. The Austrians were driven out of Transylvania; the Hungarian Görgey defeated the Austrian General Götz at Waizen (April 10) and General Wohlgemuth at Nagy-Sarlo (April 19) and relieved the key fortress of Komorn (April 22), thus menacing the Austrians in the rear.

Prince Windisch-Graetz proved in Hungary that he did not possess Radetzky's brilliant generalship. A *cunctator* without Fabius's sound strategic reason for his hesitancy, he had brought a great monarchy to grief in its struggle with one of the Emperor's patrimonial dominions. In part, his faltering policy is explained by the fact that he was more of a conservative statesman than a field-marshal. After a few military successes he hoped to be able to ban the radical spirit of Kossuth and his followers and restore Hungary, with the help of the conservative Magyar nobility, to its former position. This policy, as has been pointed out, ran diametrically

counter to that of the Prime Minister. A severe conflict between
the two brothers-in-law, brought to a climax because of the dictator's failure on the battlefield, now became inevitable. The defender
of historic constitutions based on estates and aristocratic rights
found himself in sharpest opposition to the creator of a unitary
realm to be held together by the military and the bureaucracy.[33]
Windisch-Graetz, this "Alba," this "Brennus," as he was called
during the suppression of the revolution in Austria, stopped short
of disturbing the great conservative landowners and of international
involvements. Like Napoleon, Schwarzenberg thought *en révolu-
tion le moyen le plus doux, c'est le canon,* and he did not distinguish between owners of latifundia and radical leaders unwilling to recognize Vienna's supremacy.

Upon the Prime Minister's demand, the military dictator was
dismissed by the Emperor on April 14, 1849.[34] This step caused
Francis Joseph "endless pain," but, as he explained his action to the
savior of his dynasty, it was dictated by "an imperative military
necessity and a sense of duty as a ruler." [35] Inferentially and sig-
nificantly, Schwarzenberg's policy in Hungarian affairs had triumphed over that of Windisch-Graetz. "Kinema," as the Greeks
call a military excursion into politics, had not, however, come to
an end.

In Hungary things went from bad to worse for the imperial
cause. Kossuth answered the imposition of the constitution of March
4, 1849, by convoking a rump parliament at Debreczin. In scornful
defiance of the wiser heads in the Magyar councils and of his own
generals, he proudly declared Hungary and her dependent lands an
independent state and the dynasty of Habsburg-Lorraine dethroned
(April 14, 1849). The young officers trained in the imperial army

[33] Schwarzenberg's plans for a unitary, bureaucratic, military state are discussed, *infra,*
pp. 98 *et seq.*

[34] Since his relations to Windisch-Graetz were dictated by family considerations,
Schwarzenberg informed the commander-in-chief of his dismissal in a more reserved tone
than he, the prime minister, would otherwise have done.—Müller, *Feldmarschall Fürst
Windischgrätz,* p. 232.

[35] Redlich, *Emperor Francis Joseph of Austria,* p. 55n.

continued to beat their own generals. Arthur von Görgey, a man of thirty years and formerly an officer of engineers in the Austrian army, took Budapest on May 21.

Schwarzenberg was now confronted by a momentous decision. The Austrian army in Hungary was not strong enough to suppress the Magyar revolution. The new imperial commander, Baron Haynau, who had replaced the incapable Baron Welden after Windisch-Graetz's recall, had only 60,000–70,000 troops at his disposal to break down the resistance of an army of 80,000 men. One escape from the difficulty was open to the Prime Minister. He could effect a reconciliation with Sardinia or at least order a defensive war in Italy, where Radetzky had decisively defeated Charles Albert at Novara (March 29), but Venice remained unconquered. Although Schwarzenberg's conduct of office, according to his motto *numquam retrorsum*, was distinguished by unswerving determination in the pursuit of his ends, he possessed a remarkable elasticity of mind in changing his methods to suit the occasion. Under the conditions a *volte-face* on his part would not have been surprising. In the Italian affair he considered it more expedient, however, to continue on his charted course and at once to aim at the reconquest of the whole of the Lombardo-Venetian kingdom. The distasteful alternative to this policy was an appeal to a foreign power for help. Only after some time could Schwarzenberg's pride reconcile itself to this step. Obviously a request for foreign assistance was an open admission of weakness, but since "the existence of the Monarchy was at stake," [36] he believed it necessary to take it. Which power should now be appealed to—Prussia or Russia? The crafty plan of Frederick William's aide-de-camp, Leopold von Gerlach,[37] that Austria should permit the Hohenzollern state to conclude a military alliance with the German princes in consideration of Prussia's aid with a united German force of 20,000–30,000 men in the sub-

---

[36] Schwarzenberg in the cabinet sitting of April 21, 1849. Hugo Kerchnawe, "Feldmarschall Alfred Windisch-Graetz und die Russenhilfe 1849," *Mitteilungen des österreichischen Instituts für Geschichtsforschung*, XLIII (1929) p. 369.

[37] *Denkwürdigkeiten aus dem Leben Leopold von Gerlachs*, II, 61.

jugation of Hungary was nowhere taken seriously.[38] To strike such
a bargain would not have been in harmony with Schwarzenberg's
sense of honor, nor would he have felt inclined to sacrifice Austria's
aspirations to supremacy in Germany. Thus, help could only come
from Russia, and the Russian Czar proved to be more idealistic than
the Prussians. Nicholas, who regarded himself as the God-appointed
guardian of monarchical and conservative institutions in Europe
and the protector of his young fellow emperor on the Austrian
throne, demanded no reward, not even that choice morsel Constantinople.[39] He was not guided by purely unselfish motives, however,
for he was apprehensive of the formation of a Polish legion in Hungary, a force which, joined to the Hungarian army, might in the
future menace his Polish kingdom.

On May 1, 1849, the Russian decision to grant aid was officially
announced at Vienna. The Czar's troops, 130,000 men strong, under the command of Prince Paskevitch, quickly entered Hungary
through Galicia. The numerical disproportion between the com-
batants was now too great to leave any doubt as to the outcome of
the struggle. The net was drawn in from two other sides: General
Haynau penetrated into Hungary from the west with 80,000 men,
and the Croat General Jellačić, with 35,000–40,000 men, from the
south. Haynau defeated Görgey at Zsigard and Komorn (July 11),
occupied Budapest, and, after forcing a passage over the Theiss on
August 3, routed the Hungarian army under Dembinski at Temes-
var (August 9). Görgey, unable to join the Dembinski corps with
the remainder of his troops, was hopelessly sandwiched in between
the Russian and Austrian armies. As a general, Haynau merits the
unstinted gratitude of his country, for his victorious operations had
scattered the Hungarian army and determined the result before the
Russians were actually engaged in a major battle. Austria's pride
was therefore deeply wounded when Görgey capitulated at Világos
on August 13, not to the Austrian General Haynau, but to the Rus-

---

[38] Kerchnawe, "Feldmarschall Alfred Windisch-Graetz und die Russenhilfe 1849,"
Mitteilungen des österreichischen Instituts für Geschichtsforschung, p. 331n.

[39] In 1850 Russia received from Austria 2⅓ million florins for her military assistance.
—Beer, *Die Finanzen Österreichs im XIX. Jahrhundert*, p. 20.

sian General Paskevitch, who triumphantly reported to the Czar: "Hungary lies at Your Majesty's feet." The fate of the captured Hungarian officers would probably have been milder if Görgey had not aroused Haynau's and the government's indignation. After all, it was the Austrian rule against which Hungary had revolted; it was the House of Habsburg-Lorraine that had been excluded from the Hungarian throne, and the officers and soldiers, enlisted by the Hungarian committee of national defense, had forsworn allegiance to the Austrian Emperor. "The Hyena of Brescia," Baron Haynau,[40] a son of the Elector of Hesse, a gifted, reckless general, but a sanguinary tyrant with a morbid disposition, administered terrible punishment to the captured officers and leaders of the insurrection. "The Bloody Assize of Arad" condemned thirteen generals to death, of whom four were shot and nine hanged; 386 officers were imprisoned from one to twenty years (later amnesties reduced the terms of imprisonment); 114 civilians were put to death, and 1,765 were incarcerated. Kossuth and the generals Bem and Dembinski found refuge in Turkish territory. Görgey, protected by the Czar, was banished to Klagenfurt. Among the prominent civilians executed was Count Lewis Batthyany, the first prime minister after the March revolution.[41] Throughout the conflict he had tried to mediate between the Vienna government and the revolutionary forces. No execution was more deeply resented than his; it was incompatible certainly with charity, possibly with justice, and probably with

[40] In English the name Haynau, when linked with hyena, is suggestive of a *nomen odiosum;* in German there is no unhappy correlation between Haynau and *Hyäne.* Haynau was given this epithet on account of his cruel treatment of prisoners at Brescia.

[41] See Angyal, "Der Hochverratsprozess des Grafen Ludwig Batthyany," in *Jahrbuch des Instituts für ungarische Geschichtsforschung,* pp. 354 *et sqq.* Batthyany himself seems to have been irrationally reckless about ordering hangings. When Count Edmund Zichy, Master of the Horse of the Archduke Palatin's household and custodian of the diet, wanted to have some Hungarian deputies arrested, Batthyany, apprised of the loyal Austrian's intentions by the indiscreet Archduke Stephan, told him: "You want to arrest us? We shall hang you." Naturally, Count Zichy left the Archduke's entourage at once. Wirkner, *Meine Erlebnisse,* p. 219. A statesman who had no sympathy with Batthyany's fate was Bismarck. "Can the execution of one man constitute retribution even on this earth for sacked cities, devastated provinces, and a murdered population whose blood calls out to the Emperor of Austria that God has given him the sword of authority?" he asked. *Fürst Bismarck's Briefe an seine Braut und Gattin,* p. 172.

vision. The whim of destiny—*le hasard, l'incognito de la providence*—dictated the fate of some of the captives. Count Leiningen, Queen Victoria's cousin, for instance, had asked for a transfer from Hungary to another Austrian regiment, but, his request having been refused, he was caught in the revolutionary maelstrom and paid the death penalty.

The bloodshed at Arad stirred the emotions of Western countries. In England, particularly, animosities against Baron Haynau lingered which later led to one of Lord Palmerston's indiscretions.[42] It should be recalled, however, that the Hungarian revolutionary government had acted with the same severity against its foe and, perhaps, had even indulged in more hideous doings. Its great strategist, General Görgey, had set a pernicious example by condemning Count Eugene Zichy to death for having communicated with General Jellačić. "Blood will have blood, revenge beget revenge"—indeed, the Magyars paid dearly for the folly of their intransigent leaders.

Prince Schwarzenberg informed the cabinet on October 26, 1849, that the Emperor had ordered Generals Haynau (in Hungary proper) and Wohlgemuth (in Transylvania) to put an end to executions. In principle he had approved of a severe rule in Hungary up to that date, since he considered intimidation an indispensable means of subduing Transleithania. For the same reason he advised Francis Joseph to reply to the Czar's appeal for a merciful treatment of the Hungarian officers and men that he would gladly grant pardons to his insurrectionary subjects if he could follow his feelings only, but that the welfare of the state imposed upon him harshness of action. Schwarzenberg's frequently quoted remark,[43] allegedly made at the time when clemency was recommended to him, "Yes, yes, a very good idea, but we must have a bit of hanging first," has not been substantiated. Offended by the reckless and insubordinate despotism of Haynau's warped mentality, the Prime Minister relieved him of his command in 1850. Radetzky once remarked

---

[42] See *infra*, p. 183.
[43] For instance, by Redlich, *Emperor Francis Joseph of Austria*, p. 62.

about the general when he served under him in Italy: "Haynau is like a razor; after it has been used, it should be placed back in its case." [44] Did Schwarzenberg put the "razor" away too late? As events have shown, it would have been a more enlightened policy if the advice of the German-Jewish poet Karl Isidor Beck, pleading to the Emperor for forgiveness in behalf of his adopted country, Hungary, had been adopted.

> Nun kleide dich festlich, zu werben um Minne,
> Doch nimmer im Stahl!
> Blühender, Brausender, Ununterjochter,
> Wirb um die ungrische Königstochter,
> Reich und rosig und feurig im Sinne,
> O, schön ist die Freite, herrlich die Wahl!
> Du konntest ihr Land mit Helden bekriegen,
> Ihr Herz, das musst du selber besiegen.[45]

Centralization and the Germanization of Hungary [46]

Thus, imperial authority had been effectively established in Hungary, and Schwarzenberg's aim had been attained: the country was ready to be cast into the narrow mold of a centralized unitary state. At first it seemed as if the Vienna government wanted to follow the advice of the poet quoted and "conquer the heart of the royal Hungarian bride." The preliminary administrative ordinance regulating the new order of things in Hungary was that of October 17, 1849, a lucid and well-balanced piece of work, as were all legislative acts that emanated from Dr. Bach's pen. Momentarily, old customs were respected. Baron Haynau remained as the commander-in-chief; Baron Geringer, an honorable, unostentatious civil servant, was attached to him as head of the civil administration. With the exception of the Banat, Hungary was still recognized as a unit, although the country was divided into five military districts, each

[44] Bibl, *Der Zerfall Österreichs*, II, 207.

[45] Quoted by Friedjung, *Österreich von 1848 bis 1860*, II, 324.

[46] On the Bach regime in Hungary see Eisenmann, *Le compromis Austro-Hongrois de 1867*, pp. 168–70 (a somewhat biased presentation, as it is unduly influenced by Magyar sources); Friedjung, *Österreich von 1848 bis 1860*, I, 368–438 (a well-balanced description); Rogge, *Österreich von Világos bis zur Gegenwart*, Vol. I (rabidly pro-Magyar).

with a general as its chief. The old counties were retained; members
of the old nobility were appointed to the higher administrative
posts. It was unavoidable that all civil servants and mayors were
crown nominees; they could not be elected according to old Hungarian custom in view of the unsettled state of affairs in the country. The officials were paid a fair salary; prior to the new regime they
had lived on mysteriously lucrative emoluments and court fees. The
use of the German language was made mandatory only for communications between the top administrators and the military commanders.

Soon, however, the government abandoned the principles laid
down by its own dictated constitution of March 4, 1849. No longer
was the unity of Hungary respected, nor were old institutions maintained. Through two series of measures, especially, it offended even
the old conservatives. One was the cutting up of Hungarian territory, and the other, the substitution of Austrian, chiefly German,
civil servants for Hungarian officials.

The Mur Island was given to Croatia. Three counties, annexed to
Hungary in 1836, were reunited with Transylvania. Much more
serious was the separation of southern Hungary (the Banat and Voi-
vodia) from Hungary proper as a reward, so it seemed to the enraged Magyars, for Serbo-Croatian revolt against the first Hungarian ministry.

A measure distressing for the Hungarian nobles was the importation of thousands of Austrian civil servants, the much-hated "Bach
hussars," so called after their frogged coats. A centralistic and absolutist regime had to end in the Germanization of the country. The
three policies were indissolubly interwoven; if one of the three
courses was posed as a premise, the other two followed automatically. Retained in their administrative and political posts, the nobles
might have tolerated a temporary military dictatorship. Living at
the expense of the state had always appeared a God-given privilege
to them; deprived of these prerogatives by bourgeois officials, they
were in danger of losing the means of their economic existence.
Their opposition to the Vienna government was therefore as much

dictated by class struggle as it was engendered by constitutional considerations. But Schwarzenberg thought very little of the Hungarian magnates. "What is the Hungarian nation?" "The Hungarian nobles," he remarked angrily to Ludwig von Wirkner, Metternich's adviser in Hungarian affairs; "they have always been rebels and are still rebels.—They must be annihilated, yes, be done away with forever." [47] Ruefully Count Dessewffy commented that Prince Schwarzenberg disliked everything Hungarian with the exception of a few beautiful Magyar women. The Magyar nobles became publicists. The most prominent writer of the national-liberal opposition, Baron Joseph Eötvös, Franz Deák's friend, published a much noticed pamphlet at that time,[48] in which he pointed out that strict co-ordination was impossible in a polyglot country like Austria and would lead to Babylonian confusion if the Danubian Monarchy lost its historic basis.

Although Bach adopted Fouché's motto, "on ne gouverne pas avec la rancune," he, like all men directed by mind only, was inflexible in his political calculations. His logical mind was attracted by French centralism, and so he concocted an all-pervading administration with a view to synthesizing the various nationalities into a common Austrian citizenry. In general, the country was administered in a modern spirit and with greater social justice by the "Bach hussars" than it had formerly been by the Hungarian nobility. Bach might not have created "institutions of political noonday," but he certainly discarded, in the language of Woodrow Wilson, "those of the half-light of political dawn." The best proof of the superior quality of his administrative machinery is that the Hungarian state in 1867 took over many of his innovations. The "sprawling, overlapping" bureaucracy, heretofore considered "a swarm of locusts ready to devour the country" and the source of financial distress, was even increased in number, but, as salaries were henceforth paid

---

[47] *Meine Erlebnisse*, p. 244.

[48] *Die Gleichberechtigung der Nationalitäten in Österreich*, 2d ed., p. 73. "Even if one credits our statesmen with all the skill which Archimedes imputed to himself, I cannot find that point on which the wonder shall be performed, simply because there is no fixed point."

to "national officials," dissatisfaction was resolved into contented-
ness.

The work of Hungary's amalgamation with the German-Austrian lands of the Habsburg dynasty was completed by the economic measures of the minister for economics, Bruck. The tariff
walls between the two halves of the Monarchy were abolished; [49]
the Austrian system of taxation was introduced into Hungary.
Some of these innovations were not calculated to make the Austrian
regime popular; taxes on wine and meat, for instance, had been unknown in the rural districts. The tobacco monopoly, particularly,
aroused indignation among the peasants, as they did not compre-
hend why they were no longer allowed to bring the fruits of their
labor to market.

After having scorned the co-operation of those elements of the
former governing classes which would have offered their services,
the government relied solely on its own forces, the army and the
bureaucracy. Order—"heaven's first law"—tranquillity, and material welfare should suffice to win the Hungarians for the imperial
causes, just as these three blessings should expand the greatness,
power, and glory of the entire nation. If national elements were
to be banished from the Hungarian administrative system, a bureaucratic machinery had to replace them that would work without
"grit in its huge rolling shafts and grinding wheels." That "grit"
was removed by recalling the capricious and despotic General Haynau and the prosaic and unpretentious Baron Geringer. Archduke
Albrecht, the strongest member of the imperial family, took over
the governor generalship with the title of military and civil governor. He hesitated at first to take orders from a minister of the
interior who had fought against him on the opposite side in Vienna
during the revolution. It speaks volumes for Bach's adaptability that
he understood how to gain the Archduke's full confidence. Finding
a fertile field in Hungary for his expansive ambition, the new governor was profoundly impressed with Bach's capacity as adminis-

[49] Cf. Sieghart, *Zolltrennung und Zolleinheit; die Geschichte der österreichisch-ungarischen Zwischenzoll-Linie.* The gains for Hungary are described on pp. 208-20.

trator. Thus, the name of the scion of the Habsburgs and that of the former revolutionary became closely linked during the Bach regime of 1851–1860.

A new provisional law of September 8, 1850, still left Hungary as a composite crownland with a governor general in Budapest, but Hungary proper was now divided into five administrative districts, (Ofen-Pest, Pressburg, Ödenburg, Kaschau, and Grosswardein), the creation of which had been foreshadowed by that of the five military districts. It seemed as if gradually all recollection of the original unity of the lands of St. Stephen's crown was to be destroyed and the former kingdom of Hungary was to be broken up into these five provinces, apart from the provinces of Croatia, Transylvania, and Southern Hungary. The heads of the five Hungarian districts in Hungary proper received their instructions, not from the Budapest office, but directly from the ministry of the interior, and they communicated their orders to subdivisions corresponding to the old counties. German became the official language in Hungary. Since the provisional law of September 8, 1850, was predicated on the execution of the provisions of the constitution of March 4, 1849, it obviously bore only a temporary character. The previous provisional law, that of October 17, 1849, faded into a *provisorissimum*. Naturally, the authority of the government was considerably harmed by these volcanoes of simmering uncertainties. Finally, on January 19, 1855 (after Schwarzenberg's death), the administration of the five districts of Hungary proper was regulated in definitive form. At that time the Austrian constitution had already been revoked, and thus the provisional administration had come to an end. During the era of the Bach regime Hungary was condemned to passive obedience.

If the government had shown no consideration for the Magyars, it could have found valuable ties in the nationalities previously annexed to Hungary, the Serbo-Croats, the Slovaks, and the Rumanians, who had remained loyal to Austria in 1849. They, too, however, including the most faithful of them, the German-Saxons of Transylvania—Prince Karl Schwarzenberg, Felix Schwarzen-

berg's cousin, was appointed their governor—forfeited their autonomy and were governed from Vienna just as autocratically as were
the other nationalities. The Croats had expected a reward for their
anti-Magyar stand—the fulfillment of their Illyrian dreams, a
Greater Croatia. The government was fortunate, however, in having in Marshal Jellačić, the popular leader of the Croats, a champion
of the Austrian cause who tacitly endorsed the new order. The bitter
truth of the situation is poignantly illustrated by the ironic consolation given by a Magyar farmer to a complaining Croat: "What
is meted out to us as a punishment is given you as a reward." [50]

The work undertaken by Schwarzenberg and Bach in Hungary is
known in history as the Bach regime, but the stamp is Schwarzenberg's. In Hungary hatred was turned against Bach, although the
impetus of the measures taken in Hungary emanated from Schwarzenberg's imperious will. Schwarzenberg was probably shielded
from attack because of his social position, his early death (Bach carried on the regime until 1860), and his more remote contact with
Hungarian affairs than that of his minister of the interior.

Schwarzenberg's Hungarian policy was a rule in the grand manner. It was presumptuous, however, because he trampled upon the
historic rights of the country and reduced human beings to ciphers
as in a mathematical equation. What is praiseworthy in his policy
is that he introduced modern efficiency into the country and,
through the promulgation of the new Austrian codes of procedure,[51]
gave it an administration of even-handed and unstained justice
between the large estate owners and their copyholders. In Austria
his internal policy was not without support. The middle classes in
the German-Slavic provinces were also convinced of the necessity
and the merit of a strong Monarchy, but Schwarzenberg went a

[50] Bibl, *Der Zerfall Österreichs,* II, 216.

[51] Schwarzenberg was indignant that the introduction of the Austrian civil code was
not supported by the enlightened part of the people, as, no doubt, the Austrian codification
was a great improvement over the old Hungarian law. He cited this recalcitrance as an
example of how even the best intentions of his government were misjudged. One of his
former best friends, Baron Josika, "almost threw him out of the window," so Schwarzenberg reported, when he mentioned to him his contemplated substitution of Austrian for
Hungarian law.—Wirkner, *Meine Erlebnisse,* pp. 241–42.

step farther. He did not credit the rejuvenated structure with sufficient political strength unless the entire Austrian Empire were the
universally determinant unity and unless this unity were ruled abso-
lutistically.[52] As was pointed out at that time, his disregard for
traditions and historic rights showed "revolutionary, democratic-
Jacobin" traits.[53] With regard to Hungary, he overestimated Austria's strength when he assumed that Austria could annex a country
of the size of the lands of St. Stephen's Crown. The Schwarzenberg
regime, and later the Bach regime even more, left keen resentment
in Hungary, since naturally the Magyars could not reconcile themselves to the break-up of their national life and the loss of their
old liberties. As a result, the whole Monarchy suffered from a deep
wound.

REFORM OF THE STATE

The Background: Military Autocracy and Financial Stringency

After the wild poetry of revolution, Austria was facing the prose
of practical problems. The old order had been restored only outwardly. Schwarzenberg was, with Bacon, aware of the fact that
"he that will not apply new remedies must expect new evils; for time
is the greatest innovator, and, of course, if time alters things to the
worse, wisdom and counsel must alter them to the better."

Rightly or wrongly, the Schwarzenberg cabinet initiated reforms
of the most incisive character, with the bold intent "to alter things
to the better." After the span of a few years by the feverish use of
all intellectual forces, an impressive piece of work was achieved, and
some of the worst defects of the Metternich system were eradicated:
a uniform nationality comprised all the inhabitants of the Austrian
Empire; a uniform tariff barrier encircled the Empire; the tax system and monopolies were extended to Hungary en bloc; justice was
separated from administration; trial by jury was introduced; the
civil service was overhauled; the communes were granted extended

[52] Srbik, *Deutsche Einheit*, II, 126.
[53] The critic was the Aulic Councillor Karl Hummelauer. See Schlitter, *Versäumte Gelegenheiten; die oktroyierte Verfassung vom 4. März 1849*, Annex XII.

autonomy; the peasants were relieved of the payments of feudal dues; education was lifted to a higher level.

The impression conveyed to foreign countries by Austrian emigrants of an exclusively despotically governed Austria—"a ship loaded with slaves, unhappy peoples who could only be freed after a shipwreck," as the poet Moriz Hartmann expressed it— is erroneous. It is remarkable, and cannot too strongly be emphasized, that this much-maligned "authoritarian" government undertook great reform works, some of which were of lasting value.

The vast reconstruction program of the Schwarzenberg cabinet took place in a military atmosphere and was severely handicapped by financial stringency. As Austria had been forged together by grape shot and the sword, it is understandable that the military maintained first position in the state. A martial spirit emanated from the Hofburg, to which the Court had returned in May, 1849. The Emperor invariably wore the uniform of a general. His Prime Minister and Foreign Minister had supposedly exchanged the sagum for the toga when taking office, but he, too, was in the habit of appearing in the white uniform of an Austrian general. A state of siege prevailed in Hungary, Italy (where military administration operated until 1857), Galicia, and in certain cities, such as Vienna, Graz, and Prague. Corps commanders were highly pleased with such a state of affairs. General Prince Khevenhüller, for instance, extolled the excellence of Galicia when he was transferred from Prague to the Polish province, a "splendid province . . . next to Hungary, the finest, for here not only the capital was under martial law" but also the whole province.[54] Great influence was wielded by the Emperor's supple and "high-tory" general aide-de-camp, Count Charles Grünne. As he handled all military personnel affairs—a function usually exercised by the military chancellery in a monarchy—he outstripped in power the rapidly changing war ministers of this period, Cordon, Gyulai (June, 1849–July, 1850), and Csorich (until 1855). The military governors of Vienna, Baron Welden

[54] Bagger, *Francis Joseph*, p. 212.

and after him Baron Kempen von Fichtenstamm,[55] governed the inhabitants of the metropolis as if no civil authorities were functioning.

Austria needed a huge military establishment in order to maintain her position as a great power. In Italy external and internal conditions were such that a large army had to be kept on a war footing, partly to protect the Empire from attacks on the part of Sardinia, and partly to suppress revolutions. In Hungary considerable forces of occupation had to be left to keep the country in submission. The large cities, Vienna especially, required large garrisons to enforce martial law. Prussia's aspirations to supremacy in Germany needed watching and called for a degree of military preparedness in that direction. After Schwarzenberg's death, the military situation became even more complicated, for his successor was foolhardy enough to abandon a pillar of his policy: Buol-Schauenstein antagonized Russia through Austria's Balkan policy and thus increased Austria's military engagements. Although during the decade from 1836 to 1845 the expenses for the armed forces remained stable around 50 million florins a year, in 1847 they increased, because of the revolution in Italy, to 61.2 million—about half as much as those of 1851 and 1852, 120.3 and 109.7 million, respectively.

The army of approximately 600,000 men was held together by an iron discipline. Corporal punishment was still meted out; young men were drafted into it for moral delinquency as if the army were a penal institution or a reformatory. More than at any time during the glorious history of the Austrian army, an Austrian regiment of this period was a melting pot of various nationalities and performed this amalgamation process surprisingly well. An army like that of Austria raised in this manner might have possessed the rationale of a refined race culture; yet whether the Austrian troops, composed as they were of heterogeneous and sometimes hostile elements (50,000 *honvéds*—Hungarian yeomanry—were included), would have

[55] His diary has been published under the title *Das Tagebuch des Polizeiministers Kempen von Fichtenstamm von 1848 bis 1859.*

proved reliable combat forces in actual warfare is questionable.
It must be conceded that the times demanded the upkeep of this
vast military organization, but it was run wastefully by the generals. Grünne, for example, promoted his favorite officers rapidly so
that the number of generals and staff officers swelled unconsciona-
bly. While ordinarily finance ministers dread to be challenged by
an inquisitive parliament, here the unique situation was created
that a much harassed treasury official was yearning for the creation
of the promised parliament as a curb on an epauletted octopus. With
the military in the saddle and the Emperor lending a ready ear to
their counsels, even a financial wizard could not have appreciably
relieved the financial stringency.

It is not surprising that the two revolutionary years, 1848 and
1849, ended with a budgetary deficit of 64 and 139.8 million florins,
respectively.[56] Austria had been bankrupt in 1811 and 1815, and
now she was again on the verge of defaulting on her obligations. At
the end of 1848, there were 345 million paper florins in circulation, and they drove out all metal currency. Bank notes were at a
heavy discount.[57] The instability of currency and inflation of credit
were green pastures upon which speculators and exporters grew fat,
but they were blanched deserts upon which people with fixed salaries and importers grew lean.

The budgetary deficits continued: that of 1850 was 77.2 million
florins (revenues being 180,288 million); that of 1851, 51.2 million (with revenues amounting to 205.76 million); that of 1852,
53.4 million. As outlays for military purposes made retrenchment
impossible, the other remedy was, of course, larger income. The
new revenue law of October 29, 1849, aimed at the collection of

[56] On budgetary conditions of this period see Beer, *Die Finanzen Österreichs im XIX.
Jahrhundert,* and *Die österreichische Handelspolitik im neunzehnten Jahrhundert;* Freiherr Czoernig von Czernhausen, *Österreichs Neugestaltung, 1848–1858;* Ritter von Hauer,
Über Österreichs Staatsausgaben und Verwaltung; Friedjung, *Österreich von 1848 bis 1860;*
von Pillersdorf, *Die österreichischen Finanzen;* Zugschwerdt, *Das Bankwesen und die privilegierte österreichische Nationalbank.*

[57] See on the monetary system of this time, especially, Zugschwerdt, *Das Bankwesen
und die privilegierte österreichische Nationalbank.*

higher taxes, but it was crudely conceived and fell short of expectations.[58] Only in Hungary was the tax on real estate fairly productive, because the property of the nobility was no longer tax-exempt. Increasing the floating debt and the printing of paper florins did not suffice to cover the budgetary deficits. Resort was had to increasing the funded debt. During the five years from 1848 to 1852 loans were negotiated to the amount of 344.6 million (71 million in 1849 and 85 million in 1851) [59] to establish a budgetary equilibrium, and 137.5 million for the construction of railways and investment in other capital assets. As the funded debt was 1,131 million florins before the revolution, it was enlarged by half during the Schwarzenberg era.[60] The Prime Minister's admonition, "if we regulate our finances, if we save, the Emperor will be the first monarch," remained a pious wish.[61]

Austria's financial sickness was diagnosed as exchange disturbance by Baron Charles Kübeck, the much respected ex-president of the *Hofkammer* (the predecessor of the finance ministry), under Metternich, and as budgetary-disequilibrium trouble by Finance Minister Krauss. Kübeck prescribed as cure the negotiation of a loan of 240 million florins and the gradual withdrawal of paper money. Krauss, optimistically inclined—too sanguinely in Kübeck's opinion—still hoped to balance his budget and by raising the state's credit indirectly to wipe out the formidable exchange rate. Moreover, he doubted that the floating of a new loan would be a success—*on ne prête qu'au riche,* and his treasury was poor. Where could he tap sources rich enough to pay bankers Rothschild twelve million florins in interest? [62] Kübeck's star was in the ascendancy. By December, 1850, the elder statesman had been appointed president of the imperial council, and his position, as will be shown in the later pages, threatened to eclipse that of the cabinet. As constitutional ques-

---

[58] Beer, *Die Finanzen Österreichs im XIX. Jahrhundert,* p. 235.

[59] Czoernig, *Österreichs Neugestaltung, 1848–1858,* p. 127.

[60] Friedjung, *Österreich von 1848 bis 1860,* I, 244.

[61] Kempen, *Das Tagebuch des Polizeiministers Kempen von Fichtenstamm von 1848 bis 1859,* pp. 226, 235.

[62] The argumentation between Kübeck and Krauss (also Bruck) is given in detail by Beer, *Die Finanzen Österreichs,* pp. 214 *et sqq.*

tions were also involved, Krauss resigned on December 26, 1851; he was replaced by Commerce Minister Andreas Baumgartner, who had taken over that portfolio from Bruck on May 25, 1851.[63] It would have been logical if Kübeck, the great critic of the former finance and commerce policies, had assumed the vacated posts, but he contented himself with giving general directions. Baumgartner was professor of physics, ex-director of the national porcelain factory and of the tobacco monopoly. As if these occupations were not multifarious enough, he had also been supervisor of the telegraph system and manager of the state railways. Assuredly, the new finance and commerce minister had abundant experience and vast knowledge, but, besides being weighed down by the burden of two offices, he lacked two important qualifications of leadership: independent judgment and driving power. Even if he had been a financial Titan, he would not have been able to overcome the overweening influence of the generals. In a showdown between the military and the finance ministers, the Emperor would have sacrificed the civilians and retained his officers.[64]

Schwarzenberg's and Bruck's Trade Policies and Commercial Reforms [65]

Felix Schwarzenberg selected for his minister of commerce, not a fossil civil servant, but the plucky manager of the Austrian Lloyd, Karl Ludwig Bruck, a man who looked at the world and the state through the eyes of a merchant prince. He was an ardent champion of a Greater Germany, but stressed the economic aspects of the question more than the political ones. At the same time he, born a Rhinelander, was a good Austrian patriot, imbued with a blind faith in the possibilities of his country. According to him, Austria needed only to will, and great things could be accomplished. Schwarzen-

[63] See *infra*, pp. 103, 106.
[64] Friedjung, *Österreich von 1848 bis 1860*, I, 249–50.
[65] On the Austrian commercial policy of this period see Beer, *Die österreichische Handelspolitik im neunzehnten Jahrhundert*; Charmatz, *Minister Freiherr von Bruck; der Vorkämpfer Mitteleuropas*; Delbrück, *Lebenserinnerungen, 1817–67*; Gaertner, *Zollverhandlungen zwischen Österreich und Preussen von 1849 bis Olmütz*; Lang, *Hundert Jahre Zollpolitik*; Matlekovits, *Die Zollpolitik der österreichisch-ungarischen Monarchie von 1850 bis zur Gegenwart*; Zimmermann, *Geschichte der preussisch-deutschen Handelspolitik*.

berg found in Bruck a collaborator equipped with gifts of which he himself was deficient in the economic field. But Bruck was no statesman. Although he had a keen understanding of Austria's needs and sentiments, perhaps also an intuitive insight into the nexus of economic and political affairs, as well as the future demands of European commerce, yet his grandiose schemes were not always nicely adjusted to the actual political situation. Schwarzenberg's economic policy regarding Germany, measurably colored by Bruck's idealistic ideas, lacked the sure touch of his diplomatic skill.

Bruck, prompted by his fiery ideals, at times may have transgressed the boundaries of the possible; still he deserves high praise for having directed Austria's commercial policy and monetary system into modern channels. A man of his caliber furnished a strong prop to the newly created unitary state through his boldly conceived economic measures; on the other hand, it is clear that some of his ideas could not have been put into effect, or at least not so readily, if a state of this type had not been at his disposal. Dr. Karl Hock, one of his chief assistants, the author, for instance, of a financial history of the United States,[66] acknowledged his talents in these words:

The greatness and magnanimity of his views, the creative genius of his plans, the richness of his inventive powers, his noble and mild manners, the bewitching courtesy of his company were overwhelming. The time which I passed with him, especially during his first ministerial activity, will be reckoned by me as the most fruitful of my life.[67]

In a memorandum of January 30, 1853, submitted to Count Buol-Schauenstein, Bruck incidentally revealed the program formulated by him when he took over the ministry of commerce and public works. The major planks were: abolition of the tariff barrier between Austria and Hungary; the setting up of a uniform tariff and symmetrical trade relations for Austria; abrogation of the prohibition of imports and the introduction of a modern tariff system; finally, the establishment of a customs union between Austria and

---

[66] Freiherr von Hock, *Die Finanzen und die Finanzgeschichte der Vereinigten Staaten.*
[67] Schäffle, *Aus meinem Leben,* p. 71.

the other members of the Germanic Confederation (including, if
possible, Italy and the Balkan peninsula), as the indispensable basis
of Austria's maintenance of her predominant position in Germany.[68] He attained the first objects of his program, but the crown-
ing piece of his gigantic plan, a Central European custom union,
was denied to him.

A committee was called together in April, 1849, for the reform
of the tariff. Its president was Baumgartner, later minister of finance
and commerce, and its reporter was Dr. Hock. Naturally, the old
system of a hermetically closed economy, instituted by Joseph II,
could not be changed to its opposite—free trade. A protective tariff
was worked out with these principles: all important prohibitions
were replaced by tariffs, differential tariffs and export premiums
were abolished, drawbacks were granted only in exceptional cases,
and, finally, ad valorem rates were established. The Austrian tariff
was closely adjusted to that of the German Tariff Union (*Zollverein*) with a view to bringing about eventually a merger of the
two economic systems. As the Austrian industrialists and traders
were the spoiled beneficiaries of the old regime, the new tariff program did not find the expected strong and joyous echo, except on
the part of the silk industrialists in Tyrol and the cotton manu-
facturers in Vorarlberg.[69] The tariff drafted by the committee was
submitted to a congress of experts, held in Vienna between January
21 and February 20, 1851.[70] Bruck had to use the full force of his
persuasive power to overcome the resistance of vested interests and
to win the majority over from prohibition to protection. Even high
government officials, such as Baron Kübeck, by this time already
president of the national council, and Finance Minister Krauss,
viewed the new economic system critically. It was Prince Schwarzenberg, a firm believer in the necessity of the planned economic re-

[68] Beer, *Die österreichische Handelspolitik im neunzehnten Jahrhundert*, pp. 150, 152.
[69] Gaertner, *Zollverhandlungen zwischen Österreich und Preussen von 1849 bis Olmütz*,
p. 26.
[70] Beer, *Die österreichische Handelspolitik im neunzehnten Jahrhundert*, p. 86; the
members attending the congress are given by Matlekovits, *Die Zollpolitik der österreichisch-
ungarischen Monarchie von 1850 bis zur Gegenwart*, p. 10n.

forms, who with his usual vigor drove the new legislation onto the statute books (November 21, 1851). The tariff went into effect on February 1, 1852.

Thus, the centrifugal force of reform had successfully overcome the centripetal force of reaction west and east of the Leitha. The tariff revisions in Austria made possible a tariff union with Modena and Parma. Tuscany and the Papal States became economic affiliates. Bruck, the imaginative idealist, even visualized the inclusion of Holland, Switzerland, Belgium, and Denmark in a tariff group forming a gigantic Central European commercial empire.[71]

A view that is apt to be overlooked by historians concerned exclusively with the political aspect of Prince Schwarzenberg's statesmanship, particularly when the chroniclers are circumscribed by space and sympathy, is his ardent fight for an Austro-German customs union. German historians, like Sybel and Treitschke, considering an attack on the German Tariff Union (*Zollverein*) malicious, because it frustrated the ultimate union of Germany, have treated his work in the economic field with disparagement. There cannot be any question, however, but that it would have been greatly to the advantage of German economy if Germany and Austria could have been encompassed by one tariff barrier at this time. The towering idea of a customs union was probably given to Schwarzenberg by his minister of commerce, Bruck, but Schwarzenberg's and Bruck's designs regarding the German customs union differed in emphasis. Bruck, the enthusiastic idealist and optimistic economist, did not alone consider the stabilization and expansion of the might of the

[71] The chambers of commerce received a new statute in March, 1850. Fifty-six chambers of trade and industry became small professional parliaments; in view of the lack of a political parliament, they were of importance as organs of public expression. Other important measures undertaken by Bruck referred to the Austrian railways. As Schwarzenberg does not seem to have taken a prominent part in Austrian railway building, only brief notice will be made of the fact that Bruck extended the nationalization of the Austrian railways. See *Geschichte der Eisenbahnen der österreichisch-ungarischen Monarchie*, Vol. I. The postal office was transferred under Bruck from a revenue agency to a service institution. On April 6, 1850, in the midst of grave economic controversies, an Austro-Prussian postal union was formed. It was Bruck's aspiration to extend a similar arrangement with regard to railways, navigation, coins, measures and weights; step by step, therefore, an Austro-Prussian trade union should be accomplished, if the aim could not be attained in one stroke.

Austrian Empire; he also had in view the favorable reaction of the
identity of Austrian and German interests on his country's international condition; for him the union was the spiritual and material instrument that would block the divergent tendencies of the Danubian Monarchy's individual crownlands and races. Schwarzenberg,
the sober realist and cold diplomat, on the other hand, intended to
use the customs union as a means of power politics to curb Prussia's
ambition for German hegemony and to effect a reversal of public
opinion in favor of Austria.[72] If the project could be achieved, Austria's dominating position in Germany would be permanently secured. This scheme gave birth to the idea of the creation of an empire of seventy millions. Some historians, such as Colonel Heller and
Ritter von Srbik,[73] believe Schwarzenberg to have been its origina-
tor; others,[74] especially Friedjung's disciples, assign to Bruck the
rank of front fighter in the struggle for the creation of a mighty
Central Europe. I believe that no school can advance conclusive evidence in favor of either theory. In any case, it is clear in my opinion that Felix Schwarzenberg was solely interested in the maintenance of the imperial splendor of the Habsburg dynasty and the
Austrian Empire. A customs union with Germany and the erection
of a Central European empire were only means to an end.

The fight for the common customs union may not always exhibit
the allure of the spectacular as does the political one, but it was carried on with the same doggedness, deviousness, and dexterity as the
diplomatic skirmishes. The political and economic battles were
fought simultaneously on two theaters of war, and their interrela-
tion should be concurrently visualized.

---

[72] In his polemic against Heinrich Friedjung, Colonel Heller (*Mitteleuropas Vorkämpfer: Felix Fürst Schwarzenberg,* pp. 91, 107) takes issue with the historian because of the
latter's alleged claim that Prince Schwarzenberg "did not take the tariff union seriously."
In my opinion Heller overlooks in Friedjung's narration the shift of emphasis on the part
of the two ministers. Different world outlooks and temperaments, which Heller himself
brings out, explain why the one stressed the economic aspect, the other the political side
of the problem. Of course, Felix Schwarzenberg took the tariff union "seriously."

[73] Notice Colonel Heller's title of his book, *Mitteleuropas Vorkämpfer;* Heinrich Ritter
von Srbik, *Deutsche Einheit,* II, 94.

[74] Charmatz, *Minister Freiherr von Bruck,* subtitle: *Der Vorkämpfer Mitteleuropas.*

On October 26, 1849, the official gazette, *Wiener Zeitung,* gave the first inkling of a customs union between Austria and Germany in an article written by Bruck with passion and *élan.* The unexpected alacrity with which Austria was apparently heading towards a thorough transformation of her economic system created a sensation in Europe. The complete amalgamation with the *Zollverein,* as well as with the North German group still standing outside the latter economic group, was to take place in four stages. In a second publication, a memorial of December 30, 1849, the possibility of a German customs union was again expounded, and this time the Austrian government not only tried to spread an emotional spell over Germany by influencing public opinion, but turned to the German governments as well. Bruck explained in great detail the vast advantages that would accrue to the tariff-free north of Germany. A general customs conference was suggested in order to deliberate how frontier traffic could be facilitated, how river and sea navigation could be regulated according to uniform principles, and how the exchange of the products of the individual states could be disencumbered. A uniform commercial representation abroad should be established, leading to the uniform conclusion of commercial treaties, as well as to agreements regarding postal, railway, telegraph, and steamship lines; finally a comprehensive Austro-German customs tariff should be taken into consideration.[75] Paraphrasing Jefferson's dictum, "merchants have no country," Bruck was wont to declare that "capital does not know a River Main line, nor does it respect a political dualism." [76] The great importance attached to Bruck's plan by Schwarzenberg is shown by his comment, in a despatch of January 26, 1850, to Baron Kübeck, a member of the Austrian interim committee with General von Schönhals:

In my opinion, the trade and customs union with Germany, as projected in the memorial, will be the safest basis of the German unity aspired to by Austria. At the moment it will also greatly assist in promoting an accord

[75] These two publications are reproduced, for instance, in Charmatz, *Minister Freiherr von Bruck,* Annex, pp. 157 *et sqq.,* and pp. 177 *et sqq.*

[76] *Ibid.,* p. 47.

on current problems. The earlier this memorial is brought to the attention
of the courts and of public opinion, the more easily Austria's position
towards Prussia, reinforced by the judgment of that public opinion, will
be established. It is obvious that the temporary federal committee will gain
in prestige through the conduct of this affair. At the present time, there
is, indeed, no matter better fitted to take deeper and broader roots in Germany. It is therefore earnestly recommended to the persevering assiduous-
ness of the commissioners, so that Austria may still have sufficient time to
influence public opinion before the elections to the Erfurt diet.[77]

At the beginning, the leading Prussian ministers were not inclined to take the Austrian proposals seriously. It seemed incon-
ceivable to them that commercial matters should become one of
Schwarzenberg's chief weapons of attack against Prussia. But one
man particularly viewed the matter differently: Rudolf von Delbrück, later Bismarck's right-hand man, whose unusual ability
made him an influential councillor in the ministry of commerce
when only thirty-two years of age. Upon his advice Count Bernstorff, the Prussian envoy at Vienna, was instructed to negotiate
with the Austrian government concerning a reciprocal tariff pro-
viding for the free exchange of domestic raw materials and food-
stuffs and a mutual most-favored treatment of the importation of
manufactured articles.[78] Austria was placed in a somewhat embarrassing position through this offer, because, on the one hand, she
could not rashly brush aside Prussia's advance, but, on the other, in
order to combat Prussia's Union policy,[79] she had to act as the friend
and promoter of the German middle states. Their favor would have
been lost, or at least their jealousy would have been aroused, if Prussia had come to an understanding with Austria alone. Schwarzenberg, through the communication of January 27, 1850, decided to
make it plain to the Prussian government that

involved was not a closer relationship with the *Zollverein*, but a full-fledged
tariff and trade union with Germany as a whole. Therefore, negotiations

[77] Beer, "Fürst Schwarzenberg's deutsche Politik bis zu den Dresdener Konferenzen,"
in *Historisches Taschenbuch*, p. 50; Gaertner, *Zollverhandlungen zwischen Österreich und
Preussen von 1849 bis Olmütz*, p. 38.

[78] Gaertner, *ibid.*, pp. 38–39.

[79] See *infra*, pp. 127 *et sqq.*

could not be had with Prussia merely; they had also to be initiated with
all the German confederate states. To this end the imperial government
had turned to the central organ of the Confederation and submitted proposals with a view to scrutinizing them, communicating them to the
members of the Confederation, and to inviting them to a conference at
Frankfurt.[80]

Schwarzenberg kindled no infectious enthusiasm with his note.
Newspapers friendly to Prussia, seizing upon the weak points in the
Austrian program, incidentally brought out interesting economic
facts. The *Schwäbische Kurier*, for example,[81] wrote:

Who shall watch the frontier of a few thousand miles? Not the Austrian
customs officials. They are corrupt because they are poorly paid. How shall
tariff revenues be distributed? Pro rata among the members? That would
help the impaired Austrian finances. Her customs revenues, instead of
22,000,000 florins would be doubled—at the expense of Germany, since
the two countries do not consume the same kind of products. In Austria
perhaps 15,000,000 people have never taken a cup of coffee or tea, not to
speak of a glass of foreign wine; there are people who have never used
foreign luxuries or any manufactured articles at all and, therefore, would
in no way contribute to the customs revenues.

On February 2 the Prussian minister of foreign affairs, Schleinitz,
answered the Austrian note of January 27, recognizing the importance of the matter, but asking for time to discuss it with Prussia's
associates in the *Zollverein*. In a communication to the courts of the
kingdoms, Schwarzenberg, annoyed by Prussia's dilatory methods
(tantamount to a polite diplomatic "no"), pointed to the stellar role
assumed by Prussia in all German economic interests; once again he
admonished his envoys to use all pressure on the kingdoms to foster
Austria's plans.[82] But apart from Hamburg, Stuttgart, and Darm-

[80] Gaertner, *Zollverhandlungen zwischen Österreich und Preussen von 1849 bis Olmütz*,
p. 39.

[81] *Schwäbischer Kurier*, No. 48, Feb. 24, 1850, quoted in *ibid.*, p. 40.

[82] It was Felix Schwarzenberg's custom to drive a point home by repetition. He said on
the subject to his former secretary, Hübner, later Austria's ambassador in Paris: "I have
been charged with prolixity and accused of being repetitious in my despatches. If the instructions of a directing minister to his agents were model articles of a magazine or the
outgrowth of eloquence, I would deserve this reproach. The question is, however, to im-
plant certain ideas into the heads of my agents so that they are enabled to do the same with

stadt—and their answers were noncommittal—the German governments did not react. Schwarzenberg's first diplomatic support of
Bruck's project did not meet with acclaim.

Before the month of February came to an end, it could be considered a foregone conclusion that no customs conference would
be convoked. But now political events moved in favor of Austria
against Prussia. In Electoral Hesse a change in ministry had taken
place: the Prussophile Minister Eberhard had been ousted, and the
notorious Minister Hassenpflug brought to power. On February 27
the League of the Four Kingdoms was formed; in the first article of
their statutes it was declared, in strongest contrast to Prussian policies: "As joint confederate matters are regarded . . . supervision
over mutual trade and customs affairs." The creation of the League
of the Four Kingdoms was a diplomatic defeat for Prussia. Her
political setback was heightened by the *rigor mortis* from which her
Union suffered. In the circumstances her policy was directed towards
undermining the connection of the South German states with Austria by winnowing the economic chaff from the political wheat.
In the important note of February 28, 1850, Schleinitz declared a
customs conference an inadequate means of fostering a more intimate rapport of the material interests of Germany and Austria.
Prussia, the note declared, had the contractual right to represent all
governments belonging to the Tariff Union with regard to customs
matters. He was ready, however, the note continued, to enter into
intergovernmental negotiations or to bring about discussions between the various commercial groups in Germany. The gist of
the note was, of course, a flat refusal of an Austro-Prussian tariff
merger.

At the beginning of March, Delbrück was sent to Vienna for the
purpose of preparing the way for future deliberations. Of Bruck he
thought highly. "He is a man of large views," he wrote, "engrossed
in the task which the transformation of the economic laws in Aus-

---

the foreign governments." Joseph Alexander Graf von Hübner, *Neun Jahre der Erinnerungen eines österreichischen Botschafters in Paris unter dem zweiten Kaiserreich 1851–
1859*, p. 14.

tria poses; a good Austrian, but not an enemy of Prussia; of quiet, dignified demeanor as becomes a minister of a great state." Delbrück was cordially received by Schwarzenberg, but meeting in his antechamber the envoys of the South German kingdoms, he immediately sensed the general atmosphere: it was frigid.[83] He was not the man to let such warnings go unheeded, and, in conformity with the policy that had dictated the note of February 28, he advocated countermeasures in terms of a revised tariff with alluring features to recalcitrant German states. To this end Prussia invited the members of the German Tariff Union to a conference at Cassel to take place at the beginning of July. In order to clip the commercial wings of the Prussian eagle, the Austrian cabinet answered with the memorial of May 30, 1850. Two main ideas ran through this document: (1) all German states should be united in a tariff union as of January 1, 1854, without passing through the various stages formerly contemplated; (2) a central commercial authority should be created, something which the Tariff Union did not possess. This commercial authority was to regulate not only all customs affairs but also sea and river navigation, railways and canals, the mint system, measures and weights, and, in general, all affairs declared of common interest. The first part of the Austrian memorial went as far as to outline the competence of the contemplated authority with the precision of a law. In the second part, a kind of continuation of the memorial of December 30, written in a style impelled by passion, the immense importance of the customs merger was stressed.[84] Its execution would have meant a commercial centralization under Austria's guidance, supplementing her political primacy in the confederate diet. Clearly Prussia's dominating position in the German Tariff Union was being threatened, for the focal point of German

---

[83] *Lebenserinnerungen*, I, 254.

[84] For a full discussion of the Austrian memorial of May 30, 1850, see Gaertner, *Zollverhandlungen zwischen Österreich und Preussen von 1849 bis Olmütz*, pp. 75 *et sqq.* Friedjung, *Österreich von 1848 bis 1860*, II, 48–49, states that Bruck proposed Austria's recognition of the Prussian Union provided Prussia accepted his economic project. Srbik, *Deutsche Einheit*, II, 101–2, points out correctly that such a compromise would have been acceptable to Schwarzenberg only in case the Union had been formed within the framework of the constitution of the Confederation.

commercial policy would have been transferred from Berlin to Frankfurt.

It was Schwarzenberg's strategy to have the South German kingdoms adopt the Austrian standpoint and to champion it at the Cassel Conference. He was to be sorely disappointed. At the end of October Bavaria made the motion to take as a basis for the negotiations between the German custom unions and Austria the commercial treaty concluded between Bavaria and Württemberg on May 27, 1829, on the one hand, and Prussia and Hesse-Darmstadt, on the other. Saxony declared her willingness to co-operate in the conclusion of a commercial treaty between the Tariff Union and Austria.[85] True, the Prussian tariff revision, at least in essentials, also failed,[86] but in general the outcome of the conference was not unfavorable to Prussia. The storm troops which Schwarzenberg had intended to use proved unreliable, and when threatened by Prussia with exclusion from the Tariff Union, they went over to the enemy. The South German states had just concluded the Treaty of Bregenz (October 12, 1850), and, therefore, Schwarzenberg thought himself entitled to a more hearty co-operation by his new allies. In a sharp circular of the same date, he expressed his regret at the results of the Cassel Conference, "the success of which was possible only through the narrow-mindedness of the South German governments, because, valuing momentary commercial advantages, they had forgotten the political significance of their conduct and in fact had sabotaged the Austro-Germany union." [87] The Cassel Conference had clearly shown that it depended on Prussia whether or not an Austro-Prussian customs merger could be accomplished. Moreover, the danger became manifest that influence in commercial affairs would automatically lead to predominance in political matters.

At the end of 1850, at Olmütz,[88] where Schwarzenberg won his

[85] Gaertner, *Zollverhandlungen zwischen Österreich und Preussen von 1849 bis Olmütz*, pp. 97–98.

[86] Delbrück, *Lebenserinnerungen*, p. 273.

[87] Gaertner, *Zollverhandlungen zwischen Österreich und Preussen von 1849 bis Olmütz*, pp. 95–96.

[88] See *infra*, pp. 156 et sqq.

great diplomatic victory over Prussia, no commercial concessions were wrung from the Hohenzollern state. Commercial questions, together with the political issues, were transferred to the diplomats at Dresden to be treated as interpretation, amplification, or tightening of Article 19 of the federative constitution of Germany (June 8, 1815).[89] The Dresden Conference did not accomplish anything tangible in commercial matters, just as it did not achieve anything definite in any other subject. The sitting of May 15, 1851, gave the controversy a first-class burial by passing the following resolution.

Whereas a generally reorganized organ of the allied German states has come into existence through the sending of representatives to the confederate meeting;

Whereas, further, the conviction has gained ground that all confederate states concur in their primary and ultimate aims;

Whereas, however, an immediate unconditional assent of all confederated governments cannot be attained with regard to individual points. . . .

Therefore, it is deemed expedient to close the conference.

The confederate governments, in general, approve the views expressed by the committee and obligate themselves to continue the deliberations in the confederate diet at once on the basis of the material gathered at the Dresden Conference.[90]

While Vienna was occupied with the preparation for the Frankfurt deliberations, on the strength of the foregoing *pia desiderata*, Prussia staged a master coup. She imposed upon herself and the Tariff Union a tariff with such a great inclination to free trade that Hanover and with her the Tax Union were drawn into the Tariff Union (September 7, 1851).

Austria and Prussia now vied with each other for the commercial favor of the German states. Vienna and Berlin sent out invitations to customs conferences. On January 4, 1852, Prince Schwarzenberg

[89] Article 19 reads: "The confederate states reserve to themselves the right of deliberating, at the first meeting at Frankfurt, upon the manner of regulating the commerce and navigation from one state to another, according to the principle adopted by the Congress of Vienna."

[90] Beer, *Die österreichische Handelspolitik im neunzehnten Jahrhundert*, p. 106.

opened the Vienna meeting with a speech that was matter-of-fact
in substance and conciliatory in spirit. Illustrative of the possibility
of a German trade merger, he declared, was the September agreement between Prussia and Hanover. There was no reason, he went
on, why the more comprehensive Austro-German customs union
could not be concluded, particularly as every extension of territory
favored the conclusion of such agreements by increasing their utility and cutting traffic impediments to a minimum. The present moment, he argued, was an especially favorable one: Austria, after
long preparations, had adopted a tariff system similar to the one
adhered to by the greater part of Germany. The September treaty
had convincingly shown, he continued, that the gulf separating the
northwestern coastal states from the rest of Germany was not unbridgeable. He concluded by pointing to the fact that the imminent
termination of the Tariff Union treaties offered the best opportunity
of bringing on those modifications through which an advantageous
and permanent expansion of the Union's territory could be accomplished.[91]

The best-considered plans have a way of breaking down before
the inexorable logic of economic circumstances. It was a bad omen
for the success of the Vienna Conference that Thuringia, other central German states, the two Mecklenburgs, Denmark, and Holland
in behalf of Limburg had abstained from sending delegates, because
they felt that there was no point in their joining the meeting without Prussia's participation. Austria submitted to the assembled delegates three draft agreements: Agreement A, a commercial understanding between the Tariff Union and Austria; Agreement B, an
outline of an ultimate Austro-Prussian customs merger; and Agreement C, a secret treaty between the German states and Austria
excluding Prussia. Regarding Agreement C, only Bavaria and Electoral Hesse seconded Austria's motion—of prime importance to the
Vienna cabinet—that the treaty should also become effective in case
Prussia declined to invite an Austrian representative to the Berlin
negotiations. In order to come to an understanding among them-

[91] *Ibid.*, p. 116.

selves, South German statesmen, awkwardly placed as they were
upon the horns of a provocative dilemma, met at Bamberg on March
25, 1852, and at Darmstadt in the beginning of April.

The Austrian Prime Minister died while these negotiations were
going on. As this book is concerned only with the personal share of
Felix Schwarzenberg in the great events of this period, it will merely
be recorded that the South German states, finding a good market
for their products in northern Germany, did not separate themselves from the Tariff Union and renewed their agreements with
Prussia. The whole of Germany was now comprised in the German tariff treaty, while Austria remained outside. This commercial
success, written in flame across the German sky, compensated Prussia for her political defeat at Olmütz and formed the prelude to the
era of victory beginning in 1866. In 1853 (February 20) Bruck
arranged a commercial treaty with Prussia [92] that brought about
a closer union between the two states and at the same time erected
a higher tariff against the rest of Europe. He saw in this undertaking the beginning of a complete economic union between the
two countries—a bold vision, but not to be realized. United they
would have automatically controlled the whole of the Balkan Peninsula. The march of history was different, however. In the next decades the German Empire turned from the East, looked to the West,
and started on a colonial policy, a field formerly foreign to it.

The commercial policy of the Schwarzenberg era showed a vigor
and a scope unknown to Austria before and after that time. Com-
bative and nationalistic, Schwarzenberg opened a new path for his
country's activities and potentialities. He failed in his attempt to
effect an Austro-German tariff union. Some, with an appreciation
for the spectacular in international affairs, will exalt him for his
sparkling diplomatic successes. Others, with a delicate balance of
mind, will not permit to have blotted out the quiet achievements of
the brilliant expositor of his economic ideas, Karl Ludwig Bruck,
and his collaborators, Karl von Hock, Max von Löwenthal, Karl
von Czoernig, and Siegfried Becher.

[92] Matlekovits, *Die Zollpolitik der österreichisch-ungarischen Monarchie von 1850 bis
zur Gegenwart*, pp. 28–34.

Bach's Administrative and Schmerling's Judicial Reforms [93]

The same mighty stirrings that swept through the ministry of commerce also pervaded the ministry of the interior under Dr. Alexander Bach and the department of justice under Anton Ritter von Schmerling. The ministry of the interior was an offspring of the Aulic Chamber (*Hofkanzlei*), instituted by Maria Theresa in 1749. Since this department had become too unwieldy to meet the demands of a modern state, the revolution decentralized it; later the departments of agriculture and education were carved out of it.

The position of the individual ministers had been measurably enhanced by the revolution. Formerly administrative business was transacted by means of collegiate bodies. As soon, however, as ministerial responsibility was decreed by a constitution, it had to be fastened upon definite individuals and could not be permitted to become diffused through "long, narrow, and wooden" boards. Monocratic responsibility—of the ministers, governors, and local administrative chiefs—was also demanded by Bach's absolutist doctrine entailing an organic, hierarchically constituted administrative machinery. Numerous more or less independent agencies, partly co-ordinated with and partly subordinated to the ministers, were now built into the departments. In administrative matters, the final extraordinary resort, the imperial instance—a symbol of patriarchal government—somewhat receded into the background, although the right of pardon, the grant of pensions, and the appointing power remained more than a formal prerogative under Francis Joseph.

In the Stadion administrative setup [94] the pivot of the intermediate line agencies was the county, not the governorship. The imperial decree of June 26, 1849, embodying Bach's administrative reforms, adhered to this principle. Bohemia was divided into seven counties, Moravia into two, Styria and the Tyrol into three, and the

---

[93] Cf. Beidtel, *Geschichte der österreichischen Staatsverwaltung;* Czoernig, *Österreichs Neugestaltung, 1848–1858;* Friedjung, *Österreich von 1848 bis 1860,* Vol. I; Redlich, *Das österreichische Staats- und Reichsproblem.*
[94] See Redlich, *Das österreichische Staats- und Reichsproblem,* pp. 354–82.

Coastland into two. Ethnographic considerations guided the circumscription of these counties; in Bohemia, for instance, two counties were predominantly German, three Czech, and two were German-Czech. After 1851, under the Bach regime, the internal and financial administration centered in the fifteen governors, the "bureaucratic viceroys." Since control radiated from the ministry of the interior, these outwardly powerful persons were in reality mere civil servants to whom the top co-ordinating authority issued orders for execution. As a rule, the governors belonged to the upper nobility, but it is significant that under Stadion the first bourgeois was made governor of Upper Austria. Bach's modernization of the administrative apparatus mechanized, as it were, this top-line level also by eliminating the personal and therefore the incalculable element in Maria Theresa's patriarchal government. An entirely new creation was the district, headed by administrative district chiefs and district judges, because the administrative and judicial functions of the estates ceased. Hundreds of these offices had to be created, their jurisdiction marked off, and appropriate officials selected. The employment of numerous new civil servants, the small salaries paid to them, and frugality practiced in the administration in general entailed a change in the social composition of the administrative personnel through the recruitment of a large body of petty bourgeois. Bach was not able to eradicate from his state functionaries the characteristic evils of the *ancien régime*—the sins of gentlemanly malingering and red tape—but he assiduously cultivated in them a sense of honor and loyalty to the imperial cause. His civil servants were incorruptible, singularly modest in bearing (and therefore free from another sin of the bureaucrat, as formulated by Ramsey Muir, that of the Jack-in-Office), and showed a genial understanding of popular demands.

The new administrative order went into effect on January 5, 1850. In Austria its main outlines remained in operation until the fall of the Monarchy; in Hungary the traditional county administration was re-established in 1860. The general concept of the state and of public affairs of government and of law, instilled into the

Austrian system by its renovator, crystallized itself into inde-
structible features of the Austrian administration and of Austrian
life in general. The bureaucracy, in particular, became one of the
motive powers of the state.

It had been Stadion's fundamental idea to have the county and
district officials controlled by popular assemblies. Lack of political
talent would have made it difficult to realize this magnificent structure of self-government. Bach, of a more sober and practical bent
than his predecessor in office, was, moreover, not inclined to have
his power restricted by autonomous organs. On October 29, 1849,
the execution of Stadion's communal code of March 17, 1849, was
suspended; a new order of March 7, 1850, abolished the contemplated county and district assemblies altogether.

Communes fared better for awhile. With the abolition of magisterial authority appertaining to estates, the communes had to be
reinstated in their old rights. In the administration of the communes, however, the civil authorities ran into friction with the
military commanders. Although the generals looked with a more
friendly eye at the rural communes than at the municipal communes (the latter had been hotbeds of revolution), the clash between military law under a state of siege and the civil law is
characteristic of the years 1849–1851. Illustrative of the struggle between the military and civil authorities and of Bach's switch from
mild liberalism to stark reaction is the fate of the municipal code
for the city of Vienna, of March 6, 1850. By virtue of this law, the
municipal council was elected on September 30, 1850, but when this
assembly wanted to convene, the military governor of Vienna,
Baron Welden, prevented its sessions. The minister of the interior, at
this time still liberally inclined and deeply wounded by the military infraction upon his department, had the military order can-
celled by imperial decree. Open deliberations were now allowed to
take place (March 18, 1851), but after the abrogation of the constitution, at the end of 1851, Bach identified himself with the absolutist regime and prohibited public sittings. The upshot was that
nothing was left of communal legislation except what governmental

arbitrariness permitted. In 1861, when Francis Joseph's autocratic
rule had come to an end, the Vienna municipal code of March 6,
1850, was revived, and it remained the law of the city until 1891.[95]

Since the police power exercised by the estate owners was abolished, the government required, besides the communes, additional
organs to keep peace and order in rural districts. For this purpose
sixteen regiments of gendarmerie were set up under the command of
the gruff General Baron Kempen. These gendarmes, although forming an efficient police force, were, in Byron's language, "Pagod
things of sabre sway with fronts of brass and feet of clay." It was the
pernicious system based on a fee or special reward for arrests that
led Kempen's men, suffering like all other mortals from a frail
human nature, to gross abuses of their authority. During the years
1848–1852 the police were attached to the ministry of the interior,
but was it not beneath the dignity of a three-star general to bow to
a mere civilian and a purported democrat at that? As a result, friction frequently occurred between Minister Bach and General
Kempen.[96] Soon the chief of the gendarmerie, a man of no mean
capacity and in high favor with the Emperor, had every wisp and
shred of gossip in his hands; he spied on everyone—army officers
and the clergy were not excluded. It was not until after Schwarzenberg's death that the brazen bull of Phalaris destroyed its own creator in police matters: Kempen was made the head of an independent
police ministry.

It is to the lasting credit of the Schwarzenberg cabinet that un-
qualifiedly and expeditiously it carried out, first under Stadion and
then under Bach, the land reforms bequeathed to it by the revolution through the statute of September 7, 1848.[97] On March 4, 1849,

[95] On the early government of Vienna see, for instance, "Die Gemeinde Wien," in *Wien
1848–1888*, I, 399 *et sqq.*; Tomaschek, *Die Rechte und Freiheiten der Stadt Wien*.
[96] Redlich, *Emperor Francis Joseph of Austria*, p. 239.
[97] Grünberg, "Die Grundentlastung," in *Geschichte der österreichischen Land- und
Forstwirtschaft und ihrer Industrien 1848–1898*, pp. 1, 51; the law is reproduced on
pp. 49–50, and in the same author's *Die Bauernbefreiung und die Auflösung des gutsherrlich-bäuerlichen Verhältnisses in Böhmen, Mähren und Schlesien*, pp. 495–97. Literature
on the liberation of Austrian peasant farms is given by Grünberg in *Geschichte der öster-*

the same day the new constitution was dictated, a decree was published regulating the new procedure and the amount of indemnity
to be paid for the liberation of peasant lands from feudal services.

For the purposes of redemption seigniorial rights were divided
into three classes.[98] The first class comprised the administration of
justice and police functions. Estate owners were divested of these
privileges without receiving any indemnity; on the other hand,
they were relieved of the necessity of paying the salary of an official,
learned in the law, to act for them in a judicial capacity. The second
and largest class consisted of services and dues running with the
land, and compensation for their discharge. Before the liberation of
the land in Austria 3 percent of the value of a peasant's farm was
paid, in cash or in kind, to the estates annually, farmers delivered
15 percent of their agricultural produce, and 10 percent of all
draught animals were in the service of the estates. But there was
great diversity in the various parts of the Empire, so that these
figures represent only an average. Since the peasant owned the land,
and since feudal services were not deemed equal in value to those
rendered by free labor, the estate owner received only two-thirds of
the value of such services and dues. One-half this amount was paid
by the peasant; the other half by the crownland on which the
peasant's farm was located. In Galicia, Count Stadion, while governor, decreed that this crownland was to be saddled with the whole
burden of indemnification. By this measure he was eminently successful in retaining the peasants' loyalty to the Emperor, and
thwarted the threatened rebellion of the nobles at the beginning.
Later, a decree of August 15, 1849, upheld this arrangement; even
the taxes levied on other crownlands to provide for indemnification
funds were extended to Galicia by the treasury. The third group
was made up of services which the peasant had to perform on
seigniorial estates. The statute provided that lessees in the tenure of
emphyteusis, that is, fee-farmers holding a perpetual lease of lands

---

reichischen Land- und Forstwirtschaft und ihrer Industrien, on p. 2n; and "Bauernbefreiung," in Handwörterbuch der Staatswissenschaften, 3d. ed., p. 573.

[98] Grünberg, "Bauernbefreiung," in Handwörterbuch, pp. 571–73.

and tenements in consideration of annual rent and improvements thereon, were to receive proprietary ownership, but in this instance they had to indemnify the estate owner without public assistance, again after the deduction of one-third of the value of services and deliveries. In all cases, indemnification was—roughly speaking—the annual value of dues multiplied by twenty. The amounts standing against peasant farms were recorded in the property registers as first mortgages. In 1851 credit institutions were set up, which issued to the estate owners bonds yielding 5 percent interest, to be redeemed within forty years. The liberation procedure, at the small cost of four and a half million florins, was completed in Austria proper by 1854 and in Galicia by 1857. The law of March 7, 1849, abolished the hunting right on property not one's own, except when contractually arranged for. The Austrian institution of hereditary farms, initiated by Joseph II, was left intact. In this respect the government did not follow liberal trends, with the result that peasant lands could not be alienated or divided among heirs.[99]

After the subjugation of Hungary the same reform measures were introduced in the transleithan lands (laws of March 3, 1853, and July 21, 1854), where also, for the first time, a general cadestral system of property registers was installed. Since in North Italy farms were subject to quit-rent, the land reform was not extended to the Lombardo-Venetian provinces; the government was reluctant to dispossess the *signori*.

The amount expended by the state for paying off the *corvées* was considerable. In Austria 225.9 million florins were paid to 8,000–9,000 families (half lived in Galicia alone), 34.9 million to the church, and 29 million to communes and other entities; in Hungary, inclusive of Croatia, but exclusive of Transylvania, the sum disbursed was 304 million florins. The Schwarzenberg family, or the "Kingdom of Schwarzenberg," as Friedjung calls it,[100] received for

[99] Division of peasant lands was permitted after 1868. Grünberg, "Die Grundentlastung," in *Geschichte der österreichischen Land- und Forstwirtschaft und ihrer Industrien*, p. 64. The redemption of servitudes was decreed on July 5, 1853, after the Schwarzenberg era.
[100] Friedjung, *Österreich von 1848 bis 1860*, I, 356n.

its seven main estates in Bohemia, Krumlov, Třeboň, Hluboká, Poštoloprty, Protivín, Lovosice, and Libějice 1,870,000 florins, of which 607,000 florins were allocable to Krumlov.[101]

Since the break-up of large estates was not an issue at that time, the agrarian reform outlined above completely satisfied the peasants. They were interested in their economic betterment, not in political questions. The reform implied, however, that the old legal order, built on the political and social predominance of the large estate owners, was buried. Private law no longer distinguished between owners of estates and owners of farms. In brief, the ideas of equality before the law and of economic freedom had triumphed. Karl Grünberg, the greatest authority on Austrian agrarian conditions of this time, correctly observes that "history cannot furnish an example of a more important and more incisive legal act than the one that brought about the liberation of the peasants from the restraints of a feudal agrarian setup." [102]

The government's ideals guiding the measures, upon which interests and facts must be weighed, are to be understood as sketches of an undivided whole. Schwarzenberg and his collaborator—Bismarck facetiously called them "Fiesco and his Moor" [103]—were primarily concerned with the welfare of the state and of the dynasty. They needed the largest class of the population, the peasants, for their wholehearted support of an administration which was carefully striving to protect the great social groups by means of orders and decrees, but which arrogated to itself the capacity and the right to determine what the public interest was and thus exclusively to define the general well-being from above. The protective shell required a kernel of faith in the imperial power, and that kernel was the peasantry.

The agrarian reform spelled social ascent for the middle class and social descent for the lower nobility. The status of the owners of

---

[101] Plaček, *Die österreichische Grundentlastungsoperation*, p. 13.

[102] "Die Grundentlastung," in *Geschichte der österreichischen Land- und Forstwirtschaft und ihrer Industrien 1848–1898*, p. 64.

[103] Ritter von Poschinger, *Preussen im Bundestag*, IV, 86. This volume contains more than one of Bismarck's acrimonious *aperçus* about Austrian statesmen.

entailed estates was not affected; the cash payments made by the state in consideration of the abolition of *corvées* rather added to the luster of their escutcheons. In an era when "the first society" formed the court circle, some hundreds of families, like the Auersperg, Clary, Clam, Colloredo-Mansfeld, Czernin, Kinsky, Liechtenstein, Lobkowicz, Nostitz, Schwarzenberg, Starhemberg, Taaffe, Thun, Waldstein, and Windisch-Graetz wielded an enormous influence. The lower nobility's real property, held together until 1848 and remunerative because of the peasants' feudal dues, dwindled because it was usually inherited by several beneficiaries. As a consequence, the middle and lower nobles were gradually absorbed by the rapidly rising middle class. The spokesman of the nobility's grievances was Prince Windisch-Graetz, together with another Bohemian, Count Wurmbrand, and the Tyrolese Count Wolkenstein. In a petition of February 22, 1850, their complaint to the Emperor ran as follows:

It is unfortunately a certainty that the estate owners of Austria, Styria, and Carinthia are ruined, for the orders prescribing the liberation of the peasants' lands from socage service applicable to these provinces are manifestly designed to destroy property. . . . Your Majesty will learn too late of the extent of the appalling misfortune to which thousands of the most respected families have fallen victim through the government's arbitrary acts. . . . The most rabid Communist has not dared to come forward with demands such as those which Your Majesty's government has actually put into operation.[104]

Plainly the petition was an ordinary way of seeking redress through imperial fiat, but it was also plainly an extraordinary way of depicting Felix zu Schwarzenberg as Lenin's precursor. Did pique at his dismissal by his brother-in-law dictate Windisch-Graetz's gloomily indignant outburst, not alone the defense of his class? Had the high tories "learned nothing and forgotten nothing," so that they could not in their resentment distinguish between a Coriolanus and a plebeian tribune? Just as in Hungarian affairs, however, the blast of private criticism was directed not so much against the Prime

---

[104] Müller, *Feldmarschall Fürst Windischgrätz*, p. 253; Schlitter, *Versäumte Gelegenheiten; die oktroyierte Verfassung vom 4. März 1849*, p. 70.

Minister—after all, he was one of them and considered capable of conversion—as against the minister of the interior, whose wily switch from left to right aroused their suspicion.

Besides the bureaucracy, the bourgeoisie was the gainer by the events of 1848. The liberal notion of a hierarchy in which everyone is rewarded according to his ability, epitomized by the slogan, *la carrière ouverte aux talents,* found recognition: bourgeois ministers were cabinet members. The emphasis on latent social advance assumed an eminently political character and acted as a prop to the middle-class structure of society erected by Schwarzenberg and his collaborators, Stadion-Bach-Schmerling, until in later years forces from above (the aristocracy championing national federalism) and from below (the workers imbued with Marxian ideas) undermined it. Although politically the aims of the liberal movement were attained only in a small degree, economically liberal tenets won a signal victory in three fields: the land was freed from socage service and could be acquired freely, "seigniorial" estates having been divested of their privileged character—the Bach reforms; tariff barriers, strangling trade and communications, were abolished—the Bruck reforms; the third reform, the abrogation of the old guild system and therewith the grant of free occupational choice, although contemplated even by the dictated constitution, was carried through only in 1858, after the Schwarzenberg era. The bourgeoisie, in general satisfied with the gains of the storm year, rejoiced that the bugbear of their revolution was chased away. Aristocrats and burghers have one connecting link: D'Urbevilles are determined not to sink to the condition of Darbeyfields. In the first part of the nineteenth century the upper bourgeoisie still bore a predominantly German character, even in Hungary. If a Slav became prosperous and socially prominent, he became Germanized. When in the following decades Slav petty bourgeois, peasants, and workers gained self-consciousness, they remembered their nationality and pressed the municipal patriciate into the background. The artisans were democrats and monarchists. The amorphous mass of workers, re-

garded as mere rebels even by such a liberally minded statesman as
Count Stadion, was held in restraint: the edict of December 6,
1848, dissolved workers' associations.[105]

The work done by the ministry of the interior within the span
of a few years was stupendous. Alexander Bach was an excellent
organizer and surrounded himself with an able staff. The office of
under secretary was filled by Joseph Oettl. Two former deputies of
the Kremsier diet, Joseph von Lasser (later minister under Schmerling and Auersperg) and Cajetan Mayer (Baron Mayrau) were
section chiefs. Other important councillors were Karl Beyer, agrarian reform; Weissmann, legal department; Sachse, personnel; and
Bernhard Meyer,[106] a Swiss and the head of the *Sonderbund,* police
matters (later ecclesiastical affairs).

Anton Ritter von Schmerling took over the department of justice
from Alexander Bach on July 28, 1849, the latter having carried
the burden of two departments, justice and interior, since Stadion's
sickness in April, 1849. The code of court organization on June 14,
1849 (drafted by Bach and a companion act to the code of administration of June 26, 1849), was promptly put into execution.
Judicature and administration were separated at all levels. Since
the magisterial authority of the estates had ceased, the installation
of the lowest courts, just as that of the district administrative
offices,[107] was a *novum.* In the kingdom of Bohemia, for instance,
the administration of the governorship was divided into seven
county and seventy-nine district offices. The courts started with

[105] On the social-political conditions of these times see Charmatz, *Deutsch-österreichische Politik;* Springer (Karl Renner), *Der Kampf der österreichischen Nationen um
den Staat,* and *Grundlagen und Entwicklungszeiten der österreichisch-ungarischen Monarchie.*

[106] Bernard Meyer describes (in *Erlebnisse,* pp. 334–36, 343 *et sqq.*) the brusque manner
in which he was taken into Austrian services by Schwarzenberg—the Prime Minister was
"impatient with lost causes"—and his collaborators.

[107] The cost of the civil administration rose considerably: it was 56.6 million florins in
1849, 72.8 in 1850, 92.9 in 1851, and 100.8 in 1852. The maintenance of the department
of justice cost 4.99 million florins in 1849, 10.99 in 1850, 17.53 in 1851, and 18.48 in
1852. Wagner, *Die Ordnung des österreichischen Staatshaushaltes,* pp. 46–47.

two hundred and ten district, or local, tribunals (with single
judges) ; next above them were thirteen "regional courts" or *Landes-
gerichte* (with a bench of judges), and these were capped by the
superior regional court, the *Oberlandesgericht*. At the apex stood
the supreme court, created by the law of August 7, 1850, as a symbol of the imperial and legal unity of the Monarchy. As in France
after the revolution, the spirit and complexion of criminal law
underwent a marked change: the severity of the *ancien régime* in
dealing with the common offender was mitigated. Jury trial was
introduced and operated in the Austrian lands belonging to the
Germanic Confederation from July 1, 1850. Judges were appointed
either by the minister or by imperial patent upon his recommendation. Felix Schwarzenberg's administration deserves high praise for
its selection of capable court and administrative officers from among
lawyers and estate functionaries for the thousands of new posts
which had to be filled. Nepotism and favoritism were not tolerated.
In this the Prime Minister never faltered.[108]

The court and administrative setup of 1849 formed the basis for
the organization of these branches of the Monarchy until its fall.
The immensity of the reform work undertaken by Alexander Bach
and Joseph Oettl, a labor worthy of Otos and Ephialtes, is exemplified by conditions in Lower Austria before 1848: equality before
the law was unknown; there was merely a law for the nobility and
a law for the merchant; the average subject had to be satisfied with
seigniorial or municipal jurisdiction, and only in exceptional cases
was the court of appeals available to him. Schmerling and his assistants, Würth, Hye, and Pratobevera (the latter two ministers of
justice in the cabinet of von Schmerling) executed loyally what
their predecessors had planned. The years of reaction after 1851
turned their sturdy handicraft into efforts of Sisyphus, until the
liberal legislation of 1867 reinvigorated the mentality of these re-
formers.

108 The sharp-tongued Prime Minister once said on the subject: "It is impossible for me
to give all the governorships to my six idiotic cousins."—Poschinger, *Preussen im Bundestag*, p. 22. By no means, however, were all his cousins *blödsinnig*.

Ecclesiastical Matters and Thun's Educational Reforms [109]

The imperial patent accompanying the constitution of March 4, 1849, guaranteed freedom of conscience to everyone. It further conceded to every church recognized by law autonomy in the administration of its affairs, therewith removing one of the structural pillars of church law set up by Joseph II, but subjected the churches, like all associations, to the state's supervision. So far, however, only a principle had been enunciated; of greater importance were the methods by which the new policy was pursued.

The liberal movement of 1848 played directly into the hands of the episcopate. When ordinary communes and associations were to receive autonomy, how could it be denied to the largest of them, the Roman Catholic Church? The bishops, on the other hand, understood by freedom the exercise of untrammeled dominion in religious affairs. A democratic demand for the participation of laymen in the selection of priests and bishops, as well as in the administration of the church's funds, was not the same as the episcopal demand for the removal of bureaucratic control of the Catholic hierarchy. Liberal tenets and ecclesiastical ambitions, although apparently converging upon a common goal, were poles apart.

Breaking an old tradition, the government invited the entire Austrian episcopate to Vienna for consultation in ecclesiastical matters. Twenty-seven bishops (and some other Austrian church dignitaries and Hungarian bishops) assembled in the metropolis from April 29 to June 17, 1849, under the presidency of Cardinal Schwarzenberg, the Prime Minister's brother.[110] Two men, in particular, were re-

[109] See Beidtel, "Übersicht der österreichischen Kirchengeschichte von 1848 bis 1861," in *Geschichte der österreichischen Staatsverwaltung 1740–1848*, II, 435–76, and Preface, xliv *et sqq.*

[110] The career of Friedrich Johann Joseph Coelestin Prince zu Schwarzenberg (April 6, 1809–March 27, 1885) in the Catholic hierarchy was phenomenal. He was only twenty-six years of age when, with papal dispensation, he was elected archbishop of Salzburg. On January 24, 1842, he was made a cardinal. He exchanged the archbishopric of Salzburg for that of Prague on December 13, 1849. Cardinal Schwarzenberg, benevolent, even magnanimous in later years, did not show an even-handed tolerance to the adherents of other faiths. In Salzburg he had treated the Zillertal Protestants as an implacable zealot; on the other hand, he had severely reprimanded the editor of a Catholic paper for having published an anti-Semitic article. Imbued with a mild liberalism in religious philosophy, he

sponsible for having found the way from Vienna to Rome, Count
Leo Thun and Joseph Othmar Ritter von Rauscher. The former was
a cabinet member, who at the age of thirty-eight assumed the portfolio of education and ecclesiastical affairs on July 28, 1849.[111] The
latter, a man of great learning, had taught Francis Joseph philosophy and Friedrich Schwarzenberg canon law. Cardinal Schwarzenberg paid a debt of gratitude to his old teacher by making him
bishop of Seckau-Graz. Courtly in manners, refined in his argumentation, tenacious in the pursuit of his plans, diplomatic and
tactically astute, Rauscher rendered distinguished services to his
church.[112] He well deserved to be later archbishop of Vienna (1853)
and a cardinal.

The demands of the bishops [113] were high: communication with
the Roman See and the faithful without interference from the civil
power; free intercourse of the monasteries with their superiors residing in Rome and other members living abroad; re-establishment
of the canonical marriage law and ecclesiastical jurisdiction over
marriage; transfer of the moneys obtained from the dissolved monasteries to the church; a voice in the nomination of bishops and
abbots; unrestricted conduct of theological institutions, especially
of bishopric seminaries; supervision of the national schools; and the
unabridged right of imposing penances. Even as devout a Catholic
as the young under secretary of the department of education, Josef
Alexander Helfert (1820–1910), who with unflagging energy endeavored to revive the Catholic spirit in Austria and in this vein

advocated a severely ultramontane doctrine in church policies. For the government of
Austria he endorsed a centralistic system up to 1860, and afterwards a federalistic system.
These vacillations made him inferior to forceful Cardinal Rauscher, under whose spirited
banner the concordat of 1855 was negotiated. Wolfsgruber, *Friedrich Kardinal Schwarzen-
berg*, Vol. I, 1906, Vols. II–III, 1917. See also Mörath "Friedrich Kardinal Schwarzenberg,"
Zeitschrift des Bergischen Geschichtsvereins, Vols. XII and XVI.

[111] Frankfurter, "Graf Leo Thun-Hohenstein," *Allgemeine Deutsche Biographie*,
XXXVIII, 178–212 (Bibliography, pp. 211–12).

[112] Charmatz, *Österreichs innere Geschichte von 1848 bis 1895*, I, 27. Wolfsgruber,
Joseph Othmar Cardinal Rauscher.

[113] Beidtel, *Geschichte der österreichischen Staatsverwaltung*, II, 452 *et sqq.* As Helfert
proved not flexible enough to suit Thun's ever-increasing religious fervor, Beidtel, a judge
of the court of appeals in Bohemia, was called in as a consultant in the further negotiations
with the episcopate. The term "episcopate" is not to be given a corporate connotation.

published a number of excellent books on Austria's history in the
nineteenth century,[114] considered some of the claims unacceptable
by the state. In the matter of free communication between the pope
and the bishops, for instance, he insisted on a veto by the civil authorities.

The summer of 1849 wore into winter, winter into the spring of
1850, and still the government had not reached a decision on the
episcopal program. A storm of protest had meanwhile arisen among
the state functionaries. Minister Schmerling rushed to the fray on
their side, Minister Bach playing the role of a half-hearted second.
Had not the Hungarian, the Italian, and the Polish clergy hoisted
the banner of nationalism and actively countenanced the revolutionary movement against the imperial regime? Had not Pope
Pius IX blessed the Italian insurrectionists marching against the
Habsburg Empire? Although the *curia* later sought to interpret the
pope's actions in a manner favorable to Austria, specious reasoning
did not win over to the clerical view old General Radetzky and his
officers' corps who did the stiff fighting against Rome. The bishops,
impatiently challenging decided bureaucratic and military opinion,
maneuvered to discover a makeweight in the trembling balance.
They found it in Minister Thun. He sought an audience with the
Emperor and won him over to the episcopal side.[115] For Francis
Joseph legitimacy was synonymous with Catholicism.

The Prime Minister had apparently evaded coming to grips with
the issue until his hand was forced by the imperial order to adopt the
viewpoint of the bishops. Felix Schwarzenberg was, no doubt,
deeply religious. Catholicism seemed to him as natural as the moun-
tains and rivers of his native Bohemia. On the whole, however, his
religion left no visible imprint upon his politics. He had acquiesced
in the conference of the bishops (probably upon the entreaties of
his brother, the cardinal), he allowed the recall of the Jesuits and
the Liguorians, it is true, but it may be questioned whether the

[114] For example, *Geschichte Österreichs vom Ausgange des Wiener October–Aufstandes,
1848,* and *Geschichte der österreichischen Revolution im Zusammenhange mit der mitteleuropäischen Bewegung der Jahre 1848–1849.*

[115] Reports of Count Thun to the Emperor of April 7 and 13, 1850, *Reichsgesetzblatt,*
1850, pp. 103–24.

strong list of his conscience would have yielded to absolutism the categorically clerical complexion which it assumed after his death under the guidance of Archduchess Sophia and Cardinal Rauscher.[116] Nevertheless, the foundation was laid for a new church policy during his era by the two imperial decrees of April 18 and 23, 1850. These epitaphs of Josephism, offsprings of direct imperial will, deeply influenced Austria's cultural life and church law until the end of the Monarchy.

The decrees permitted the Holy See to communicate and correspond freely with the bishops; papal bulls and pastoral letters could be published without governmental restrictions, subject only to the submission of a copy to the department of education. Therewith the *placet* was abrogated. Ecclesiastical disciplinary powers were re-established. The bishops were now empowered to impose ecclesiastical punishments on clerics and laymen alike. In addition, the temporal powers of the bishops over the clergy, like suspension of salary and incarceration, were restored, and the state obligated itself to execute these sentences, provided they were certified to as being in conformity with canon law. On the other hand, the state could proceed against a cleric, for instance, for political reasons. Catholic priests were therefore under the dual jurisdiction of the episcopate and the government, with no appeal from one power to the other. The regulation of the divine service was left to the bishops, under abrogation of the order of 1783 issued by Joseph II. The theological faculties of the universities still remained under the direction of the state, but concerning the nomination of the professors the bishops were to be consulted; seminaries were subject solely to the bishops. Thus the Catholic Church was no longer detached from Rome: priests no longer had the status of state functionaries.

The coping-stone of the church policy was the concordat of August 18, 1855, with the Roman See which practically fulfilled the remaining demands of the bishops set forth in 1849. It handed all the supervision of the national schools to the bishops and gave

---

[116] Schwarzenberg refused, for instance, to reinstate the ultramontane official historian, Friedrich Hurter, who had lost his position as biographer of Ferdinand II in 1847, but he granted him a pension.

to the church the decision as to the legality of Catholic marriages. All secular officials were instructed to sustain the censorship and moral precepts of the church. Promises to restore the estates confiscated by Joseph II were held out. It is safe to venture the opinion that if Felix Schwarzenberg had still been foreign minister he, the incarnation of the power state and the skilled diplomat, would not have bound himself by a state treaty to conditions so unfavorable to the Austrian state, putting it under the sweeping influence of Rome.

"To a Minister of Education" Grillparzer sent his often-quoted epigram: "I must inform you of a suicide. The minister of ecclesiastical affairs has killed the minister of education." It is natural that liberals or conservatives imbued with the ideas of Joseph II, like the poet, severely criticized Minister Thun's new church policy. In later years, in the Austrian house of lords, another poet, of a more leftist texture than Grillparzer, Anastasius Grün (Count Anton Auersperg), called the concordat "a printed Canossa." In the chamber of deputies Baron Pratobevera, Schmerling's assistant, stigmatized the church legislation as "a cancerous growth that had to be extirpated." Many of Thun's untiring endeavors to transfer border-line jurisdiction from the civil to the ecclesiastical authorities, successfully carried out through the treaty with the Holy See of 1855, were swept away by the liberal tide rising against Francis Joseph's autocratic regime of the first decade of his reign. Thun resigned as minister when this era came to an end in 1860; the concordat was no longer in force after 1870. But Austria's renowned poet and epigrammatic annotator of political events did an injustice to Leo Thun when he accused him of rendering his own educational reform work nugatory by his ecclesiastical measures.

Thun was made up of paradoxes; he was a member of a centralistic government, yet he was a federalist at heart; he devoted himself to the rebirth of Czech literature with lavish efforts, yet he did not object to the Germanization of Hungary and Galicia; he was friendly to the Czech national cause while head of the civil government in 1848, yet he faithfully collaborated with Marshal Windisch-Graetz. Similarly, with "a Catholic heart and a Protestant mind,"

he defended his school reform against ecclesiastical encroachments
and salvaged the work of his assistants, Professor Franz Exner and
the ex-Prussian gymnasium teacher Hermann Bonitz.[117] These men
created for the Austrian state permanent values deserving the un-
alloyed commendation of impartial observers. University and gym-
nasia were thoroughly overhauled after the Prussian model. New
textbooks were introduced; libraries were enlarged. The law cur-
riculum, the basis of Austrian civil servants, was strengthened.
Colossal as this reform was, it stopped short of the national grammar
schools. To educate the masses and thereby to raise potential revolutionaries seemed dangerous even to a lofty idealist. Ethical and religious emotions distinguished Leo Thun, not an analytical mind.
"Two souls, alas! were dwelling in his breast."

THE ABROGATION OF THE CONSTITUTION OF MARCH 4, 1849 [118]

The tide of the 1848 revolution was receding quickly, leaving
the people clinging to the rock of the Habsburg Monarchy, with
only a few landmarks swept away. A counterrevolutionary movement was not slow to set in. It gathered head under the military
surrounding the Emperor, the aides-de-camp, and thence spread
irresistibly through the army, the civil servants, and Vienna society.
Large circles of the population, renouncing ambition and valuing
general tranquillity, began to long for the re-establishment of Austria's old authorities and old order of life. Sentimental values and
class interests inclined the leading strata of society, at that time
still the substantial elements among the German-Austrians, to the
maintenance of a strong executive. According to their absolutist
ideology, Austria could only exist as a great power if she were supported and held together by a strong monarchy.

Vienna returned to its proverbial joviality and bohemianism,

[117] See Frankfurter, "Graf Leo Thun-Hohenstein, Franz Exner und Hermann Bonitz,"
in *Beiträge zur Geschichte der österreichischen Unterrichtsreform.*
[118] Freiherr von Andrian, *Denkschrift über die Verfassung und Verwaltung in Österreich,* and *Zentralisation und Dezentralisation in Österreich;* Freiherr Czoernig von Czernhausen, *Österreichs Neugestaltung;* Friedjung, *Österreich von 1848 bis 1860;* Freiherr
Kübeck von Kübau, *Tagebücher,* ed. by his son, Max von Kübek, and *Metternich und
Kübeck;* Redlich, *Das österreichische Staats- und Reichsproblem,* pp. 382 et sqq.

which Aeneus Sylvius, later Pope Pius II (1458–1464), had already praised while nuncio to imperial headquarters. The bachelor Emperor, in spite of heavy work, went hunting and riding and danced the cotillion with Countess Elizabeth Ugarte at Archduchess Sophia's balls. The world-famous salons of Princesses Liechtenstein, Schönburg, and Eleanore Schwarzenberg (the Prime Minister's sister-in-law) were reopened. The diplomatic corps resumed its rounds of entertainment, Lord Westmoreland, the English envoy, dazzling his colleagues by the sumptuousness of his parties.[119] The period of *inter arma silent Musae* was at an end. The Imperial Opera played Auber and Thomas, Donizetti and Verdi, Flotow and Meyerbeer. The exquisite Strauss orchestra was continued, after the death of Johann Strauss (September 25, 1849), under the baton of his son; excellent regimental bands provided cheap and delightful musical entertainment. Heinrich Laube, appointed director of the *Burgtheater,* received full authority directly from the Prime Minister to revive the glory of this famous institution. Director Carl and his author-comedian Johann Nestroy amused the public at the theater in the *Leopoldstadt;* director Pokorny was his keen competitor at the theater in the *Josephstadt.* Their vehicles were popular plays, typically Viennese productions, in which the Viennese recognized himself on the stage, albeit in somewhat flattering and sometimes persiflaged form. But even in normal times, when Vienna was Vienna, not all was music, art, and graciousness; in these days of restoration the pretense of having recaptured the genial spirit of that ethereal city required a good bit of self-deception. Pent-up emotions burst forth in the extravagantly gay carnival of 1851. Keen observers of the trend of public opinion not incorrectly discerned in these manifestations of popular behavior a desire for order and concord, regardless of the fact that these blessings were imposed by an unshakable authority.

The counterrevolution, initiated at the time of the change in sovereigns and the installation of the Schwarzenberg cabinet, remained closely tied to the military and diplomatic events of the times. The

---

[119] Andlaw, *Mein Tagebuch,* II, 184.

subjugation of the Hungarian rebellion in the summer and autumn
of 1849 and the successful termination of the struggle waged by
Prince Schwarzenberg against Prussia for the renewal of the Germanic Confederation and the re-establishment of Austria's primacy
in this Confederation were the presuppositions that allowed the absolutists to drop the constitutional cloak in Austria's domestic affairs. But it was not Felix Schwarzenberg who was the leader of
neo-absolutism. The darts against the constitution were shot from
another side, and they were not launched against him directly. The
nonofficial military and court protagonists of the abrogation of the
governmental and administrative institutions, partly created and
partly promised by the Schwarzenberg cabinet, concentrated their
hostility on the bourgeois members of the ministry; they feared that
the liberal ministers might persuade the Prime Minister to continue
the "provisional" constitutional regime, along sham liberal lines
adopted by the Manteuffel ministry in Berlin, or worse, swing him
over to putting the constitution of March 4, 1849, actually into
operation.

The Confessions of a Soldier, a spirited pamphlet written by Major von Babarczy,[120] one of the Emperor's aides-de-camp, opened
the crusade of the conservative nobility against the still existing
constitution and therewith against the onrushing bourgeoisie. Ministers in office were openly censured; Alexander Bach was especially
singled out for criticism on account of his democratic past. Clearly,
a person in the Emperor's immediate entourage would not have
dared to drive his sword deep and surely into the heart of his adversaries with all the jaunty flourish of a popular matador if he had not
been assured of support in the highest quarters. Count Franz Hartig, another champion of absolutism, epitomized the credo of the
absolutists in the telling maxim: "The Emperor listens, examines,
orders—subjects wish, discuss in consultative local committees, and
obey." [121]

[120] See *Licht- und Schattenseiten aus dem Soldatenleben und aus der Gesellschaft,*
pp. 67, 343.
[121] *Zwei brennende Fragen in Österreich,* p. 86.

Since Prince Windisch-Graetz's star had gone down and since Prince Metternich, still living in Brussels, declared himself physically unable to steer the ship of state, the ex-president of the Aulic Chamber, Baron von Kübeck, the much admired and much criticized favorite of Emperor Francis, a man of seventy years, but still in full possession of his high mental qualities, became the fulcrum of the high-tory reaction. This tailor's son from Iglau in Moravia had made a spectacular career in the Austrian civil service with high purposes, hard work, and great erudition. Originally a liberal, influenced by Josephine ideas, he viewed the violent temper of the revolution with so much apprehension that he turned to stark absolutism. He was held in highest esteem by the imperial family and was consulted on the occasion of Francis Joseph's accession to the throne. Schwarzenberg withheld the portfolio of finance minister from him at Olmütz, and after Stadion's death he preferred the more tractable Bach to the opinionated old baron. In the following period he exiled him discreetly to the honorific post of head of the joint Austro-Prussian confederate committee at Frankfurt. With Schwarzenberg's revival of the Germanic Confederation, Kübeck's mission came to an end. On his return to Vienna, the appointment to the presidency of the council of the Empire (Reichsrat) awaited him (December 5, 1850), much to his own and everyone else's surprise, because this institution was not even in existence. The nomination was, as events were to prove, crucial.

After Prince Schwarzenberg had won his victory over Prussia at Olmütz at the end of 1850 and Hungary and Italy had again been placed under imperial rule, he deemed the time propitious to place his constitutional house in order. Since all the leading ministers of his cabinet believed a unitary Empire could be securely anchored only through an imperial parliament, he had the choice of either separating himself from his most talented colleagues, if he wanted to eliminate that "drollery, a representative government," or of finding an instrument capable of dealing an indirect death blow to the constitution and acting as a counterweight to his recalcitrant ministers. Perhaps the Reichsrat would be that organ standing outside

his ministry that would lift the ancient Habsburg tower and battle-
ment high and dry above the rising and roaring tide of democracy.
But now a great surprise was in store for the omnipotent Prime
Minister. The new president of the Reichsrat entertained entirely
different views regarding the functions of the body to be created.
Whereas, naturally, the ministers were unwilling to relinquish their
powers and therefore proposed to erect the Reichsrat only as a
supreme administrative court in the image of Napoleon's *conseil
d'état,* Kübeck postulated that the council of the Empire, not the
cabinet, should represent the imperial will. Long and bitter discussions took place between Kübeck, on the one side, and Bach, Krauss,
and Schmerling, on the other. The Emperor, himself, in the ministerial council of March 3, 1851, under his presidency, acted as
arbiter. For the first time in his reign he acted against the advice of
his ministers—a breach of the doctrine of ministerial responsibility
still surviving from the revolution—by deciding the main issues
in favor of the Kübeck thesis: the law of April 18, 1851, authorized
the Reichsrat to give an opinion on all legislative matters, not only
on those submitted by the cabinet, with the privilege of offering
counterproposals. The president of the council of the Empire was
surrounded with an aura of dignity; he was placed on the same
footing as the cabinet.

The severe conflict organized by the statute of April, 1851, between the aristocratic, pre-March civil servants, appointed to the
Reichsrat, and the new bourgeois-liberal bureaucracy, led by Alexander Bach in the ministry, was bound to continue. The new course
was revealed to the public by the sudden and rather ungracious dismissal of Minister of Justice Schmerling (January 24, 1851), who
had strenuously and openly criticized the maintenance of a state
of siege, the strengthening of the police system,[122] and a series of
administrative measures, especially against the press.[123] Irked by the
criticism leveled at his economic measures, particularly by the con-

---

[122] Cf. on police arbitrariness, Rogge, *Österreich von Világos bis zur Gegenwart*, pp.
252 *et. sqq.*

[123] See on the press "Die Wiener Presse," in *Wien 1848–1888,* pp. 411 *et sqq.* Of 306
Austrian political newspapers in 1841, only fifty-nine remained in 1852 (p. 424). The
leading newspapers of this period were August Zang's *Die Presse* (as liberal as feasible in

demnation of the high cost of the Semmering Railway, Bruck, the minister of commerce, resigned on May 23, 1851. Schmerling was replaced by the vice-president of the supreme court, Karl von Krauss, a brother of the finance minister, and Bruck, by Andreas Baumgartner.[124]

The April statute was only the first thrust in the duel between Kübeck and the ministry. In June, 1851, the president of the imperial council thought the time ripe to force a decision. Two memorials, June 15 [125] and July 2, laid the groundwork for his massive sally. Meanwhile the methodical old baron had aroused the Emperor's excited sympathy for making him an absolute ruler: the pupil became more impatient than his mentor to execute the proposed plans. The crisp comments in Kübeck's diary patently reveal the telling effect of his conversations with the Emperor and the almost fanatical thoroughness of the proponent.

January, 1851
9. Call to the Emperor, who becomes more and more open. Great hopes in that fine young man! May they unfold successfully!
18. Prince Schwarzenberg's jealousy has been roused . . .
20. So much is clear: Emperor full of confidence in Schwarzenberg, who depends on Dr. Bach while imagining he leads him.

June, 1851
17. Called to the Emperor, who declares he wishes to proceed with my proposals but will confer first with Prince Schwarzenberg as is due to him.
23. The Emperor, to whom I am called, is apprehensive of the possible resignation of Prince Schwarzenberg with expressions of pained concern; but declares that he is nevertheless determined on the step advised.[126]

---

the teeth of censorship), Ignatz Kuranda's *Österreichische Presse* (mildly liberal), and Edmund Warren's *Lloyd* (opportunistic). The Augsburg *Allgemeine Presse*, of Baron von Cotta, the leading paper in Austria in Metternich's times, lost in circulation. The strict censorship had its good sides: it trained newspapermen to a fine, weighted journalistic style by smuggling into their feuilletons and reviews delicate shades of meaning which would have been stricken out by the censor in the political columns.

[124] See *supra*, p. 68.
[125] The memorial of June 15 is reproduced by Schlitter, *Versäumte Gelegenheiten*, pp. 209 *et sqq.*
[126] Redlich, *Emperor Francis Joseph of Austria*, pp. 83–85.

Kübeck's two memoranda were a sharp rebuke to constitutional monarchy. The great body of the Austrian population, he asserted, wanted nothing else but a strong and intelligent monarchical authority, not the numerous new-fangled institutions (copied from French models by the Schwarzenberg cabinet), because they were unintelligible to the people and essentially inappropriate for Austria. Attacking more the system than the ministers, whose courage in combatting the revolution was gratefully acknowledged, he demanded the revocation of the constitution of March 4, 1849. After all, he declared, it would be better to acknowledge openly an error than to jeopardize the welfare of the state; correlatively, the "liberal" laws enacted in the last years and the new organic institutions should be given a strictly monarchical tinge. The crux of his complaint was the avowal of ministerial responsibility by the present regime. Since no political authority was in existence to which ministers could be responsible, that sort of ministerial accountability was, in his opinion, a sham, obscured the exalted person of the Monarch and led to ministerial despotism. Ministers should only be departmental heads, the irresponsible executioners of the imperial will. The Reichsrat, supervising the ministers, was to become the supreme imperial legislative organ.

It is, indeed, astonishing that Kübeck, the great critic of patriarchal absolutism, an experienced administrator of high talents and advanced age, advocated putting the whole executive power unreservedly into the hands of an inexperienced youth of twenty years. His idea of establishing neo-absolutism, a government relying on the military, the bureaucracy, and the clergy, not the nobility, resembled more Schwarzenberg's view than that of the aristocratic Fronde. Why, then, did he so bitterly attack Schwarzenberg's regime? He saw that the Prime Minister was directing all his thoughts and actions toward the restoration of the ancient imperial splendor of the Habsburg dynasty. He could not accuse the Prime Minister of believing, like Madame de Staël, that, if the weather was bad, it was only because the English constitution had not been everywhere introduced.[127] Did sheer jealousy prompt him to try to jockey the

---

[127] Metternich-Winneburg, *Memoirs of Prince Metternich*, ed. by Prince Richard Metternich, III, 506.

Prime Minister out of the saddle? The high character of the president of the Reichsrat would not support such a base assumption. The only plausible explanation for Kübeck's puzzling action is that his low opinion of Emperor Ferdinand's phantom monarchy and his ghastly impressions of the revolution drove him to the advocacy of that new type of absolutist rulership of Austria which he was successfully to instill into the mind of the young Emperor. Evidently he credited his master, despite his youth, with the faculty of filling the role of autocrat.

Schwarzenberg handled a perplexing situation in a manner that is symptomatic of his flexible intelligence. Of course he was irritated by the precipitate attacks of "persons who withdrew while there was danger and now censure men of saving deeds." [128] After all, it was his masculine instincts and all-steel will that had stamped out the revolution, not the mandarinesque theorizing and intellectual flatulence of his adversary. Evasion of reality was not foreign to him, but when called to heroic action, he, the man of force rather than the man of opinion, could easily enough ride roughshod over every obstacle. No divorce from democracy had to be granted to him; he had flirted with democracy, but he had not married it. Was there any reason for a powerful and self-contained personality, who, like William Pitt, the Elder, to George II, could have said to Francis Joseph: "I knew that I can save the country and that no one else can," to cede the first place as the Emperor's counsellor to an officious zealot? Schwarzenberg converted a delicate situation into a strategic success. He signified to the Emperor his acquiescence in Kübeck's proposals in principle and asked his august master to charge him with the detailed task of abolishing ministerial responsibility and revoking the constitution. He only requested that the proposed measures be not made public before a contemplated treasury loan was launched in order not to disturb the money market. The Emperor remained under the spell of the strong and fascinating personality of the Prime Minister. It is only abstract justice that Francis Joseph a few months later, after his death, deeply moved, said of him: "Since the beginning of my reign he assisted me with

[128] Müller, *Feldmarschall Fürst Windischgrätz*, p. 256.

self-sacrificing faith in blind loyalty, with iron perseverance, and with inexorable energy." [129] A memorable ministerial council took place on August 17, 1851.[130] At the opening of the meeting the Emperor announced his demand that the cabinet submit to him the draft of a new basic law, since "all discerning and loyal people had recognized the impossibility of applying the so-called Anglo-French constitutional principle to the Austrian Empire and therefore also the impossibility of executing the imperial constitution of March 4, 1849, as being at variance with the unity of the Monarchy and the true needs of the peoples." The Prime Minister, rising first, declared his unequivocal acquiescence in the proposed measures and his willingness to serve the Emperor unconditionally in this matter and in any further matters, "as long as the Emperor would graciously bestow his confidence upon him." Minister of the Interior Bach, Minister of Agriculture Thinnfeld, and Minister of War Csorich also expressed their accord with the projected plan. Minister of Education Thun asked for and received permission to think matters over. Only the minister of finance, Philip Krauss, sprang a surprise by declaring that although he realized the shortcomings of the constitution of March 4, 1849, he felt himself bound by his oath to uphold it. Baumgartner, the minister of commerce, and Karl Krauss, the minister of justice, happened to be absent from the conference; the first voted for the project, the second against it, but Karl Krauss and also Thun later withdrew their objections. The only minister, then, insistent on his resignation was Philip Krauss, who had more religious scruples than his devoutly Catholic colleague Thun.[131]

After Kübeck's dramatic appearance on the stage, the minister of the interior, Alexander Bach, had been placed in a situation that amounted to a *mise en demeure;* either he had to pursue his liberal ideas, whatever was left of them, or he had to shift over to the cause of autocracy. After some soul-searching he found that the "lust of

[129] Schnürer, *Briefe Kaiser Franz Joseph I. an seine Mutter 1838–1872,* p. 176.
[130] Redlich, *Das österreichische Staats- und Reichsproblem,* p. 127.
[131] The ministerial sitting of August 17, 1851, is described in fuller detail in English by Bagger, *Francis Joseph,* pp. 184–85. Incidentally, I surmise that Mr. Bagger would have treated the various characters of *Francis Joseph* with more gallantry, had he written his book a decade and a half later, after he had witnessed recent events in Europe.

government was his greatest lust!" Moreover, it was unpleasant to climb down from the dazzling social heights to which his protector, the Prime Minister and mightiest lord in the realm, had led him. Schwarzenberg and Bach, "Fiesco and his Moor," different as their characters were, splendidly complemented each other's faculties. Schwarzenberg was the organ of direction; Bach, the organ of execution. The cordial relationship between the two extended even to the social sphere. Schwarzenberg invited Bach frequently to the Ballhausplatz, where Bach played "hostess" when Princess Mathilde, Schwarzenberg's sister, did not preside over men's parties. They both went to the theater and to parties arranged for them by Princess Schönburg, another sister of the Prince. Bach, "the renegade," was scornfully treated by his former liberal friends, but the nobility, too, looked with haughtiness and suspicion upon the parvenu who had divested himself of democratic trappings (even outwardly by shedding his "democratic" beard). Schwarzenberg's support of Bach's ministerial ambitions and social aspirations gave a minister, finding himself attacked from two sides, security in office and social standing. On the other hand, Bach brought to his Prime Minister the qualifications of trained intellect and a brilliant legal mind. The teamwork between the two men was admirable.

On August 20, 1851, the Emperor signed four orders, one patent and three rescripts. The imperial patent contained the by-laws of the imperial council, modifying the corresponding paragraphs (96–98) of the constitution of March 4, 1849. One of the three rescripts notified the president of the imperial council of the change in status of that body, as well as in that of the ministry. Once again it was laid down that the Reichsrat was to be heard before the promulgation of every new law; now its opinions were even to be submitted in all cases to the Emperor, not to the ministry. Another rescript, addressed to the Prime Minister, declared the ministers exclusively responsible to the monarch and the throne, not to any other public authority. Ministerial counter-signature henceforth merely signified that the imperial will was correctly expressed in the text. The third rescript, also addressed to Schwarzenberg, ordered the cabinet "to give the urgent question of maintaining and executing the constitution of March, 1849, its mature and minute consideration." The last rescript was tantamount to a death certificate of the March constitution, but formal funeral services were still to be arranged. From September on, the civil servants took an oath of loyalty to the Emperor, just as the army had been sworn in to the Emperor since November 27, 1850, and no longer to the constitution. A commission consisting of three ministers and three imperial councillors under Kübeck's chairmanship was appointed to draw up the report on the "revision" of the constitution. Alexander Bach made a last attempt to prevent the return to naked absolutism. To this end he submitted a memorial—and one wonders whether he gave advance knowledge of its contents to his Prime Minister. In it he wrote:

The people are honestly convinced that a purely bureaucratic and military government will not be in harmony with the present needs and conditions of the Monarchy and the general situation in Europe, and that, if the throne shall be founded securely, and Austria's influence shall extend far beyond her boundaries, another foundation must be laid . . . It is undeniable that the absolutist system will not be approved even by moderate, discerning, and loyal subjects. They consider it inadequate and view it with misgivings. Consequently, public opinion being in opposition, co-operation and a just appraisal of even the wisest and best-intentioned measures of the government cannot be relied upon.[132]

He then advocated the creation of diets for the various crownlands and a consultative imperial college, a sort of shadow parliament, but even these modest proposals did not find an echo.

In November the mixed commission finished the report in six sittings. It passed the Reichsrat in one sitting, with one dissenting vote; in the ministerial council, however, it met unexpected resistance. In seven meetings no final decision could be reached. The Emperor, influenced by President Louis Napoleon's *coup d'état* on December 2, 1851, grew feverishly impatient. The French dictator's action was entirely in harmony with the Austrian Emperor's credo that a sovereign must not only reign but also govern. In these circumstances Francis Joseph decided upon a step as simple as it was

132 Friedjung, *Österreich von 1848 bis 1860*, I (Annex), 510–12.

decisive, and acted in this instance with military resoluteness just as he was to do repeatedly and fatefully in later years. He ordered a joint sitting of the Reichsrat and the cabinet; the prepared bills were read, and the Emperor asked if anybody had any objections. Since there were no exceptions, the task of abrogating the constitution of March 4, 1849, was terminated. The bills received the imperial sanction on December 31, 1851, and were at once announced to Austria's peoples.[133]

The patent of New Year's Eve, 1851, consisted of three parts. The first abrogated the March constitution. To forestall popular agitation a proviso was inserted that equality of the citizens before the law remained in force, as well as the liberation of the peasants from feudal dues. The second part abolished the bill of rights that had been granted as an annex to the constitution of March 4. A reservation was made in favor of "all churches and religious services, for the autonomous administration of their affairs, and for the possession and enjoyment of institutions, endowments, and funds necessary for their religious, educational, and eleemosynary needs, subject, however, to the general state laws." The third part, in form of a rescript addressed to Prince Schwarzenberg, laid down in thirty-six paragraphs the principles for the legislation to be enacted.

"The lands, united to the Austrian Empire under their old historic or under new names and forming inseparable parts of the imperial hereditary Monarchy" were divided into four sets of local division, as heretofore: governorships, counties, districts, and communes. In the communes the confirmation, eventually even the nomination, of officials was reserved to the government. Large estates were taken out of communal areas and immediately subordinated to districts. The hereditary nobility was promised favorable legislation with regard to entailed estates. One fundamental change in the setup of the districts was decreed: administration and judicature were combined in the lowest instance, a step back to seigniorial jurisdiction, with the distinction, however, that the Vienna central

---

[133] Redlich, *Das österreichische Staats- und Reichsproblem*, p. 394. The Emperor wrote to his mother: "We have thrown overboard what we had of constitutionalism, and Austria now has only one master. Henceforth I have to work still harder." Schnürer, *Briefe*, p. 166.

government had become the seigniorial lord of the whole realm.
Trial by jury was abolished. A press law of June 6, 1851, had already
permitted the suspension of a newspaper for three months by the
governor and its suppression by the minister of the interior.[134]
The Austrian civil and penal codes were to govern for the whole
Monarchy. Therewith Stadion's contemplated measures concerning
local government and Schmerling's court and procedural reforms
were swept away.

The patent of December 31, 1851, said nothing about the statutes
for the crownlands which had been elaborated by Bach in 1850 for
all of them save Hungary.[135] These statutes were now laid aside,
just as the constitution was shelved—"sincerely and without reserve."

The aggregate execution of the thirty-six principles laid down
by the imperial rescript of December 31, 1851, forms what has
been comprehensively called "the Bach system," that is, an order of
the absolutist unitary state. It was a severely administrative order,
conceived and constructed as an instrument serving the supreme
will of the Emperor and operated by ministers acting as the hand-
maids of their imperial master. The systematized new order of life—
neo-absolutism—differed from the patriarchal imperial regime of
Francis II and Ferdinand particularly in the inclusion not only of
all the cisleithan lands and Galicia but also of Hungary and her
partes adnexae. The equipment of this Empire with new, generally
uniform institutions is the work of Alexander Bach, whom Francis
Joseph, soon after Schwarzenberg's death on April 5, 1852, made
chairman, but not prime minister, of the council. The political and
administrative principles of neo-absolutism were, however, the intellectual property of Baron von Kübeck. As president of the
Reichsrat he forced his ideas on the committee on the revision of the

[134] *Wien, 1848–1888*, p. 422.
[135] The electoral system in the crownlands was based by Bach on a three-class system,
a system taken over later by the constitution of 1861. The 1861 constitution gave large
estates a privileged position, while the projected system of 1850 placed large estate owners
in the same category as the highest taxpayers. The second class of electors supposedly consisted of deputies from the cities, and the third class of deputies from the rural communes.

constitution and impregnated with his philosophy all administrative renovations and imperial ordinances founded on the proposals of this council. Only after Kübeck's death on September 11, 1855, did Bach become the guiding spirit of Austria's internal policy. Therefore the responsibility before history for the creation of a premature self-reliance in the young Emperor and for the erection of an absolutist state rests on Baron von Kübeck rather than on Alexander Bach. Historians would come nearer the truth if they spoke of the "Kübeck system," or at least of the "Kübeck-Bach system."

As long as the quick rhythm of the startling diplomatic and military successes that characterized the Schwarzenberg regime lasted, people with no political rights could be satisfied with a non-party government that brought them, or at least promised them, economic prosperity. When Schwarzenberg's powerful hand no longer guided Austria's destiny and external reverses set in, foreign affairs made imperative the overhauling of a domestic system that the Prime Minister had desired in principle, although he had only tolerated its precipitate creation. No doubt the Prince was a firm believer in absolutism, at least as far as the Habsburg Empire was concerned. A few months before his death (April 5, 1852) he wrote to the King of the Belgians: "One has only a choice between the principles of authority and total dissolution of society. Any intermediate measures merely mean empty words and impractical utopias, the adherence to which will lead sooner or later to ruin." [136] Although Prince Schwarzenberg was not directly responsible for the abrupt change in the political course in 1852, his general conceptions of the nature and premises of statesmanship were deeply inculcated upon the mind of his student in political science, the Emperor Francis Joseph.[137] These tenets remained the mainspring of the political thinking and actions of the Emperor until his death. In this sense Felix Prince zu Schwarzenberg still ruled from the grave.

[136] Heller, *Mitteleuropas Vorkämpfer*, p. 192.
[137] Redlich, *Emperor Francis Joseph of Austria*, p. 104.

3

GERMAN POLICY

THE GERMAN PROBLEM [1] was one of the matters which at once claimed the attention of Schwarzenberg when he first came to power. He approached it as a neophyte, since until the time when he assumed his new high office, he had never had occasion to give it his attention.[2] He was not well-informed about the views of the national assembly, and, mistakenly, he believed the Administrator of Germany, Archduke John, and his minister, von Schmerling, to be in league with the ultra-national party. "Schmerling is ultra-German," he wrote to his brother-in-law, Prince Windisch-Graetz, on November 3, 1848, "and, as far as I know, he is too much Archduke John's man to be our man." [3] Possessing only meager knowledge regarding Prussia's intentions and the attitude of the other German courts, he had to consider all

[1] The basic material for this chapter is furnished by Friedjung's *Österreich von 1848 bis 1860*, I, 166–200, II, 1–134. Other main works relied upon are: Beer, "Fürst Schwarzenberg's deutsche Politik bis zu den Dresdener Konferenzen," in *Historisches Taschenbuch*, 1891; Bibl, *Der Zerfall Österreichs*; Friedjung, "Fürst Felix Schwarzenberg und Graf Albrecht Bernstorff," in *Historische Zeitschrift*, September, 1911; Freiherr von Helfert, *Geschichte Österreichs vom Ausgange des Wiener October–Aufstandes 1848*, Vols. III–IV; Ritter von Srbik, *Deutsche Einheit*; von Sybel, *The Founding of the German Empire by William I*, tr. by Marshall Livingston Perrin.

[2] Prince Schwarzenberg did not at first have the good fortune to be surrounded by first-class advisers on German affairs. Baron Joseph von Werner, an official of vast experience, but lacking in independent judgment, the head of the German section of the *Staatskanzlei* under Metternich for sixteen years, had been made an under secretary and no longer handled this important phase of the department. His successor was Aulic Councillor Baron Thierry, a nervous bureaucrat of limited capabilities. His only assistant, Alfred Ritter von Arneth, in his pleasing memoirs, *Aus meinem Leben*, I, 276–78, gives a tragi-comic account of the agony through which the wretched Thierry passed while drafting, redrafting and then again redrafting despatches before he could satisfy his exacting and imperious master. Later, the Hessian Baron Biegeleben, who had entered the Austrian service, a man of great culture and an excellent stylist, was called in for fruitful consultation.

[3] Helfert, *Geschichte Österreichs*, Vol. III, Annex 27.

eventualities, even the possibility of a united Germany having merely international relations with Austria.

Schwarzenberg's first statement touching upon the German question was made in the opening declaration of his cabinet, read to the parliament at Kremsier on November 27, 1848. This program included the following paragraph:

Austria's continuance as a union is a German as well as European necessity. Convinced of this, we look forward to the natural development of the transformation which has not yet been completed. When Austria and Germany, both rejuvenated, are fairly settled, each in its new and firm form of government, then it will be possible to determine officially their mutual relations.[4]

Heinrich von Gagern, the new head of Archduke John's ministry at Frankfurt, read into the Prime Minister's words an endorsement of his own system of a restricted German union in alliance with Austria. In consequence, he asked the Frankfurt parliament for power to negotiate with the Austrian government concerning a future confederation as if Austria were a foreign state. Such a procedure would have implied the immediate severance of the centuries-old union of German-Austria and the rest of Germany. Schwarzenberg, as events were to show, would have dared a war rather than relinquish Austria's position in Germany. The pertinent phrase in the Kremsier ministerial declaration was for him *une façon de parler* to a despised assembly—nothing more.

While the Austrians and their friends in the Frankfurt parliament faithfully labored to overcome the unfavorable impression created by the Kremsier ministerial declaration and to defend the supremacy of the House of Habsburg in Germany, Schwarzenberg, as the ministerial champion of the Austrian cause, was engaged in negotiations with Berlin. Here he found unexpected encouragement for his policies. Especially welcome was the message transmitted by Graf Brühl, who accompanied Prince Charles of Prussia to Olmütz as Frederick William's bearer of congratulations on the

[4] Sybel, *The Founding of the German Empire by William I*, I, 301–2.

occasion of Francis Joseph's accession to the throne.[5] Guided by his romantic feeling for the concept and grandeur of the Imperium, the Prussian King implored Austria not to leave the Germanic Confederation and to co-operate with Prussia in solving the German question.

The new head of the Austrian government was too occupied with domestic affairs subsequent to the change in sovereigns to assume a definite stand in Austro-Prussian affairs from the beginning. Two important statements with regard to the German question were, however, made by him. One is contained in a letter addressed to Archduke John, dated December 4, 1848.

Austria's relationship to Germany is very difficult to determine exactly at present. The Emperor has clearly expressed his willingness to go hand in hand with Germany, to act in conjunction with the central authority, to serve with vigor their many joint interests in dealing with foreign powers, and to fulfil faithfully his obligations to the Confederation. For the moment, no more should be demanded of Austria.

The other was made in the cabinet council of December 12, 1848, where he declared:

While withholding the idea that all the provinces belonging to the Austrian Monarchy are to remain inseparably united in a great Empire, a union of the purely German-Austrian territories with Germany, which would lead to the dismemberment of Austria, would be out of the question. Neither would Austria as a whole have to enter the Germanic Confederation as a really great European power, in its own interest and in the obvious interest of Germany.[6]

The Prime Minister returned Frederick William's compliments by declaring the most intimate relationship between Austria and Prussia to be the sole possible basis for solving the German problem. Only on such a foundation, he continued, with a view to gaining the Prussian King for the Austrian point of view, could be realized the longing of all the German tribes to be united in a pow-

---

[5] Beer, "Fürst Schwarzenberg's deutsche Politik bis zu den Dresdener Konferenzen," p. 5; Sybel, *The Founding of the German Empire by William I*, I, 310.

[6] Heller, *Mitteleuropas Vorkämpfer: Fürst Felix Schwarzenberg*, pp. 242, 230, quoted according to the translation given in the manuscript of the book, *Austria—Yesterday and Tomorrow; the Austrian Problem and Post-War Settlement*, by Dr. Ernst Hoor.

erful national state. Schwarzenberg proposed that Germany should
be reconstituted, not as a federal union which would annihilate the
individuality of the different states, but as a confederation. In order
to carry out the idea of a confederation—and this plan was somewhat contradictory—he advocated a stronger executive than formerly; a body formed of delegates of the princes should take the
place of a popular assembly. Union of the economic interests of the
German tribes and a universal military system were his next proposals. For the maintenance of peace in Germany he recommended
the support of the central government in Frankfurt, provided,
however, that it would conduct the current affairs of the Confederation within the framework of its competence. All the preparations for attaining the objects outlined should be undertaken with
the greatest secrecy. Bavaria should first be acquainted with this
plan, and then the courts of Hanover, Dresden, Stuttgart, and Cassel
should be persuaded to concerted action. Insurrection in Germany
should be put down by force of arms, and to this end Austria, in
view of her engagements in Italy and Hungary, would pledge a
"symbolic" representation of troops.

In his memorandum Schwarzenberg admitted the alternatives of
a close or loose Austrian coherence with Germany, but on one condition: Austria would not consent to an ambiguous dual position
of her German provinces or to a virtual separation of these provinces as to legislation and administration from their inseparable
unity with the non-German lands. Otherwise, an Austrian participation would be condemned by public opinion, and he declared
that his government had neither the desire nor the power to oppose
a universally voiced national wish. At any rate, Germany would
have in the new-born Austrian Empire the most natural and loyal
ally for all times; she would have a stronger support through Austria's strengthened and undivided forces than individual parts of
that Empire, torn from their natural integration, could ever render.[7]

[7] Beer, "Fürst Schwarzenberg's deutsche Politik bis zu den Dresdener Konferenzen,"
pp. 7–9; Friedjung, Österreich von 1848 bis 1860, I, 173–74; Sybel, The Founding of the
German Empire by William I, 305.

SCHWARZENBERG'S FIRST PLAN TO SOLVE THE GERMAN PROBLEM

Although occupied with the reconstruction of his Empire and with Hungarian affairs, the Prime Minister was soon forced by events to formulate a more concrete plan. At this juncture, King Max of Bavaria implored the Austrian cabinet not to withdraw its protective hand from Germany, giving the assurance that he would never willingly recognize a Prussian hegemony. Schmerling, who had hurried from Frankfurt to Vienna to report that the Gagern program would probably be rejected by the Frankfurt assembly, urged Schwarzenberg to prompt action in the unification work of Frankfurt if the House of Habsburg were not to be cast aside by all Germany. Thus, Schwarzenberg's first plan concerning the future constitution of Germany emerged. Considering the circumstances in which it was conceived, it is understandable that it was not the fruit of ripened thought. Two principles guided the Prime Minister: unity of the Monarchy and the abolition of politico-economic and legislative barriers between the individual parts of the Austrian Empire and, secondly, maintenance of the centuries-old position of Austria as the first power of all the German territories of the former Holy Roman Empire.

As Count Albrecht von Bernstorff, the Prussian envoy at Vienna,[8] shared the anti-Austrian views of his foreign minister, Bülow, Frederick William sent Brühl, his aide-de-camp, a second time to Olmütz to conduct further negotiations. Schwarzenberg availed himself of a plan submitted by Frederick William in 1840 and in April, 1848, and now repeated, but he remodeled it according to Austria's special requirements. He proposed dividing Germany and Austria into six groups: Austria and Prussia with their territories and the other four kingdoms, Bavaria, Saxony, Württemberg, and Hanover. Each of the six groups, which, upon Brühl's suggestion, were given the sonorous title "imperial military dukedoms" in order to appeal to the strong historical feeling of his king for the medieval empire, should have a chamber of deputies from the estates, its own

[8] On Bernstorff's mission to Vienna see Bernstorff, *The Bernstorff Papers*, by Karl Ringhoffer; tr. by Mrs. Charles Edward Barrett-Lennard and M. W. Hoper, I, chaps. iii–v.

finances, and its own army. The whole should be headed by a directory under the presidency of Austria. The lesser states were to suffer a subordination to these kingdoms, or a "quasi-mediatization," which Schwarzenberg, despite his passionate championship of conservative stability, considered unavoidable, "since life cannot be maintained by artificial means when the inner forces have died." [9] Naturally, what the Prussian ministers did not like in their own king's scheme, since it ran directly counter to Prussia's ambition and the national desire for unity, Schwarzenberg found excellent from his Austrian standpoint. Why should he be more Prussian than the Prussian king?

That the Prussian ministers were highly displeased with Schwarzenberg's plan is not surprising. To the King, however, a rupture with Austria was unthinkable. Believing that the Austrian statesman had misinterpreted his intentions, the romantic on the throne drew up with his own royal hand a reconstituted Roman-German empire patterned on modern lines (note of January 4, 1849). Only with difficulty could his ministers induce the King to delete the concluding sentence, in which he had formally offered the predominating position in Germany to Austria. Count Brühl was despatched for the third time to Olmütz with this note.[10]

Schwarzenberg had previously doubted that he could successfully carry out his idea, but now he thought the King strong enough to overcome the opposition of the ministers. His note of January 17, 1849, drafted by his then secretary, Josef Alexander Hübner [11] (1811–1892, Count von after 1888), skillfully adapted itself to the King's reasoning by emphasizing the points of agreement and glossing over significant discordant passages in the memorial. As the King's note had been silent on the question of the imperial crown and the Prussian king's position as hereditary commander-in-chief,

[9] Beer, "Fürst Schwarzenberg's deutsche Politik bis zu den Dresdener Konferenzen," p. 10.
[10] The ensuing interview between Schwarzenberg and Brühl is given by Sybel, *The Founding of the German Empire*, I, 310–18.
[11] The author of *Ein Jahr meines Lebens, 1848–49*, and *Neun Jahre der Erinnerungen eines österreichischen Botschafters in Paris unter dem zweiten Kaiserreich 1851–1859.*

Schwarzenberg did not have to commit himself on these delicate subjects. He endorsed again the formation of six military dukedoms, even allocating to them more powers than Frederick William had done. The King's fear of revolution was nourished by approvingly referring to the "Utopian ideals of the assembly in the Cathedral of St. Paul" and painting in even more glaring colors "the confusion of Above and Below"—expressions which the King had used. Schwarzenberg wanted to make sure that the favorable attitude taken by the Frankfurt parliament towards a Prussian hereditary empire would not prompt the King to change his mind regarding the despised assembly. But while the King desired to have the work of the parliament come to an end peacefully, and only afterwards come forth with his plan regarding the league of six kingdoms, the Austrian statesman suggested having the parliament dissolved at once by military force. For the preparation of meeting a possible revolt, an army of 20,000 Prussians, 10,000 Bavarians, and 10,000 Württembergers under the supreme command of the king of Württemberg should be assembled in the vicinity of Frankfurt; Austria, considering her other military engagements, would contribute a thousand men for the re-enforcement of the garrison of Mayence. Nothing was said concerning the central government or Austria's relation to the federation.[12]

Prince Schwarzenberg's first plan to solve the German problem was not destined to become Germany's constitution. This time the Prussian ministry offered resolute and unanimous opposition to the King's cabinet policy. When the Prussian cabinet with its advisers had almost given up hope of drawing the King to their side, the highly gifted but mentally affected sovereign suddenly veered around and assented to a circular note, despatched to all the German governments on January 23, 1849.[13] Now, for the first time, Prussia, though in guarded terms, officially supported Gagern's program of a restricted union under her leadership. Nothing definite was said as to the acceptance of the imperial dignity;

[12] Sybel, *The Founding of the German Empire by William I,* I, 328–29.
[13] Beer, "Fürst Schwarzenberg's deutsche Politik bis zu den Dresdener Konferenzen," p. 13.

rather it was left to the members of the proposed union to decide what position they deemed most expedient to take on the
question of the headship of the federation. The contents of this
circular harshly clashed with the Prussian declarations formerly
made in Vienna. Schwarzenberg had good reason to be enraged at
the course taken by the Prussian cabinet. True enough, the Prussian
ministers finally had to take a firm stand if the Prussian state was
not to suffer irreparable harm. But they should have resorted to
more energetic action before and, especially, prevented the King's
note of January 4. As a result, the King was now compromised, and
although Bülow had never failed to reveal his own sentiments
through his envoy Bernstorff, still he had failed to keep his promise
to come to an understanding with Austria before Prussia should
embark on a new policy.[14]

The Prussian incongruities called for strong Austrian action.
Schwarzenberg vented his ire in a letter to the Austrian envoy at
Berlin, Count Trauttmansdorff, dated January 24, 1849.

The [King's] ministry, the mouthpiece of a powerful party in Prussia,
unperturbed by the royal will, follows its own way and assigns the royal
words to the limbo of *pia desiderata*. The declarations made to Your Excellency by Counts Bülow and Brandenburg are in complete contrast with
those of the King's. Consequently, Count Brühl's journeys to Olmütz have
not promoted an understanding in the constitutional question. At best—
if that was necessary—they have thrown a regrettable, but glaring light
on the King's impotence and his minister's attitude. . . . The King has
repeatedly given us his solemn promise that he would never aspire to the
first place in Germany, knowing very well that that place will always
belong to Austria. Who will give us the guarantee that also on this point
other influences, the impulse of events, some bold stroke from anywhere,
will decide His Majesty, reluctantly, but resignedly, to have the Imperial
German Crown pressed on his head? . . . [But] His Majesty as Emperor
of Austria is the first German Prince. This is a right, sanctified by tradition and the course of centuries, by Austria's political power, and by the
wording of treaties on which the federal relations, still in force, are
founded. His Majesty is not willing to renounce this right.[15]

[14] Bülow resigned. His place was taken by Count Arnim, who had been envoy in Vienna
before 1848 and was of pro-Austrian complexion. Valentin, *Geschichte der deutschen
Revolution von 1848–49*, II, 365.
[15] Friedjung, *Österreich von 1848 bis 1860*, I, 181–82.

In a letter to his brother-in-law Windisch-Graetz he revealed himself as a true Austrian patriot. "The King of Prussia," he wrote,

could not withstand the intrigues around him. His cabinet left us in the lurch; we must now follow our own path and alone. I confess, that I, as an Austrian, am not greatly concerned. . . . We see a great danger and a hindrance to our consolidation and our progress in the so-called relationship with the contemplated reconstituted Germany.[16]

The circular note of January 15, 1849, strengthened the hearts of Prussia's friends in Frankfurt. On the other hand, the position of the 120 Austrian deputies (the Slavs of the Monarchy had refused to elect deputies, so that the quota of 190 allotted to Austria was never filled) became more and more precarious. On the fourteenth of January the question of the supreme authority in Germany was placed on the agenda of the Frankfurt parliament. After five days of discussion the advocates of the Prussian hereditary empire succeeded, by a vote of 258 to 211, in forcing a motion through the first reading that the dignity of the imperial supreme authority should be conferred upon one of the reigning princes. The majority of the deputies (263 to 211), the friends of Austria, in alliance with the democratic Left, however, rejected a hereditary imperial office. National ideals reached from Frankfurt to Austria, but not from Austria to Frankfurt.[17]

The Austrians had weathered the first reading, but a second reading of the article dealing with the supreme authority might be disastrous for them. Schmerling, therefore, desired a forceful reply from Prince Schwarzenberg to Prussia's circular note. He was advised to play a waiting game, but the master in the art of gliding over difficulties by means of noncommittal and pliant phrases uttered with an apparent glow of warmth regarded the present situation as prohibitive of further delay. In repeated reports he urged his Prime Minister to come forth with a positive plan to meet the

[16] Beer, "Fürst Schwarzenberg's deutsche Politik bis zu den Dresdener Konferenzen," p. 13.

[17] See Schüssler, "Die nationale Politik der österreichischen Abgeordneten im Frankfurter Parlament," *Abhandlungen zur mittleren und neueren Geschichte*, Heft 51, pp. 19, 32; see also Telle, *Das österreichische Problem im Frankfurter Parlament im Sommer und Herbst 1848.*

Gagern proposal. On February 4, 1849, Schwarzenberg gave Josef von Würth, Schmerling's collaborator of tested mettle, a note for the temporary guidance of the adherents of an entire Germany, in which he aimed to gain time and tried to persuade the members of this group to continue to exert themselves in behalf of Austria and her inclusion in Germany. He assured them that his government felt Germany's need of rejuvenation through a closer association of the individual states, but he declared a unitary Germany, now under discussion at Frankfurt, to be unacceptable to Austria and undesirable for Germany, because "such a union would infringe upon German moral and material interests, age-honored customs, and claims on the future." [18] What he advocated in his note was a Germany powerful against the outside world, internally strong and free, organically articulated, and yet composite. In this Germany, the German states, as well as their non-German parts, should have no difficulty in finding their place. Interestingly, the last sentence contained the first allusion to the creation of a great empire in Central Europe, a grandiose plan about which more was soon to be heard.

Although the note of February 4 was primarily designed to put off the Frankfurt assembly, it was intended at the same time to influence the royal courts. The Austrian envoys were instructed to declare to the kings to whom they were accredited that while Austria would not hold aloof from a new union of kindred peoples she was by no means willing to be relegated to a minor role therein. Regretting that at the moment he could not render effective assistance, Schwarzenberg invited the German kings to stand firm and not to surrender to an imperial supreme authority. His adroit scheme was successful. Bavaria's note of February 16, 1849, expressed the conviction that only a union inclusive of all parts of Germany and therefore also of Austria would answer the mighty national striving for unity and guarantee the strengthening of the whole fatherland. Württemberg, in a note of February 24, characterized a potential severance of Austria from the whole German

[18] Bibl, *Der Zerfall Österreichs*, II, 200.

state as self-mutilation of the fatherland and spurred the imperial
government on to an accord with the national assembly.[19]

In a note of February 27 Schwarzenberg instructed Ritter von
Schmerling to proceed with the latter's plan concerning a directory
for the empire and to come to an understanding with the delegates
of the royal courts thereon. It seemed as if he was now ready to lend
a willing ear to the suggestions of his plenipotentiary at Frankfurt.
The draft submitted to him in answer to his request clung to the
idea of a directory, but proposed a presidency of Austria and Prussia alternately. On this basis an amicable settlement of the German
question might perhaps have been reached; possibly the assent of the
national assembly could have been obtained if the former hostility
to a popular assembly had been dropped. The Austrian "minister of
drastic effects," however, willed differently: in his dictated constitution of March 4, 1849, and its commentary of March 9, 1849,
contained in a note to the Frankfurt assembly, he had prepared two
thunderbolts.

Thereby he cleared away the bog of equivocation with categori-
cal directness and his usual robust will power. Now he thought the
time ripe for forceful diplomatic action. The centralized constitution of a Greater Austria radically eliminated the possibility of Austria's subordination to a Greater Germany, and especially, to a German parliament. His note, in addition, refused Austria's secession
from Germany.[20] But the greater novelty of the note consisted in
his demand of the admission of the whole of Austria, Hungarians,
Poles, and Italians included, that is, some thirty million non-
Germans, to the Germanic Confederation. The Confederation
should be headed by a directory in which Austria and Prussia each
had two votes, Bavaria one, and all other states four in all. The presidency of the directory was to be reserved exclusively for Austria.

[19] Beer, "Fürst Schwarzenberg's deutsche Politik bis zu den Dresdener Konferenzen,"
p. 16.

[20] "Austria . . . cannot tear its German provinces out of that close inner union which
makes of the monarchy a united whole. *If Germany will not recognize this requirement,
we shall regret it, but we shall not on that account give up the very prerequisites of our
existence.*" Heller, *Mitteleuropas Vorkämpfer*, p. 50, Hoor's translation.

Army and foreign affairs were left to the individual states, while the directory had the decision as to war and peace of the Confederation, as well as the conduct of economic affairs. It was to be assisted by an assembly of seventy deputies sent from the chambers of the individual states in the ratio of one deputy to every million inhabitants, so that thirty-eight would be allotted to Austria and thirty-two to the rest of Germany.[21]

The projected union would have been tenuous. Instead of the old Confederation of sovereign states, guided gently, yet firmly, by Metternich's resourcefulness, there would have been a powerful directory that threatened to mediatize not only the petty German states, but all of them, Prussia included. Could the Frankfurt parliament, could even a romantic king of Prussia agree to such a plan? Was not the idea that a Pole or a Czech might be the leading figure at Frankfurt frightening enough to the feverish imagination of a Junker of the Mark of Brandenburg to instill in him an intense dislike for Austria? Yet the idea of an empire of seventy million people was not without grandeur.[22] It was the conception of a mighty Central Europe offering advantages to both Austria and Germany. The plan had been suggested to Schwarzenberg by his minister of commerce, Bruck, who hoped in this manner to erase the party lines between great and little Germans. On the one hand, the unitary state excogitated by Schwarzenberg and Bach could be realized only through a closer union with Germany; on the other, Germany was vitally interested in the maintenance of Austria as a German state and in her cultural mission of erecting an impassible barrier against the Russian colossus in the East. But Schwarzenberg, like Metternich, focused his policy on the West, with this difference: whereas his cautious predecessor had avoided a quarrel with Prussia, the impetuous successor did not take alarm at the thought of settling accounts with his country's rival at a double-quick pace.

[21] On the note of March 9, 1849, see, for example, Beer, "Fürst Schwarzenberg's deutsche Politik bis zu den Dresdener Konferenzen," pp. 17 et sqq.; Sybel, The Founding of the German Empire by William I, I, 340–42; Valentin, Geschichte der deutschen Revolution von 1848–1849, II, 370.

[22] Bibl, Der Zerfall Österreichs, II, 204.

Schwarzenberg's imperious demands dispelled the illusion that all German states could be preserved on a national basis. The Austrian deputies, who had on more than one occasion shown that an ideal, Austrian national sentiment, could be formed through a common political history and the centuries of living with alien races in the same state, lost their stoutness of heart. Only some time later did most of them feel themselves again to be Austrians first and Germans second, just as do Austrians nowadays. Schmerling, humiliated because he had not been notified of the momentous steps taken by his government, sent a dignified letter of resignation to Schwarzenberg on March 12. The Prime Minister, though vexed to see his policy disapproved, was impressed by the jurist's unsullied sincerity, and before long he gave him a cabinet appointment as minister of justice.

The gulf between the Austrian government and the Frankfurt assembly was unbridgeable. Two factors, however, retarded the showdown between the great and the little Germans: King Frederick William and his ministers, who were never certain whether they should welcome or loathe the offer of the imperial crown, and the arbitral role of the democratic Left, holding the balance between the two major parties, for whose benefit the prerogatives of the crown were whittled down to a phantom. Finally the parliament aroused itself to give a telling answer to Schwarzenberg's enunciation by declaring the hereditariness of the supreme authority on March 27 by a vote of 267 to 263, four "faithless" Austrians voting in favor of the measure. On the following day 290 members of the assembly elected King Frederick William of Prussia Emperor of Germany.[23]

When on April 3, 1849, the Prussian king declined "the crown of mud," as he called it, the Austrian government was relieved of an irksome worry. Now Schwarzenberg deemed it expedient to liquidate part of the German enterprise. As in his eyes the national assembly no longer existed, he peremptorily ordered the Austrian deputies to return at once. He recalled Count Trauttmansdorff from his

[23] Valentin, *Geschichte der deutschen Revolution von 1848–1849*, II, 372–73.

post in Berlin and replaced him by Baron von Prokesch-Osten, a famous orientalist and writer, as well as one of the best diplomats of
his day, of whom he expected more vigorous action.[24]

PRUSSIA'S ATTEMPT AT LEADERSHIP AND THE INTERIM

The scene shifted from Frankfurt to Berlin and opened with Prussia's proposal for the future imperial constitution. In spite of her
serious mistakes in policy, new possibilities to assume leadership in
Germany presented themselves to Prussia in the spring and summer
of 1849. Prussian regiments had suppressed insurrections in Saxony, in the Palatinate, and in Baden, and although some of the German princes might prefer Austria to Prussia, they had to subordinate their pride to the prowess of Prussian arms. No help could be
expected from Vienna, since Hungary was still in the turmoil of
rebellion. In these circumstances Frederick William's advisers urged
him to seize the supreme power in Germany. Count Arnim, the
pro-Austrian foreign minister, was dismissed on May 2, and General
Joseph von Radowitz, an intimate friend of the King's, became the
guiding spirit of Prussia's new tactics. Count Brandenburg, and
later Freiherr von Schleinitz, took over the vacant portfolio. If
Radowitz had been endowed not only with unselfishness, patriotism,
and great intellectual gifts but also with daring, ambition, and
practical sense [25] he could have anticipated under a clear sky a large
part of the work that Otto von Bismarck had to perform under
thunder clouds. The sole thought of the King, however, was, now
as ever, that his plans should be achieved peacefully; no force should
be used against the princes to underwrite the Radowitz constitution.

General von Canitz was sent to Vienna to lay the Prussian pro-
posals, contained in a note of May 9, before the imperial cabinet:
Austria should allow Prussia a free hand to form a federal union in
Germany, exclusive of the Habsburg Monarchy; as a compensation
Austria was offered an eternal alliance in a German union, so that

---

[24] His reports to Prince Schwarzenberg on the Berlin situation are excellent. Some of
them were published by his son; see *Aus den Briefen des Grafen Prokesch von Osten*
(*1849–1855*).

[25] Sybel, *The Founding of the German Empire by William I*, I, 372.

the whole of Germany would have been committed to Austria's defense of her possessions in Hungary and Italy; while the German federal union and the Austrian Empire should remain two independent sovereignties with their own legislatures, they should form an indissoluble union towards foreign states; finally, Austria should at once give her assent to Prussia's assumption of a provisional central government, a control which, obviously, Prussia, with her troops stationed in Suabia and the Upper Rhine, could have exercised ever so much more effectively than the powerless Archduke John.[26]

Prince Schwarzenberg was not for a moment doubtful what attitude he should take towards the Prussian proposals. He possessed grace not only in salons but also under pressure; he had courage. Could a statesman of his caliber be expected meekly to renounce his proud Empire's historical position in Germany? In his reply to the Prussian document (May 16, 1849), couched in polite terms, as external circumstances demanded, he admitted that Germany was threatened with great danger, primarily because national feelings and political exigencies had crystallized into illegitimate claims whose unconditional acknowledgment would entail a regrettable disturbance of natural and legal relationships. Austria was fully convinced of the necessity of Germany's reconstitution, he argued, but in order to attain this aim the new constitution should respect vested rights and lay down as first principle the safeguarding of the various states' interests. He suggested for the conduct of a provisional central government a college, consisting of Austria, Prussia, and one of the lesser kings chosen by the latter from their own midst. In conclusion, he flatly rejected a restricted federal union and a wider international alliance, the German Union. At any rate, he contended, how could he be called upon to give his consent to a constitution presented only in draft form? He followed his note of May 16 by a formal protest of May 19 against any resolutions taken in Berlin in violation of existing treaties and Austria's claims resting thereon.[27]

---

[26] Beer, "Fürst Schwarzenberg's deutsche Politik bis zu den Dresdener Konferenzen," p. 19, citing *Denkschriften des Freiherrn von Canitz*, II, 277; Sybel, *The Founding of the German Empire by William I*, I, 376.   [27] Sybel, *ibid.*, 377-78.

The Prussian government based its right to the creation of a federal union on Article XI of the old Act of Confederation, which granted the Germanic states the privilege of entering into separate alliances. Schwarzenberg, ever ready to pounce on an enemy when he discovered a vulnerable spot in his armor, denied the cogency of the Prussian argument with irrefutable logic: of course Article XI did not envisage the creation of a new state, a German Empire, tantamount to the sundering of the Germanic Confederation.

In spite of Austria's opposition, the League of the Three Kingdoms, Prussia, Hanover, and Saxony, was formed on May 26, 1849.[28] With regard to the courts of Munich and Stuttgart, however, Schwarzenberg's artful calculations that forceful action would buoy up the opponents of Prussia's supremacy in Germany proved correct; they stood aloof. Dresden and Hanover, fearful of the revolutionary forces in their states, reluctantly yielded to pressure. Adherence to the League implied assent to the Radowitz constitution of May 28, which was given with the reservation that the two courts would no longer hold themselves bound to the League if, at the time of the election of the contemplated diet, Bavaria and Württemberg had not become members. The covenant did not grant the crown of Prussia the title German Emperor, yet it conferred upon the Prussian king powers not dissimilar from those granted to William I in later years. Schwarzenberg exerted every influence upon the other German courts to keep them away from a German realm in which Prussia would combine the leadership of the common army with that of its tariff union; however, he succeeded only in causing a long deferment of their decisions: twenty-seven of the thirty-five German states, that is, all except Austria, Bavaria, Württemberg, Hesse-Homburg, Liechtenstein, Frankfurt, Denmark for Holstein, and the Netherlands for Luxembourg and Limburg joined the League, headed by an administrative council, under Radowitz's presidency, in Berlin.[29]

The incessant negotiations and wrangling between Austria and Prussia continued during the summer of 1849. Credit for having

[28] Beer, "Fürst Schwarzenberg's deutsche Politik bis zu den Dresdener Konferenzen," pp. 23 et sqq.; Sybel, ibid., 382 et sqq.   [29] Sybel, ibid., 396–97.

found the formula for a temporary understanding between the two powers must be given to Archduke John's under secretary of foreign affairs, Baron Biegeleben of Darmstadt. Germany's dignified administrator of a thankless office had in April expressed the wish to resign. Only because Prussia had claimed the central government for herself in the summer did he, the Habsburg Prince, cling to his duties, but in the fall he had definitely decided to turn his back on Frankfurt. On the other hand, Austria had heretofore always insisted upon the participation of the lesser states in one form or another in a temporary government, but was now ready to drop her demand. Bernstorff believed that he scored a diplomatic success [30] by signing "The Compact of the Interim" [31]—so-called because it was to last no longer than May 1, 1850—since the agreement provided for the double rule of Austria and Prussia with equal rights conceded to each contractant. The pact was ratified on October 13, rather belatedly, as it was accepted by the Prussian ministry only after some hesitation. The necessity of submitting the agreement to the administrative council of the German Union of May 26, 1849, served as an excuse for the Prussian tardiness.

The concord of the two rival powers remained patchwork. Its existence did not deter Prussia from pursuing her former policy regarding her Prussian-German federation with unabated vigor. On October 19, 1849, she caused its administrative council to issue writs for the election of a parliament at Erfurt on January 15, 1850.

AUSTRIA'S COUNTERMEASURES TO COMBAT PRUSSIA'S AMBITIONS

As Saxony and Hanover had vetoed the calling of elections and therefore all the kingdoms stood apart from Prussia's undertaking, her provocative action could not be construed in Vienna as anything other than a peremptory challenge to Austrian claims. Schwarzenberg saw in Berlin's conduct the exploitation by the Hohenzollern dynasty of a national movement through a legislative assembly to

[30] Friedjung, "Fürst Felix Schwarzenberg und Graf Albrecht Bernstorff," in *Historische Zeitschrift*, September, 1911, p. 546.
[31] Beer, "Fürst Schwarzenberg's deutsche Politik bis zu den Dresdener Konferenzen," pp. 25–26; Sybel, *The Founding of the German Empire by William I*, I, 397.

feed its lust for undisputed leadership in Germany. Moreover, the German middle states were powerful pawns in his diplomatic game. He needed them in his play against Prussian ambitions, just as Napoleon I had made effective use of the kingdoms in checking both Austria and Prussia.[32] He was consequently willing to sacrifice the lesser states and, if need be, to mediatize them; even the Czar was now ready to abandon them as structures too weak to stem a revolutionary tide.

The protest of November 28, impregnated with a measure of acerbity uncommon in diplomatic documents between nations in peacetime, was the depository of Schwarzenberg's rage. In it he declared the projected Prussian-German Union to be wholly illegal, as violative of the 1815 Acts of the Germanic Confederation. Changes in these Acts, so Schwarzenberg proceeded to argue, could be introduced only with the assent of all governments; a separate league, as was now contemplated, would be a permanent threat to the security of the states not represented at Erfurt. Then he added a veiled threat of a declaration of war: should the Prussian Union disturb peace and order in Germany, Austria would with her united forces protect every state injured by Prussia's action.[33]

Baron von Schleinitz, the Prussian foreign minister of natural and sterling insignificance, replied by a calmly worded despatch of December 12, 1849. He declared that his cabinet could not deviate from the policy adopted, as this would be a breach of loyalty towards Prussia's associated states. The action of his country, he maintained, was in full accord with the Act of Confederation and the Vienna Final Act: the Austrian protest could not therefore be recognized as valid. The safety of any member of the Confederation would be strengthened rather than weakened, and consequently Prussia could await any claims on the grounds of injury with complacency. This was the official version, but Prokesch-Osten reported to Vienna that the Prussian ministers Brandenburg and Schleinitz apparently de-

[32] Napoleon III, too, was aware of the importance of the Middle States for France. See Lebey, *Louis Napoléon Bonaparte et le ministère Odilon Barrot*, p. 569.

[33] Beer, "Fürst Schwarzenberg's deutsche Politik bis zu den Dresdener Konferenzen," pp. 32–33; Sybel, *The Founding of the German Empire by William I*, I, 403–4.

sired to find in the Interim the golden bridge leading to an understanding between Austria and Prussia.[34]

Although Prince Schwarzenberg had attacked Prussia by invok-
ing the Confederation of 1815, he was far from wishing, in terms of
a favorite phrase of his, to reconstitute "the old, thoroughly shaky,
and very wobbly *boutique*, ready to collapse at the next blow from
inside or outside." [35] His present intention was to advance the creation of a Central European empire of seventy millions not only by
admitting Austria into the Germanic Federation but also by merg-
ing the whole of Austria and Germany into an all-embracing trade
and tariff union. Concomitantly with a customs union, a political
union was considered by Prince Schwarzenberg of utmost necessity
to energize his German reform projects. He was sorely irritated by
the confused actions of the Prussian cabinet, split into a majority,
headed by Prime Minister Brandenburg, siding with General Radowitz, and a conservative minority, represented by Foreign Minister
Schleinitz, Minister of the Interior Manteuffel, and War Minister
Stockhausen, adhering to the traditional alliance between Austria,
Prussia, and Russia. The King, upon Radowitz's promptings, redeemed his pledged word by the decree of February 16, 1850: a
German parliament, at first adorned with the majestic title "imperial assembly," was convoked at Erfurt for March 20. Bernstorff,
the Prussian envoy at Vienna, after an interview with Schwarzenberg, reported the Austrian Prime Minister's stinging criticism of
the Prussian measures under date of February 23 in these words:

I am convinced that your declarations and the assurances made upon orders
from your government are bona fide. But what shall I say when all your
despatches undertake that Prussia will hold the old Confederation sacred
and will do nothing running counter thereto, while all her actions are in
direct disagreement with these undertakings? How can I have confidence in your government or any faith in the declaration of your cabinet? [36]

[34] Sybel, *ibid.*, 404–5.
[35] Bibl, *Der Zerfall Österreichs*, II, 217–18.
[36] Friedjung, "Fürst Felix Schwarzenberg und Graf Albrecht Bernstorff," in *Historische
Zeitschrift*, September, 1911, p. 552.

Schwarzenberg's political plan "for the beginning of the permanent unity of Germany" had as a basis a Bavarian draft [37] of a
new German federal constitution, which he remodeled according
to Austrian ideas. The covenant finally agreed upon, usually called
the "League of the Four Kings," was entered into between Bavaria,
Württemberg, and Saxony at Munich on February 27. Austria acceded to the pact; Hanover, fearing Prussia, refused to sign it, but
withdrew from the League of May 26 in order to demonstrate her
neutrality between the two rival camps. Attached to the agreement
was a constitutional draft containing these provisions. A federal
government, consisting of a directory of seven (Austria, Prussia,
Bavaria, Saxony, Württemberg, Hanover, and the two Hesses) was
to be set up. Its presidency was by implication reserved to Austria.
The other twenty-eight states, as a kind of castigation for having
joined the Prussian-German League, should be so divided that the
seven directing states would vote for them also. A national assembly
should be elected by the chambers of the individual states, one
hundred from Austria, one hundred from Prussia, and one hundred
from the remaining states. The main Austrian wish was therewith
fulfilled: the admission of the entire Monarchy into the Federation
and the formation of a tariff union.

Austrian statesmen were skeptical regarding the creation of
February 27, offered in such glittering phrases to the German governments. The dean of the elder statesmen, Metternich, at the time
living in Brussels, disapproved the wide deviation of the League
from his work, the Confederate Acts of 1815. He held Schwarzenberg, "a disciple of his diplomatic school, a man of firm character,
solid courage, and clear insight," in high esteem, but his German
policy met with his keen disapprobation. Although "he disliked to
mix in current affairs," he went so far as to give his successor in
office his "impressions on the Prusso-Teutonic imbroglio" in a private letter of March 27.[38] Kübeck, this *fine fleur* of the old bu-

---

[37] Sybel, *The Founding of the German Empire by William I*, I, 406.
[38] Beer, "Fürst Schwarzenberg's deutsche Politik bis zu den Dresdener Konferenzen,"
p. 72.

reaucracy, left without instructions in Frankfurt, found the new policy "erratic." Even Schwarzenberg's secretary, Hübner, generally an ardent admirer of his master, was rather frigid towards the late Austrian course in German matters. But Schwarzenberg moved on unperturbed; he was preparing to strike another decisive blow at Prussia.

On March 20, 1850, the Erfurt assembly, ill-starred as it proved to be, like most undertakings of the talented and irresolute Prussian king, convened, and on April 15 it accepted the constitution of the German Union with a supplementary act. Its sessions were concluded on April 29 amid general recognition of dignity and patriotism. Prussia had journeyed to her German empire as the pilgrims go to Echternach, Luxembourg, by taking three steps forward and two to the rear; bellicose defiance was hurled at Vienna, at once followed by a declaration of friendship. Thus, despite the zig-zag course of the Prussian cabinet, Schwarzenberg had not succeeded in forcing Prussia, through coercive diplomatic measures, to give up the Union.[39] But the Prussian-Austrian drama moved on, inexorably guided by the principle of logical, interior action. Its main character worked towards the aim of the plot: to prevent Prussia from seizing the supreme power in Germany. *Avilir puis démolir,* his intentions toward Prussia were said to be, but the epigram, probably first imputed to him by his Prussian counterplayer, General von Radowitz, is a myth both as to substance and to form. The logic of events might have provoked an armed showdown, but the stage was not yet set for a military display. The arbiter between Austria and Prussia, the Russian Czar, disapproving of Austria's desire to enter the Germanic Confederation with all her lands, declared that he did not wish to frustrate his brother-in-law's designs in the German constitutional question. Realizing that without Russia's assistance Austria's flanks were exposed in Italy and Hungary, Schwarzenberg had to await more favorable days and to continue to play a diplomatic game.

"The Interim," the central authority in Germany assumed by

[39] Friedjung, *Österreich von 1848 bis 1860,* II, 39.

Austria and Prussia, was about to expire at the end of April, 1850. Bavaria, on March 30, and other German courts following her, stated that she would not consent to a prolongation of the central government as constituted and that she expected a share in the administration of confederate affairs. Prussia demanded a continuation of the Interim in the present form until the enactment of a definitive constitution for the whole of Germany, and this demand implied Austria's tacit consent to the Prussian Union. Schwarzenberg, on the other hand, desired, even as a temporary instrument, the creation of a directory of seven and the installation of his group system. A Nassau privy councillor, Forsboom-Brentano, who was held in high esteem by both Schwarzenberg and Schleinitz, was called in as a mediator between these two irreconcilable views. Bernstorff, too, had many conversations with the Austrian Prime Minister on the subject. As late as April 12 the Prussian envoy was under the impression that an accord could be reached.[40]

A rude awakening from a complacent attitude was in store for the Prussian cabinet. On April 19 Schwarzenberg gave notice, by a circular despatched to all the German governments except Prussia, that no agreement had been reached with Prussia concerning a provisional central authority and that therefore Austria, as the presidential power under the Confederate Acts of 1815, felt herself constrained to reconvene the federal diet at Frankfurt for the purpose of establishing in common such a new authority.

This incident led to a rupture between Schwarzenberg and Bernstorff. Schwarzenberg intimated that the Prussian envoy had consented to his *démarche* provided Prussia were treated "gently." Bernstorff's sense of honor was aroused; in an irate letter he protested to Schwarzenberg against the use of the latter expression. Originally an admirer of Schwarzenberg, he became his embittered foe. Henceforth pique grew into mordancy, and mordancy into venom in his reports to Berlin about the "obstinacy and the inaccessibility to any reasonable arguments" of the "mad" Austrian.[41]

[40] Concerning the interview of April 12 see Freidjung, "Fürst Felix Schwarzenberg and Graf Albrecht Bernstorff," *Historische Zeitschrift*, pp. 554–55.

[41] *The Bernstorff Papers*, pp. 146, 148, 161.

The Prussian foreign minister, Schleinitz, unwilling to provoke a break between the two powers, accepted the holding of a congress, but attached conditions which if approved would have been equivalent to recognition of Prussia's Union. The decision of the General-Minister was instantaneous: he moved up heavy artillery. On April 26 a new Austrian circular invited all the German governments, inclusive of Prussia, to send plenipotentiaries to Frankfurt on May 10, threatening delinquents with punishment for any violation of their confederate pledges.[42]

The boldness of Schwarzenberg's document becomes apparent when its flimsy legal basis is discovered. The Austrian government had announced the extinction of the confederate diet after the latter had dissolved itself on July 12, 1849. Moreover, the full assembly of the confederate diet could be convoked only when summoned by the close council, now represented by the central committee of the Interim, Austria and Prussia. But was the Austrian move more "unlawful" than the Prussian had been on May 28, 1849, the day of the declaration of a constitution for a "German Empire" against Austria's, Bavaria's, and Württemberg's objections? After all, there had recently been a confederate diet, but no "German Empire" that could be resurrected.

The glove that was thrown down by Schwarzenberg was picked up by Prussia. Frederick William's honor was wounded, and while he still shrank from severing the ties of friendship binding him to an old confederation ally, the value of the Prussian Union increased in his eyes in direct proportion to Austria's challenge of his creation. The King invited all his allied princes and free cities, twenty-seven in number, to a meeting in Berlin in order to mobilize them against the Austrian policy. There was much external pomp and much internal friction in the Prussian capital. Finally, Prussia's allies agreed on the prolongation of the Union until July 15, 1850, because the lesser states were motivated by the fear of mediatization on the part of Austria's royal sympathizers. With regard to the representation at Frankfurt, it was resolved that all the states of the

[42] Sybel, *The Founding of the German Empire by William I*, I, 421 et sqq.

Union should present themselves as one unit, Prussia casting her votes in the name of all the states. Thus the Union, with the exception of the two Hesses, which reserved an independent vote at the Frankfurt congress, was not a closely-knit whole; still it offered a fairly united front to Austria.[43]

As might be expected, Schwarzenberg was not intimidated by the performance at Berlin. In defiance of Prussia, the diet of the Germanic Confederation was reopened at Frankfurt in the name of the "Imperial Presidential Power" on May 10. Only ten states were represented: Austria (by Count Friedrich Thun, chairman); the four kingdoms of Bavaria, Württemberg, Saxony, and Hanover; Hesse-Cassel; Hesse-Homburg; Liechtenstein; the Netherlands in behalf of Luxembourg and Limburg, and ironically enough—the king of Denmark was still at war with some members of the Germanic Confederation—Denmark for Holstein. The Union states had sent envoys to Frankfurt, but they were not admitted to the assembly, since Prussia demanded to preside over the diet with Austria alternately, and Count Thun, with Schwarzenberg's full approbation, rejected the Prussian condition.

Thus, Schwarzenberg, to Metternich's great rejoicing, had resurrected the confederate diet, despite Prussia's opposition, but what could he accomplish through a rump assembly? Should he ride roughshod over the resistance of the Union states, have the dissolution of the Interim formally decreed, and initiate the constitution of a new central government? But what would happen if Prussia and her allies—and this had to be expected—took exception to these aggressive steps? Could the Austrian Minister then proceed to coercive measures against Prussia as he threatened to do in conversation with Bernstorff? A war between Austria and Prussia would have been inevitable in the circumstances, and for this clash Austria was not sufficiently armed. The crescendo in Schwarzenberg's inimical actions against his rival was unmistakable: from a protest against the Union he had moved to the formation of a counter-league, and from the League of the Four Kings he had advanced to the Frank-

---

[43] *Ibid.*, pp. 423–27; Friedjung, *Österreich von 1848 bis 1860*, II, 45–46.

furt confederate diet. His machinery of power politics, nicely adjusted to his policy of might in Central Europe, ran on ceaselessly. The next link to be added to his diplomatic mechanism would have been a military one—war. Austria, however, had only 30,000 troops in Bohemia; nor were Prussia's assembled reinforcements in Silesia impressive. Logically, therefore, both camps turned to the power that had enough mobile reserves to provide a necessary make-weight in the national German struggle. The following scene opens at the temporary imperial Russian headquarters at Warsaw.

NEW RIVALRIES BETWEEN AUSTRIA AND PRUSSIA

On May 28, 1850, Prince William of Prussia and Prince Felix Schwarzenberg arrived at the palace of Skierniewice, near Warsaw, to lay each country's case before the judge of appeal in Central European affairs. Emperor Nicholas, a man of a lucid mind but limited by lack of knowledge, of an iron will but fettered by Slavic emotionalism, held to his original conception: Prussia had fostered liberalism (liberalism, radicalism, constitutionalism, republicanism —all were of the same brand to him) by her convocation of the Erfurt assembly and her whole constitutional procedure, and thus was subject to censure; on the other hand, Austria's confederate diet appeared to him to be of conservative and therefore legitimate character as flowing from the principles of the Acts of 1815. Nevertheless, he did not deem Prussia's action so condemnatory as to warrant an Austrian declaration of war on her; nor did he consent to send an envoy to the Frankfurt confederate diet, as at that time he still sternly disapproved of Austria's desire to join the Confederation with all her provinces.

The Czar, effulgent with a sense of authority derived from recent successes, gave a verdict not in favor of Austria or of Prussia. He called the Austrian policy "irresolute and wily, although politically prudent, because it sought to gain time." [44] When it was the Prussian prince's turn to defend the case of his country by describing Prussia's action as in accordance with the articles of the Act of

[44] Sybel, *The Founding of the German Empire by William I*, I, 446.

Confederation, the Czar interrupted the pleader with this admonition: "Do not talk to me about Articles of Confederation, I beg
of you; I do not understand their meaning."

In constitutional questions the Emperor Nicholas found a more
acceptable response from the Austrian. "It is true that the Constitution has been granted but many things may happen to change it.
Its execution is still a long way off." [45] This is the first known public statement which hinted at the resurrection of absolutism in Austria. Despite the Austrian's congenial pliancy on a subject so dear
to the heart of the Russian autocrat, the main issue was not decided
in harmony with the purpose of his mission. When he asked the
Czar point blank what Russia intended to do in case of a war between Austria and Prussia, Nicholas serenely replied that he wanted
to have peace preserved at any price and that he would turn against
the attacker. He construed "attacker" to mean, as Baron Meyendorff, the shrewd Russian envoy at Berlin, explained, not only the
breaker of peace, but also the party that would give legitimate cause
of declaring war. [46]

The stately mission of the two princes did not obtain the objec-
tive sought for by either side: Russian aid was denied to an "attacker." This was a discordant note which rang unpleasantly in the
ears of the tempestuous Austrian statesman when he drove home
through the fine palace park. The shrill word "attacker," uttered in
Warsaw, deserved to be pondered over. It had its effect.

While in Warsaw no immediate tangible results had been achieved
for either Austria or Prussia, momentous decisions were soon to
come from the Czar in the Schleswig-Holstein affair. After two
successful campaigns, Prussia had concluded an armistice with Denmark on July 10, 1849. As the Schleswig-Holsteiners had cleared the
foreigners from their soil and had an army strong enough to defend
themselves against the Danish king, the Czar, as the champion of
legitimacy, threatened, if the Germanic Confederation did not
subdue the "rebels," to restore Denmark's overlordship with his
own troops. England, too, sided with Russia in this question. The

[45] *Ibid.*, p. 447.   [46] Friedjung, *Österreich von 1848 bis 1860*, II, 55.

British foreign minister, Palmerston, Austria's implacable foe, unblushingly meddled in Austro-Italian affairs in the name of liberty
as a possession common to all peoples. With regard to Schleswig-
Holstein, however, the warm sympathies of his cosmopolitan idealism were chilled by the cold considerations of British materialism:
for English maritime interests it was more profitable to have the
ports of the two duchies in Danish hands.[47] In espousing the Danish
cause "the dreadful old man" as usual pursued a policy different
from that of the court. Since the Prince Consort favored the hegemony of Prussia over a confederated Germany, the Queen, for whom
he was wisdom incarnate, of course, held the same view. But Palmerston had "the satanic gift of making royal flesh creep; he did worse
than criticize the august husband of his young Queen—he just
ignored him."

France played a double role. Officially she supported England and
Russia. The Prince-President Napoleon, however, entertained the
idea of destroying the spirit of the Holy Alliance by expanding
the existing discord between Austria and Prussia and of constitut-
ing himself the arbiter between the two rival parties. Naturally, he
expected to be a lucky fisherman in troubled waters. In opposition
to his foreign minister, General Ducos de la Hitte, the crafty prince
held out to Prussia the alluring bait that he would further her ends
in Germany provided he received as *quid pro quo* Prussia's assent to
breaking up Austria's power in Italy and to acquiring the part of
Bavaria lying on the left bank of the Rhine. The French envoy in
Berlin, M. Fialin de Persigny, a man of "apostolic pride," and more
of a buffoon-journalist than a diplomat, was unable to convince the
Prussian ministers of the stability of his master's regime.[48] Frederick
William treated these French advances with disdain. How could he
hammer out, on the hot anvil of German public opinion, his newly
forged Union based on a national idea when he was called upon to

[47] Srbik, *Deutsche Einheit*, II, 9.
[48] On these French schemes and M. de Persigny's inglorious mission to Berlin see Rothan,
"Souvenirs diplomatiques," *Revue des deux mondes*, May 1 and 15, 1889, and *Souvenirs
diplomatiques: L'Europe et l'avènement du Second Empire*, 2d ed.; Lange, *Frankreichs
Preussenpolitik in den Jahren 1849 und 1850*.

surrender German lands to a foreign power? Besides, he was brought
up in the atmosphere of brotherly alliance with Russia and Austria
and of violent antipathy to the upstarts in the Elysée.

Prussia was faced with the cruel choice of either acceding to the
Russian-English demands respecting Schleswig-Holstein or of aban-
doning her sanguine hopes in Germany in order to placate Austria.
The Prussian cabinet, under the influence of General Radowitz, decided in favor of an understanding with Russia. Prussia, therefore,
concluded peace with Denmark on July 2, 1850. The Schleswig-
Holsteiners were bargained away like cattle for political reasons.
That statesmen traded the duchies like international merchandise in
1850 was an "act repugnant to all feelings of justice and morality"
in the language of the high-minded British Queen,[49] but not astonishing when even nowadays the claim to national self-determination
is decided only by the side with the stronger battalions.

The Danish peace might have brought on that understanding
between Prussia and Russia which was the *raison d'être* for its conclusion on the part of Berlin. In that event the Prussian Union
would have been secure, and Schwarzenberg's policy would have
been defeated. All the Austrian statesmen whom the Prime Minister
consulted on the question of "finding a way out of the German
labyrinth" [50] were unanimous in their demand for the abolition of
the Prussian structure. Schwarzenberg, feeling uneasy about the
Russo-Prussian situation and confronted with an empty treasury,
resorted to a risky maneuver, but a remarkably dexterous feat of
his many-sided statecraft. An interview with Count Bernstorff,
July 8, 1850, gave him the opportunity of setting forth his startling
proposal. After the Prussian envoy, upon instructions from the Berlin cabinet, had admitted to him the "infeasibility" of the constitution of May 26, although he had not been empowered to concede its
"abrogation," Schwarzenberg declared the distinction to be a soph-
ism and angrily remarked: "Again you hand out a hollow bundle of

[49] *The Letters of Queen Victoria,* ed. by Arthur Christopher Benson and Viscount Esher,
II, 295.
[50] Beer, "Fürst Schwarzenberg's deutsche Politik bis zu den Dresdener Konferenzen,"
p. 77.

straw for us to thresh." Thus, Bernstorff at first encountered rough usage at the hands of a sarcastic adversary. It would be difficult to conceive of two men having less similar methods of diplomatic technique: Schwarzenberg, galvanic and then serene, aggressive and then suave, ironical and then captivating; Bernstorff, always stiffly reserved, meticulously correct, and hypersensitive about the honor of his king. After the biting question, "Are you still arming?" which the envoy answered with the cool observation, "We are armed," [51] the Prime Minister did the striking and surprising: he submitted to Prussia a plan of conciliation. This project, the so-called "six-point program," turns up time and again in subsequent negotiations in this or that form. It reads as follows: [52]

1. Germany shall be united into a confederation of seventy million people, headed by a strong central executive in the hands of Austria and Prussia, exclusive of the other states.
2. The duties of the executive proper shall devolve upon Austria and Prussia in common, and the two great powers shall be on equal footing in the Confederate diet.
3. Prussia may preside over a restricted union of those states which choose to join it, with the proviso, however, that this union shall not form the base of a German empire.
4. Austria shall be admitted with all her provinces into the Confederation, for the protection of her sovereignty in Italy and Hungary.
5. A tariff-union between Austria and Germany should be initiated.
6. A popular representation shall not exist in the Confederation.

Through the foregoing proposals Schwarzenberg had made a lavish offer to Prussia. He had dropped a favorite idea of his, the strengthening of the German kingdoms with the concomitant system of groups, in favor of an equal participation of Austria and Prussia in confederate affairs. For the nullification of the constitution of May 28 there was an equitable equivalent: the dissolution of the recently resurrected confederate diet. From the beginning, Schwarzenberg had been doubtful of the success of his tender, but he considered its submission necessary, for "as long as Austria and

---

[51] Friedjung, *Österreich von 1848 bis 1860*, II, 62; *The Bernstorff Papers*, pp. 141, 145.
[52] Sybel, *The Founding of the German Empire by William I*, I, 458; Friedjung, *ibid.*, pp. 67–68.

Prussia do not come to an agreement, neither party will attain anything; the present wretched state of affairs will continue and terminate in general exhaustion from which only the enemies of order
and the enemies of Germany will benefit." [53] His main purpose in
forging his diplomatic master stroke was, however, to conciliate
Russia, to convince her that he was not an "attacker." [54] He succeeded brilliantly. Czar Nicholas for the first time consented to
Austria's admission into the Germanic Confederation with all her
possessions. It was a rich reward for having dared to come to terms
with the detested Prussian Union.

The minority of the Prussian cabinet, led by Baron Manteuffel,[55]
stood for acceptance of the Austrian proposals and the nullification
of the May constitution. General von Radowitz, however, fought
for his problem child with utmost doggedness, arguing that Prussia
was not only answerable to the princes alone, but to the whole nation as well, and, as the Erfurt parliament had adopted the constitution, that this fundamental law could be set aside only by a
parliament. He hoped, of course, to be able to drag the German
constitutional problem on until a day when the sun would shine
brighter for his adopted country; after all, there might soon be

[53] Letter to Count Thun, November 22, 1850; Heller, *Mitteleuropas Vorkämpfer*,
pp. 102–3.

[54] Heller, *ibid.*, pp. 102 *et sqq.*, is convinced of the sincerity of Schwarzenberg's offer to
Prussia, while Friedjung, *Österreich von 1848 bis 1860*, II, 64, 67, is inclined to believe that
Schwarzenberg's plan was, so to speak, an expert *coup de théâtre*. Heller, basing his arguments on the Thun letter referred to, cites three reasons for his opinion: (1) Schwarzenberg's desire to conciliate Russia; (2) his wish to come to an understanding with Prussia;
and (3) to brush the "unreliable" German kingdoms aside. Friedjung, grounding his view
as to Schwarzenberg's gamble on Prussia's nonacceptance of his proposals on a later letter to
Thun (July 7) and on a message of July 10 to Prokesch von Osten, assigns as motive for
Schwarzenberg's action his wish to propitiate the Czar and to placate his ministerial colleagues. Schwarzenberg, well-informed about the temper of the inner circles in Berlin, as
the opposition ministers had the unorthodox penchant to pour out their innermost thoughts
to the Austrian envoy, was undoubtedly entitled to consider Prussia's rejection of the
program a foregone conclusion. The question of diplomatic morality cannot therefore be
raised. Should Prussia have accepted Schwarzenberg's suggested arrangement against all
expectations, he would have taken her decision philosophically according to his motto,
chaque jour a sa peine, and proceeded on his path to attempt to procure the Habsburg
domination over his planned empire of seventy millions.

[55] See Manteuffel, *Unter Friedrich Wilhelm IV.*, ed. by Heinrich von Poschinger (Berlin, 1901), pp. 228 *et sqq.*

trouble again for the Austrians in Italy, and Louis Napoleon might then come to the assistance of the Italian nationalists.

On July 18 Bernstorff acquainted Schwarzenberg with Prussia's refusal to adopt the proposals of July 8. The Austrian Prime Minister, expressing extreme displeasure, at once declared that Prussia's adherence to the League of May 26 prevented any discussion about the confederate constitution in open conferences, as proposed by Berlin. On the very same day Schwarzenberg invited the confederate diet to constitute itself in definitive form as of September 1, 1850, and to install the close council as the executive central body.[56] The tenacity with which Prussia clung to her Union of twenty-one states was impressive evidence for Schwarzenberg that she desired at a propitious moment to unite all Germany under her scepter. From now on he was firmly resolved to resort to extreme measures. Thus, the unusual and startling was even outwardly abandoned in favor of the continuation of consistent, inward action.

Other situations arose which caused fresh quarrels between the two rival powers. Prussia entered into military covenants with some of the lesser states by which their contingents were taken into her own army; by agreement with Baden she stationed Prussian troops in the grand duchy for a like amount of rebellious Baden troops held in her garrisons. Prince Schwarzenberg protested against these arrangements upon the ground of the old confederate rights. But as Prussia had originally marched her troops into Baden to quell a rebellion, her cause was excellent in the eyes of Czar Nicholas and solid enough to gain Russian support in this matter. Consequently, this line of attack had to be abandoned by Austrian diplomacy.

The assault on Prussia through the Baden gate having been beaten off, Schwarzenberg selected a front entirely acceptable to Emperor Nicholas. This was again the Schleswig-Holstein question. After Prussia had concluded peace with Denmark, July 2, 1850, the boisterous sea of liberty in the duchies still showed waves of resistance. The Schleswig-Holsteiners, forsaken by the rest of Germany, con-

[56] Beer, "Fürst Schwarzenberg's deutsche Politik bis zu den Dresdener Konferenzen," p. 77; Sybel, *The Founding of the German Empire by William I*, I, 461.

ducted a war of their own against an abhorred foreign prince. When they had lost Schleswig after the battle of Idstedt (July 24–25, 1850), they continued the struggle in Holstein, and Denmark was not strong enough to overcome the opposing forces of a heroic people. There was another complicating factor. In order to guarantee the indissoluble integrity of the Danish monarchy—and to thwart Germany's expansion in the north—Russia, England, and France recognized a successor to the childless King Frederick VII in the person of Christian of Sondersburg-Glücksburg. In Schleswig-Holstein, however, the conviction prevailed that the laws of succession of the duchies favored the house of Augustenburg. The gulf between *cratos* and *ethos,* between craving for power and the infringing sense of moral responsibility, had not been covered by a consultation of the estates of the duchies. Nicholas imperiously demanded the accession of Austria, Prussia, and the Germanic Confederation to the London Protocol. As German public opinion was enraged at the interference of foreign powers in German affairs, approbation of the protocol was a hazardous undertaking for any German government. In this situation Schwarzenberg experienced unexpected annoyance at the hands of the four kingdoms; they did not dare to run counter to the liberal sections of their population. The matter of restoring law and order in the duchies was delayed. Czar Nicholas became impatient, even vehement, in his demand that Holstein should be pacified. Schwarzenberg thought for a moment to brush Russia aside and to arrive at a reconciliation with Prussia, using Bernstorff's intermediaries, again the Nassau Privy Councillor Forsboom and this time also the Danish envoy, Baron Heeckeren,[57] but he soon found it more expedient to come to an understanding with Russia. When the Russian chancellor, Count Nesselrode, and Baron Meyendorff, the new Russian envoy at Vienna, arrived at Ischl, where Emperor Francis Joseph and Prince Schwarzenberg happened to be, the latter could please the Russian diplomats with the news that he had already signed the treaty on August 23. More-

---

[57] Friedjung, "Fürst Felix Schwarzenberg und Graf Albrecht Bernstorff," *Historische Zeitschrift*, pp. 557 *et sqq.*

over, he could promise them that the close council of the Confederation (at that time the Confederation consisted of thirteen states
and eleven million of other Germans, while the Prussian Union embraced twenty-one states with only five million other Germans)
would at once debate the form in which the pacification of the
duchies should be taken in hand. Prussia, on the other hand, refused
to accede to the protocol on August 25. Thus the two imperial
courts had come to a mutual understanding directed against Prussia: Holstein was to be handed over to the Danish king by the Confederation as sheriff.

Fate placed another trump card in the hands of Schwarzenberg
—the controversy between Frederick William of Hesse-Cassel and
the estates of the electorate.[58] The cause of the trouble was the
refusal of the Hessian parliament to vote taxes and the civil list of
this shrewd but wretched prince unless a budget was presented in
accordance with constitutional provisions. When the Hessian Minister Hassenpflug, a fanatical absolutist, decreed a state of siege,
although the temper of the country was serenely tranquil, the civil
servants flatly refused to take part in this infraction of the constitution, and nine-tenths of the corps of officers resigned their commissions. That officers became "rebels" was not only an atrocious
crime in the eyes of the Elector and his minister but was also an act
dangerous to their lives. They fled to Frankfurt and petitioned the
confederate diet to subjugate a revolting population. On September
12 Prussia demanded that the case be submitted to the court of arbi-
tration at Erfurt, in conformity with the provisions of the League
of May 26, of which Hesse-Cassel had professed herself still to be
a member at the conference of the princes in Berlin. Even conservative Austrian statesmen condemned the insolent maladroitness and
cowardly rashness of the pettifogging ex-judge and Hessian minister.[59] Nevertheless they regretfully conceded the necessity of granting this admittedly incompetent government moral and military
support because the revolutionaries, violators of the monarchial

[58] Srbik, *Deutsche Einheit*, II, 56 *et sqq.*
[59] Beer, "Fürst Schwarzenberg's deutsche Politik bis zu den Dresdener Konferenzen,"
p. 96.

principle, were on the Prussian side. Prokesch-Osten went farther: he jubilantly spoke of the Hessian affair as a godsend for Austria. Indeed, Schwarzenberg and his resurrected diet had the golden opportunity of appearing in shining armor before the Czar as the saviors of law and order by suppressing the Cassel revolution. Moreover, as the confederate diet declared the refusal of the Hessian parliament to vote the finance law to be illegal, the Austrian statesman acquired a legal title to the expansion of his influence into Prussia's domain proper, northern Germany.

The new situation was fraught with mortal danger for the Hohenzollern kingdom. As long as the Hessian military roads with their halting-stations were in the hands of a friendly state, Prussia's connections between the East and the West, between Berlin and Cologne, were safe. But if a power inimical to her should occupy this vital territory, if Austria and the southern kingdoms should march their troops into Hesse and beyond Hesse into Holstein, a military crisis would be created that would call for drastic action. In the circumstances the not very courageous Baron Schleinitz was replaced as foreign minister by the real leader of the Prussian policy, Austria's adversary, General von Radowitz. The cinematographic succession in the Prussian foreign office—Bülow, Arnim, Schleinitz, Radowitz—is the best proof of Prussia's instability in her Austrian policy. One of the first moves that Radowitz forced on the ministry was a vigorous protest against any interference in Hesse by the confederate diet. Even War Minister von Stockhausen then remembered Frederick the Great's dictum that "diplomacy without armaments is like music without instruments," aroused himself out of lethargic indecision, and half-heartedly undertook various military measures. Yet Radowitz was by no means in a warlike mood. He proposed negotiations with Vienna about the questions in dispute through commissioners and conferences, but did not budge as far as the maintenance of his cherished Union or the clearance of Hesse-Cassel from confederate troops was concerned. Thus the King and Radowitz steered Prussia into a position in which she was either compelled to fight for an impracticable object, the Union, or to

come to dishonorable terms with her enemies on account of the very
infeasibility of her object. Still, there would have been an obvious
egress out of the impasse: she could have joined the confederate diet
with all the members of the Union and attempted to wrest the leadership from Austria. In that event the other German kingdoms
would have interposed no objections to Prussia's restoration of
legitimacy in the electorate of Hesse, nor would they have blocked
a Prussian expedition in Holstein. But the Prussian king, despite his
readiness to settle all controversies with Austria in an amicable way,
conjured up his honor again in magnificent incantations and declined to deal with, let alone join, a body unlawful in his eyes.[60]

The Prussians were poor psychologists when they believed
Schwarzenberg to be still in the mood of playing with dilatory com-
promises through diplomatic formulae. Assured of Russian support
in the Hessian question, he was now prepared to come to a showdown with Prussia on the issue of the Union and its accompanying
problems.

Austria encountered no difficulty in drawing Bavaria and Württemberg to her side in the Hessian question. The monarchs of the
two kingdoms and their prime ministers, von der Pfordten and
Baron von Linden, met Emperor Francis Joseph and Prince Schwarzenberg at Bregenz, and on October 12 they concluded an offensive
and defensive alliance against Prussia. At the banquet warlike
speeches were exchanged. To the king of Württemberg's toast,
phrased in the language of an Austrian vassal, "When the Emperor
gives the word, we are ready to march," Francis Joseph replied: "I
am proud to march against the enemy with such comrades." [61] The
toasts were ceremonial expressions of the treaty stipulations. The
preamble declared in unmistakable language that the three monarchs "were compelled to consider any obstacle that might be raised
against the execution of measures decided upon by the Confederation a revolt against the legitimate authority of the supreme confederate authority and consequently a breach of the Confedera-

---

[60] Sybel, *The Founding of the German Empire by William I*, I, 484–85.
[61] *Ibid.*, I, 489.

tion." It was left to Bavaria to take the first steps. Article One of the treaty provided:

When the confederate diet, in accordance with the demand of the elector of Hesse, resolves to take action on the basis of the confederate laws, the Royal Bavarian government declares its readiness at once to place the necessary troops at the disposal of the Confederation. These troops will be joined by the Imperial-Royal Austrian Fourteenth Battalion of Chasseurs stationed in Frankfurt on the Main, and this battalion will be replaced in Frankfurt by Bavarian troops.[62]

Article Three was designed to counteract Prussia's opposition to these undertakings.

Should Prussia, as the wording of her relevant communications gives cause to apprehend, resort to active resistance against the execution of the confederate resolutions regarding the electorate of Hesse, a breach of the Confederation is regarded as being therewith committed, which must be met not only with protests but also with confederate execution. To this purpose His Majesty the Emperor of Austria will, as the initial step, assign 150,000 men within three weeks; His Majesty the King of Bavaria, 50,000 men; and His Majesty the King of Württemberg, 20,000 men as soon as possible.

Hanover considered the matter too dangerous, and therefore the treaty, in Article Four, merely invited her, as well as the Royal Saxon and Grand-Ducal Hessian governments, to accede to the agreement.

In conformity with this treaty, Emperor Francis Joseph ordered the mobilization of four army corps under the command of General Count Wratislaw. Three of these were assembled in Bohemia, eventually to strike at the heart of the enemy through the Elbe valley. Naturally, Prussia took countermeasures, but she concentrated her troops in a secondary theater of war, in the west against Bavaria, and omitted to prepare for counterblows against her main foe, Austria.

Prussia now occupied not only the Hessian military routes but also the territory lying between them, in violation of the Prusso-

[62] Friedjung, *Österreich von 1848 bis 1860*, II (Annex), 549.

Hessian agreements. The confederate diet answered this infraction of international law on October 26 by directing the Bavarians to march into Hesse. Besides, after some hesitancy it ordered the Holstein government at Kiel to refrain from further hostilities under threat of severe penalty. The noose around Prussia became uncomfortably tight. The all-important question Prussian statesmen had to ask themselves was: "Could Prussia still rely on her old friends from the days of the wars of liberation against Napoleon, the Russian czars, to extricate her from a precarious situation?" [63]

SCHWARZENBERG'S TRIUMPH OVER PRUSSIA [64]

On October 17, 1850, one week before the Czar's Austrian guests, Emperor Francis Joseph and Prince Schwarzenberg, were to arrive, the Prussian prime minister, Count Brandenburg, arrived in Warsaw for the purpose of impressing the referee in Austro-Prussian affairs with the soundness of Prussia's position. In the German constitutional question he was instructed to convince Emperor Nicholas of the impossibility of Prussia's recognizing the German confederate diet as revived by Austria; he was to propose the solution of the Hessian and Holstein questions through commissioners appointed by Austria and Prussia with the approval of all the German governments. Nicholas, in his final decision on October 22, declined to mediate the German controversy. His refusal left the Austrians free in their negotiations with Prussia—an advantage for them—and consequently any negotiations at Warsaw pertaining to this subject had to be carried on by these two powers alone. In the two other questions he expected, even exacted, of Prussia unconditional submission to Austria's demands.

On October 26, the same day when the confederate diet ordered the Bavarians to invade Hesse, the Austro-Prussian conversations commenced. Emperor Francis Joseph left the conduct of the negotiations to his minister, formulating the Austrian standpoint only

[63] *Ibid.*, II, 79–81.
[64] On this phase of the Austro-Prussian dispute see especially *ibid.*, II, 81–117; Sybel, *The Founding of the German Empire by William I*, II, 1–82; on Olmütz see also Srbik, *Deutsche Einheit*, II, 56–91.

in a few pregnant phrases. He expressed the earnest hope that a satisfactory understanding would be reached, but made it abundantly clear that he would not abandon the legal basis of the treaties on which he and his government founded their claims. The ensuing discussions between the two ministers were marked by an affable, passionless tone. A spectator would have taken the negotiating statesmen as two old friends engaged in good-natured banter rather than two exacting adversaries playing a dangerous game of power politics with their hands on their hilts. With regard to the German question, the six-point program [65] was taken as the foundation of their conversations. Schwarzenberg accepted the points agreeable to Austria: the formation of a confederate council of seventeen votes, having functions similar to those of the old confederate diet; no popular representation; and the admission of the entire Austrian Monarchy into the Confederation. He rejected the points favorable to Prussia and formulated counterproposals: the equal authority of Austria and Prussia in the presidency (Schwarzenberg reserved the decision on this point to all the members of the Confederation); the assignment of the executive power proper to Austria and Prussia (instead, he proposed the establishment of a "powerful executive" without further concrete definition); and the recognition of the principle of free unions among the German states on condition that their constitutions be not in conflict with that of the Confederation (in lieu thereof, he acknowledged the right of forming unions only if not directed against the spirit and the purpose of the Confederation, that is, its security, and if sanctioned by Article XI of the Act of Confederation).

As the Prussian Union was in Schwarzenberg's eyes founded in violation of Article XI, it should be dissolved. In consideration of Prussia's renouncing the Union, Prince Schwarzenberg, upon Russian pressure, expected Prussia merely to leave the confederate diet unmolested without insisting, however, as before, on Prussia's formal recognition of that body. As a concession, he further agreed to a reformation of the Confederation in free conferences by ministers

[65] See *supra*, p. 140.

of the German states. In analogy to the 1819 precedent, he proposed Vienna as the place of these conferences, while Brandenburg
suggested Dresden. The final settlement of the meeting place was
left in abeyance. Thus, Prussia found herself in a worse bargaining
position than Tarquinius Superbus. At least, he had to pay Amal-
thaea of Cuma for three books of prophecies not more than the
former asking price of six. But Brandenburg, although three points
were granted to him, was still called upon to pay an additional price
in the Hessian and Holstein affairs.

The adjustment of the latter two problems was governed by Russian influence. On October 28 an agreement of utmost importance
for the Habsburg dynasty was concluded between Austria and Russia. In reply to Schwarzenberg's note asking what Russia intended to
do in case of war between Austria and Prussia, the Petersburg cabinet drew a distinction between the Holstein and the Hessian case.
Should Prussia resist a confederate corps sent to Holstein for her
subjugation, Russia declared that she would regard such opposition
as a *casus belli;* with regard to Hesse, Russia promised only benevolent neutrality and friendly support.[66] The booty which Schwarzenberg brought home from Warsaw was substantial. He was fast
approaching his goal of forcing Prussia to acknowledge Austria's
military and diplomatic supremacy. With superb skill he had finally
gained Czar Nicholas for his cause by means of arduous diplomatic
labors extending over many months. Prussia had been maneuvered into a position wherein she would be waging a war in the
most unfavorable circumstances if she persisted in her former
policy.

No one was now more convinced of the worthlessness of the Prussian objects at the risk of mortal peril than was the Prussian Prime
Minister Brandenburg. In the Prussian ministerial councils, held
under the presidency of the King at the beginning of November,
he conceded his former self-deception with admirable fortitude
and relentlessly battled for a new Prussian policy against the bitter
opposition of General von Radowitz. As long as Prussia had con-

[66] Srbik, *Deutsche Einheit,* II, 67.

fessed the impracticability of the Union, why not take the logical step in giving the straightforward declaration of its abolition, he argued. Why not permit the entry of confederate troops into Hesse, provided Prussia should receive a binding pledge from Austria that the occupation of Hesse served no other purpose than the restoration of the legitimate authority—a design entirely in harmony with the royal wishes—and that the Prussian military roads would afterwards be re-established as covenanted—guarantees which the Russian Chancellor Nesselrode had underwritten at Warsaw? And as to Holstein, why strain at gnats—adhering to technicalities—while potentially swallowing camels—risking a hopeless war according to the analysis of the military situation by War Minister Stockhausen—when Prussia was ready to inform the ducal government of the withdrawal of her protection? As Frederick William, the confirmed nonbeliever in ministerial responsibility, had mysteriously left the decision to his ministers, a despatch was sent to Vienna on November 3, in which the Berlin cabinet gave up the Union and acquiesced in the confederate execution in Holstein and Hesse. Brandenburg, the son of Frederick William II of Prussia and his morganatic wife, the Countess of Dönhoff, a noble character, was barely able to sign the despatch; he was suddenly seized by a high fever and died on November 6. Radowitz, the stormy petrel of aggressive Prussian policies, had already folded his wings and resigned on November 2, after the defeat of his motion for the mobilization of the Prussian army. Before the conservative Otto Freiherr von Manteuffel could liquidate a burdensome heritage, he had first to clear away some unexpected new obstacles.

It was far from Prince Schwarzenberg's intention to launch a war jauntily against Prussia.[67] He has often been accused of Prussophobia; some of his contemporary Prussian adversaries charged him bluntly with the will to demolish the Hohenzollern kingdom. No proof can, however, be adduced that he desired to wage war as an end in itself. He was an implacable foe of the plan to solve the German problem in accordance with the doctrine of the "little Germans"

[67] *Ibid.*, p. 70.

(exclusion of Austria from the Confederation), and he would have unhesitatingly combatted any attempt to do so by force of arms. On the other hand, he consistently regarded a full-fledged collaboration between the two great powers as the proper answer to the German question in the sense of the "great Germans" (retention of Austria in the Confederation), with the allocation of the leading role to the Habsburg dynasty in an economically independent and revolution-proof Central Europe.[68] In order to attain the latter aim, the Prince deemed it necessary first to demonstrate unequivocally Austria's supremacy to Prussia. With this end in view, he drafted his reply of November 6 to Brandenburg's despatch of November 3. He flatly refused, though in impeccably courteous phrases, to comply with Prussia's wishes. Instead of acceding to an immediate holding of a congress for the reform of the Germanic Confederation, he made the evacuation of the Hessian territory, which the Prussian troops had meanwhile occupied, a condition precedent to the redemption of his pledge given at Warsaw. He softened this stipulation, however, by granting the guarantee demanded by Prussia with respect to the duration and the purpose of the occupation of the electorate, thus promising to safeguard her military roads in the end.

The Prince had plucked Prussia's ambitions like an artichoke: leaf by leaf. That now even the last leaf, and an unpalatable one at that—the subjugation of a population which had (mistakenly) greeted the Prussian troops as "liberators"—should be forced from her seemed to her king and his ministers unbearable. The mobilization of the Prussian army was ordered (November 6), curiously enough, less with a view to anticipating force by force, but rather for the purpose of permitting the King, "helmeted," to adhere to his pacific intentions and to preserve Prussia's honor untarnished by conducting further negotiations "under arms."

Presently the episode of "The White Horse of Bronzell" occurred to fill Foreign Minister Manteuffel with fresh apprehension lest his peace efforts should be wrecked. The confederate army under the

[68] *Ibid.*, I, 388–89.

command of the Bavarian Prince of Thurn and Taxis approached
the Prussian positions at Bronzell near Fulda on November 8, 1850.
Prussian outposts fired at the advancing vanguard. The shots were
returned: [69] a few Austrian soldiers were wounded, and a Prussian
(white) horse was killed. The officers on both sides quickly separated
their fighting squads, but the fact remained that Austrian blood
had been spilled. Prokesch-Osten had on November 2 been instructed to leave his Berlin post in just such an emergency, and now,
on the top of the grave Bronzell affair, Schwarzenberg sent him
on November 9 this imperious telegram: "Inquire whether and
when Prussia evacuates the electorate of Hesse. In case an answer is
in the negative, ask at once for your passports." [70] Ripe reflection
and deep courage were required of the Austrian envoy to be temperate when the impetuous voice of his prime minister and foreign
minister called for perilous extremes. A narrow interpretation of
Schwarzenberg's orders might have entailed the immediate opening of hostilities. Self-possessed Prokesch-Osten, preferring Schwarzenberg's firm but courteous procedure of November 6 to his head-
long action on November 9, continued to grope for a diplomatic
formula productive of the maintenance of peace. He sought an
interview, first with Manteuffel, then with the King. The Prussian
foreign minister at once expressed his sincere regret at the unfortunate occurrence (November 9) and showed him a despatch to
be sent from Berlin to Vienna on that day in which the dissolution
of the Union and the unhindered march of confederate troops to
Holstein were reaffirmed.[71] With regard to Hesse, the despatch requested a guarantee not only by Austria but also by all her con-
federates; Manteuffel added orally that he had not the slightest doubt
as to the smoothing away of this point also, to the satisfaction of

[69] At first it was unknown which side started the skirmish. Count Nesselrode, the Russian chancellor, on this occasion, repeated the story told about the famous singer Sophie
Arnould. Interviewed by M. de Sartine as to the parenthood of the child to whom she had
just given birth, she answered: "Eh! Monsieur, quand on tombe dans un buisson d'épines,
on ne sait jamais laquelle s'est enfoncée la première."—Lettres et papiers du chancelier
Comte de Nesselrode 1760–1856, Paris, 1911, IX, 325.

[70] Friedjung, Österreich von 1848 bis 1860, II, 95.

[71] Prokesch von Osten, Aus den Briefen, pp. 179–81.

both parties. King Frederick William consented to the evacuation of Bronzell and the withdrawal of his troops to the military roads. Although the way to Cassel was not as yet opened, the retreat before an "undisciplined horde of Bavarians on a penal expedition" was felt as a severe humiliation by the Prussian army. Prince Schwarzenberg, in his counter despatch of November 13, "cordially acknowledged to have found, in the Prussian communication of November 9, the language characteristic of an old and faithful ally"; still he inexorably insisted on his demand for the evacuation of all Hesse by Prussia.

In answer, the temporary Prussian prime minister, von Ladenberg, induced the King to convoke the Prussian chambers on November 21. In an address from the throne, the King declared that Prussia would adhere to her position in the Hessian affair and take up the question of a constitution for the entire fatherland in conjunction with the reform of the Germanic Confederation. As had been expected, there was an upsurge of national feeling. But since prestige had to be defended and since the things supposedly to be secured—constitutionalism and liberty in a united Germany—rested on false premises, the outburst of patriotism was blind and irrational. That the liberal-national elements rejoiced at Prussia's armaments especially dismayed Frederick William. Distrustful of the progressive parties since 1848, he had no desire to wage war for Germany as a prize, let alone liberty.

A special Prussian envoy, a Count Westphalen, a diplomat belonging to the Manteuffel school, was not able to break the deadlock between the two powers. Prussia held to her demand for the occupation of Cassel and the Hessian military roads, although she had received the most sweeping guarantees for her safety in these regions from the confederate diet on November 20, the diet having voted on these guarantees on November 15; Austria insisted just as firmly on evacuation. In the meantime, the circle around Prussia was closing tighter and tighter. Saxony had acceded to the Bregenz League on October 22, 1850, and Hesse-Darmstadt was on the point of following her example. Prince Gortschakoff's arrival in Frank-

furt to announce officially the Czar's recognition of the confederate
diet as the highest authority in Germany had been symbolic of his
master's complete sympathy with the Austrian policy.

As time passed, the Austrian and Bavarian troops in the vicinity
of Fulda found themselves in an increasingly difficult position. The
region was too poor to furnish supplies to the confederate corps.
The Prince of Taxis had either to beat a dishonorable retreat or to
advance. In the circumstances, Prince Schwarzenberg, believing
with Burke that "there is a limit at which forbearance ceases to be a
virtue," decided to cut the Gordian knot. On November 24 he instructed Prokesch-Osten to present Prussia with an ultimatum. The
Austrian envoy announced November 27 as the time when hostilities would begin unless Prussia agreed to the advance of the confederate troops, without opposition, towards Cassel.

The strangely contradictory personality of Frederick William
avoided a war. On November 24 he sent another special envoy,
Count Eberhard Stolberg, to Vienna to extend Manteuffel's invitation for a personal meeting between him and Schwarzenberg, but
the Prince had rather tartly declined the request, because Prussian
troops had not yet departed from Cassel. The King hit now on the
expedient of using moral pressure. On November 26 he instructed
Manteuffel to communicate to the unyielding Prince that Prussia's
foreign minister was being sent to meet him as the bearer of two
royal autograph letters, one from him to the Emperor, and one from
the Prussian Queen to her sister, the Archduchess Sophia. Manteuffel, anxious to see the shadow of war hovering over Prussia recede
and to save his country from a seemingly threefold mortal danger,
telegraphed Count Bernstorff even before receiving an answer, that
he was leaving for Olmütz and that Schwarzenberg's answer might
reach him there on the twenty-seventh. Later, on the same day, the
anxiously awaited telegram arrived in Berlin, with the announce-
ment that Prince Schwarzenberg, at the orders of the Emperor,
would arrive at Olmütz on November 28. Writers differ as to
whether he went to Olmütz on his own volition [72] or against his

---

[72] Heller, *Mitteleuropas Vorkämpfer*, pp. 119–20; Srbik, *Deutsche Einheit*, II, 80.

will by superior orders.[73] Whatever Prince Felix's own opinion in
the matter might have been, to my mind it has always been clear
that he quickly and keenly sensed the pacific atmosphere flowing
from the Hofburg. Although he was no fawning courtier, dynastic
fealty was in view of his family tradition inseparable from his nature. Emperor Francis Joseph would not have imposed his will on
his Prime Minister's dominating authority or have altered his decisive influence on the policy of the Empire, but the manifest imperial
resolve to maintain peace no doubt tipped the scales in favor of
Schwarzenberg's decision that was to prevent another Armageddon.

Manteuffel was directed by the King and his ministers to obtain
from Austria her assent to (1) the six-point program as formulated at Warsaw, (2) the immediate convocation of a general congress, and (3) a decision of the Hessian and Holstein questions by
this congress. With a heavy heart he set out on his somber journey
to Olmütz, but he did not expect to be obliged to pass under the
Caudine Forks in order to preserve peace for his country.

The climactic scene is laid in the Hotel *Zur Krone* at Olmütz. It
is November 28, 1850, six o'clock in the afternoon. The Austrian
and Prussian foreign ministers meet and at once begin their conferences. It is Prince Schwarzenberg's "superior presence" that governs
the interview; [74] it is he who brings the Austro-Prussian drama to
an effective end and stamps it as a *pièce bien faite*.

On the first day the two ministers did not make any headway.
The Prince unflinchingly insisted on unconditional acceptance of his
demands in the three controversial subjects. Manteuffel was left with
the alternative of either bringing a declaration of war back to Berlin or of acknowledging Austria's and the confederate diet's superiority. By the time the session reopened after ten o'clock in the
morning of the following day (the previous conferences had lasted
until the small hours of the night), the Prussian foreign minister
had made up his mind to transgress his instructions and to bow to

[73] Redlich, *Emperor Francis Joseph of Austria*, pp. 72–73; Sybel, *The Founding of the
German Empire by William I*, II, 89.

[74] Manteuffel's secretary, Privy Councillor Abeken, remarked later: "Prince Schwarzenberg is a splendid man, noble through and through. I wish we had *him* as minister." *Manteuffel, Unter Friedrich Wilhelm IV.*, p. 336.

Schwarzenberg's unrelenting attitude in military matters.[75] He
fully realized Prussia's hopeless international situation.[76] In the
Hessian affair she was opposed by the armies of Austria, the four
German kingdoms, and Russia; in the Schleswig-Holstein contest
she was completely isolated as she was confronted with the opposition of England and France also. In the face of this crushing superiority of power, discretion at the right time involving the welfare
of his country seemed to Manteuffel heroic virtue. Moreover, the
Prussian, unequal in stature to his adroit adversary, lost his independence before a statesman who, "like Bismarck and Cavour, was
a master in the assessment and exploitation of diplomatic and political forces." [77]

With respect to the confederate diet he found the Austrian more
tractable. At its expense Schwarzenberg stretched a point in the
Holstein conflict and half a point in the Hessian quarrel in favor of
Prussia. The execution of the measures to be taken against the former
country was left to commissioners appointed by Austria and Prussia, and not by the truncated assembly at Frankfurt. Accordingly,
Section B of paragraph 3 of the "Agreement between the Austrian
and Prussian Ministers Respecting the Affairs of Holstein and Hesse-
Cassel," of November 29, 1850, provided:

After consultation with their allies, Austria and Prussia will send to Holstein, and that as speedily as possible, joint Commissioners, who shall demand of the Stadtholdership, in the name of the Confederation, the cessa-
tion of hostilities, the withdrawal of the troops behind the Eyder, and the
reduction of the army to one-third of its now existing strength—threatening common execution in case of refusal. On the other hand, both Governments will endeavor to prevail on the Danish Government not to
station in the duchy of Schleswig more troops than are necessary for the
preservation of the tranquillity and order.[78]

As to Hesse, Schwarzenberg allowed the presence of Prussian
troops on the military roads and one Prussian battalion at Cassel.
The crux of the controversy was, however, resolved in accordance

[75] Friedjung, Österreich von 1848 bis 1860, II, 119.
[76] Sybel, The Founding of the German Empire by William I, II, 79.
[77] Friedjung, Österreich von 1848 bis 1860, II, 169.
[78] British and Foreign State Papers, XLI, 978–79.

with his wishes: about forty thousand Prussians had to beat an inglorious retreat before the advancing Bavarians. The relevant section (Section A of paragraph 3) stipulated:

In Electoral Hesse, Prussia will oppose no impediment to the action of the troops called in by the Elector, and, therefore, will issue the necessary orders to the Generals in command there, to allow a thoroughfare by the military roads occupied by Prussia. The two Governments of Austria and Prussia will, in concert with their allies, call upon His Royal Highness, the Elector, to give the consent for one battalion of the troops called in by the Electoral Government, and one Royal Prussian battalion, to remain at Cassel, in order to maintain tranquillity and order.[79]

Concerning the German constitutional question, the two ministers were unable to reach an accord. The Prince did not relinquish his views held at Warsaw; on the other hand, he did not coerce Prussia to join a confederation dominated by Austria. He was probably mindful of the note which Nesselrode had handed him at Warsaw on October 28.

Le Cabinet Impérial de Russie entend que l'Autriche s'engagera de son côté envers la Russie à ne point appliquer les décrets de la Diète aux Etats Allemands qui ne l'ont pas encore reconnue. . . . une . . . extension donnée à la compétence de l'assemblée de Francfort ne serait pas conforme à la position actuelle de la question allemande et ne s'accorderait point avec les règles d'une saine politique.[80]

The reform of the German constitution was left to free conferences, but Schwarzenberg made a concession to Prussia by accepting Dresden as the place of holding the conferences. Thus paragraph 4 of the agreement declared:

Ministerial conferences will immediately take place at Dresden. The invitation to them will be issued by Austria and Prussia conjointly, and will be so arranged that the conferences may be opened about the middle of December.[81]

One harsh condition was imposed by Schwarzenberg on Manteuffel before he signed the agreement: the Prussian Foreign Minister

[79] *Ibid.*
[80] Heller, *Mitteleuropas Vorkämpfer,* p. 128.   [81] *British and Foreign State Papers.*

had to consent to an immediate demobilization of the Prussian troops, even before the Dresden congress would assemble, while he conceded only the disbandment of the fourth battalion of every Austrian infantry regiment, leaving Austria all her cavalry and artillery, the troops engaged against Hesse and Holstein, and the soldiers of the lesser states. Even from his own conservative point of view, prompting him to re-establish the old friendly relations with Austria, Manteuffel must have had the gravest misgivings regarding the wisdom of exposing his country to the good will of a foreign power. He realized, however, that Schwarzenberg, distrustful of the palpable divergence in Prussia's ministerial councils and the excursive imagination of her king, leading him to lame endeavors undertaken with a half mind, would never have consented to the agreement but for the inclusion of this clause. In a letter to Prokesch-Osten, dated December 1, 1850, Schwarzenberg characterized the instability of conditions in Prussia in these words:

If the course of policy in the most decisive moments depends on the caprice of a visionary, the clamor of a frenzied chamber, the ambitious dreams of a prince [Prince William], or even the shouting of a milling crowd, how can one foresee or calculate anything?

With Manteuffel personally, I have been quite satisfied, but in the circumstances one or even three sensible ministers are not helpful . . .

The two Manteuffels [the foreign minister and his nephew, an officer, who accompanied him to Olmütz] will testify to the fact that I have in all sincerity expressed my humble opinion on the miserable *boutique* in Berlin.

The King's letter to the Emperor is a pathetic product. Every honest man, reading it, must be filled with deep compassion. The letter is sentimental, insincere, and inane . . .[82]

Frederick William ratified the agreement on December 2. He had for months persisted in an outwardly liberal policy by combatting the confederate diet with its avowed punitive design, yet when threatened with war against Russia and Austria, he yielded to the innermost reactionary wishes of his heart, the re-establishment of legitimacy in Hesse and Holstein. Idealism in the Hohenzollern kingdom, diffuse among the common people, was trampled to the

[82] Friedjung, *Österreich von 1848 bis 1860*, II (Annex), 534; see also p. 120.

flatness of its own shadow through the Olmütz agreement. Prussia's prestige sank low in the scales of the world. She had been administered a severe diplomatic defeat and subjected to fearful humiliations.

Prince Schwarzenberg returned to the Austrian capital like a Roman triumphator of old. He is reported to have remarked on his arrival in Vienna: "War would perhaps have been better and would have brought peace lasting fifty years . . . perhaps. Ah! what an embarrassment is a conscience." [83] A number of cities made him their honorary citizen, among them, Vienna, happy to continue to live in tranquillity and comfort and gladly paying a large amount for the diploma as a token of its appreciation of the preservation of peace. The sentiment of the common people was shared by high aristocrats, who felt that a conflict between the two conservative powers would encourage the liberal elements in the country. To the generals the idea was repellent that they might eventually be compelled to fight their old comrades-in-arms of 1813. Old Field Marshal Radetzky, the designated commander-in-chief in case of the outbreak of war with Prussia, had only reluctantly separated himself from the charms of sunny Italy and the arms of dazzling Giuditta Meregalli, and he was delighted to be able to return to his two loves. Marshal Nugent, a genial gentleman of eighty years, probably the most intellectual, though not the most successful, among the Austrian generals expressed himself in this way:

L'unité allemande, c'est l'union entre l'Autriche et la Prusse; l'Autriche c'est le mari, la Prusse c'est la femme, et une femme trop coquette parfois, aimant à mettre des rubans nouveaux à son bonnet; que diable! il faut s'entendre et ne pas se quereller pour un ruban. La paix une fois rétablie entre les deux époux, ceux-ci parviendront bien à ramener à l'ordre les enfants grands et petits, la Saxe, la Bavière, etc.[84]

Only the educated class among the German population of the Habsburg Monarchy showed signs of sustained interest in the continuation of Austria's stay in Germany.

[83] Vitzthum von Eckstädt, *Berlin und Wien in den Jahren 1845–1852*, pp. 304–5.
[84] *Ibid.*, pp. 265–66.

It would be a gratuitous blunder to venture a prophecy on the possible outcome of a war between Austria and Prussia at that time. From what has been said in preceding pages, however, it may be assumed that Austria would probably have been victorious, although there were factors in the equation working against her, such as the greater *élan* of the Prussian troops, the insecure position in Italy, and the unreliability of the *honvéds*, the Hungarian yeomanry. Even in the opinion of the Prussian generals, an advance by the energetic Austrian chief-of-staff, Baron Hess, as far as Berlin would have been within the realm of possibilities, but whether his entrapment in the vicinity of the capital could have been effected as hoped for by the Prince of Prussia might have depended on the emergence of another military genius such as Frederick the Great.[85] Perhaps there is some truth in Manteuffel's famous saying that "war between Prussia and Austria would be like an ancient Japanese duel in which each of the participants ripped open his own bowels." [86]

At Olmütz, Prince Schwarzenberg forged the last link of the chain that connects the denouement with the beginning of the dramatic Prussian-Austrian struggle. Diplomacy during the conflict was often "dark, dreary, desultory, drivelling." Thorns were planted that choked the seeds of nationalism and liberalism. A romantic king provided for declamations and gesticulations, for action that was not infrequently mere turmoil and carried with it few if any real accomplishments. It was an Austrian statesman, the main character on the political scenes, who in these days worked out the salvation of the Danubian Monarchy by the driving force of his superior character—passionate pride in Austria as a great power. He showed that Austria possessed vast reserves of strength and unsuspected resilience and that the Monarchy was the expression of these qualities. Seldom did the Habsburg dynasty owe so

[85] The general opinion is that the odds were in favor of Austria—"ten to one," in Radetzky's estimation, as acquiesced in by King Frederick William's chief aide-de-camp, von Gerlach, *Denkwürdigkeiten aus dem Leben Leopold von Gerlachs*, I, 586, but Colonel Heller, *Mitteleuropas Vorkämpfer*, pp. 125 *et sqq.*, holds to a less sanguine view. He argues that the Western powers, even in case Austria had been the victor, would not have allowed a crushing defeat of Prussia.

[86] Sybel, *The Founding of the German Empire by William I*, II, 81.

much to one man. When the curtain fell, Felix Prince zu Schwarzenberg, to the astonishment of a world envious of the cluster of his
victories, had re-established Austria's supremacy in German lands.

THE DRESDEN CONFERENCES

Olmütz had successfully demolished the Prussian schemes. A war
had been avoided, but Prussia, although humiliated, had not been
conquered, not even essentially weakened. Nevertheless, Prince
Schwarzenberg had no doubt but that he would also accomplish a
tariff union and via this bridge would create an empire of seventy
millions under the political control of a united Austria. The Dresden Conferences were to lead to this goal.

There were some good but more bad omens for Schwarzenberg's
undertaking. After Olmütz, Manteuffel wrote the Prince a servile
letter of thanks, rather unmanly in tone for the minister of a great
power. "I ask your Serene Highness," the conclusion read,

> to accept my sincere and dutiful thanks for the courtesy shown to me and
> the confidence bestowed upon me at Olmütz. Whatever the future may
> bring, I shall always cherish the memory of those hours during which I had
> the privilege of discussing with your Serene Highness Austria's and Prussia's
> interests—interests incapable of being pursued in opposition to each other
> without gravely endangering Germany.[87]

Manteuffel also acquiesced in the recall of Count Bernstorff from
his post. The Prussian envoy, querulously reproving Schwarzenberg's mentality and character, had become *persona non grata* in
Vienna. He had not been invited to the discussions at Olmütz; special envoys had to be sent from Berlin in the last months of the year
1850 when critical negotiations were being conducted. It was therefore logical that he was replaced by a diplomat of pro-Austrian
stripe, Count Arnim-Heinrichsdorff, who hastened to join the Ballhausplatz household as a servile member like the Saxon envoy,
Carl Friedrich Graf Vitzthum von Eckstädt, who chronicled the
Viennese diplomatic and aristocratic world of his days in letters not
devoid of literary charm despite their naïveté in political judg-

---

[87] Friedjung, *Österreich von 1848 bis 1860*, II, 123.

ment.[88] In Berlin, where Schwarzenberg was received most graciously by the King after the opening of the Dresden Conferences, nothing definite was settled, it is true, but the cordial tone of the Austro-Prussian conversations entitled the Prince to the entertainment of high hopes for the possibility of sincere co-operation with Prussia. The great question remained, however, whether Prussia would be satisfied with the role of concert master or even first violinist in the Habsburg orchestra, comprising Hungarians, Poles, Czechs, Italians, and other nationalities, under the baton of Prince Schwarzenberg. Or had Manteuffel, after all, sacrificed Prussia's present at Olmütz only in order to save the future? [89]

On the other hand, the German middle states showed keen resentment at the handing of an olive branch to Prussia without their participation. Munich, Dresden, Stuttgart, and Darmstadt either feared Prussia's direct ascendancy over Germany or they were apprehensive of a dualistic government to be established in Germany by Austria and Prussia. Moreover, these jealous guardians of their sovereignties were not inclined to grant to the Habsburgs what they had denied to the Hohenzollerns. Beust, the choleric Saxon minister, considered it necessary, so he declared, *ni avilir ni démolir mais contenir [la Prusse]*,[90] but Schwarzenberg's estimation of his frame of mind (and that of his colleagues in other German capitals) comes nearer to the truth in his remark to his Saxon host in Dresden: "You would have preferred to see us come to blows." Beust, in his memoirs, adds these words: "So would have I." [91] The author has good reason to believe, however, that Beust misunderstood or misinterpreted Prince Felix's last sentence. In confidential commu-

[88] *Berlin und Wien in den Jahren 1845–1852.*
[89] On December 19, 1850, Schwarzenberg wrote to Prokesch von Osten: "The official [Prussian] interpretation of the Olmütz punctations, which we have read in the newspapers, is a wretched piece of work; it contains neither truth nor honesty. . . . We at least are more candid and tell the world: yes, we have made concessions in order to arrive at an understanding with an old ally and to maintain peace, and because we hope that Germany will be the gainer thereby. If Berlin continues to speak in various languages, to say this to the right side and that to the left, it will be soon evident that the harmony established is illusory."—*Aus den Briefen des Grafen Prokesch von Osten*, p. 192.
[90] Beust, *Aus Drei Viertel-Jahrhunderten*, I, 121.
[91] *Ibid.*, p. 122.

nications of December 6, 1850, addressed to his envoys in Munich
and Dresden, Counts Valentin Esterhazy and Kueffstein, Schwarzenberg attempted to show that Austria's cool and sedate reflection
in the Prussian matter was preferable to the heat and rashness of
Bavarian or Saxon perturbation.[92] The lesser states, fearful of losing even their roles as drummer boys in the Schwarzenberg orchestra, as usual, grouped themselves around Prussia for protection
against mediatization.

In the matter of Austria's joining the Germanic Confederation
with all her provinces, the Austrian statesman had to figure on the
opposition of France and England. The two Western powers filed
a formal protest against the Austrian plan on the ground that it
violated the Acts of 1815 and clashed with the national character of
the Confederation. It is easy to discover the true reason for the
antagonism that lay behind the legal façade: the foundation of a
powerful Central Europe synthesizing the component states into
a common political and economic unit would have created an unwelcome rival; solicitude for German liberty or the independence
of the German pigmy states was a pretext shielding the intended
impediment of Germany's inner consolidation.

At a solemn ceremony Prince Schwarzenberg as president delivered the introductory speech to the conference of ministers assembled in the Brühl palace at Dresden on December 23, 1850. The impressive act reflected the grandeur of the position conceded to the
Austrian Prime Minister by the leading German statesmen as a matter of course. At that moment the prediction would have been
justified that he was likely to meet with good fortune because he
had put himself in its path. But Petrarch proved to be right: "Dame
Fortune is never more treacherous and dangerous than when she
caresses."

The Austrian and Prussian foreign ministers attended the Dresden congress only for major conferences. During this period Manteuffel's attitude towards Austria was vacillating as usual. At Ol-

[92] Heller, *Mitteleuropas Vorkämpfer*, Annex, pp. 245–55.

mütz he had been outright timorous; yet he was not convinced of
Austria's intrinsic strength and predicted the disintegration of the
Danubian Monarchy. Naturally, the Olmütz defeat rankled in his
soul. It was not in Schwarzenberg's nature to expect consideration
from his Prussian colleagues—for that he had too much contempt
for average humanity—but it would have been wise for the Austrian statesman if he had remembered the words which Schiller puts
into the mouth of Tell's wife:

> He trembled then before you? Woe the while
> You saw his weakness; that he'll never forget.

Even the mediocre Manteuffel managed later in the year (September 7, 1851) to outwit the astute Schwarzenberg by inducing Hanover to join the Prussian tariff union, but it was left to a man
destined to occupy a seat of the mighty in this world, Otto von
Bismarck, not to "forget." When at Dresden, both ministers were
quartered in an annex to the royal palace, while even the Bavarian
Baron Pfordten, much to the dismay of Munich, had to be satisfied
with a less imposing residence. In outward appearance the representatives of the two great powers were thus on a par, but the sur-
roundings did not equalize their bearing: Schwarzenberg, with
perfect ease and freedom, portrayed the elegance of the Austrian
grand seigneur; in contrast with this magnificence, Manteuffel displayed simplicity of manners in the ceremonious style of a top-
ranking civil servant.[93]

The permanent Prussian delegate was Count Alvensleben-
Erxleben. This gruff ex-finance minister, whose natural roughness
had been offensive to Frederick William, extricated Prussia from
many a difficulty by his consummate flexibility; from the beginning
of the conferences he ingratiated himself with the petty states and
became their recognized leader. His counterpart on the Austrian
side, Count Buol-Schauenstein, had been called from his ambas-

---

[93] Bismarck, in his "Reflections and Reminiscences" (*The Man and the Statesman*, I,
84), expressed it this way: "Prince Schwarzenberg on the first-floor with his liveries,
silver-plate and champagne" and "the Prussian Minister with his clerks and his water-
bottles one pair higher."

sadorial post at St. Petersburg to substitute for his chief and protector. While Alvensleben was firm and sedate, the polished Buol
was stiff and given to outbursts of rage. Metternich compared Buol
to a knife having a sharp point but a dull edge. The metaphor was
felicitous in the light of Buol's later ministerial activity—he succeeded Schwarzenberg (after his death) as minister of foreign affairs
but not as prime minister—for Austria's policy under him was often
piercing, but it seldom cut across. In Beust's language,[94] he stirred
up much bad blood but did not carve out anything worth while.
Schwarzenberg, who groomed him for his successor, overestimated
his abilities. He took his haughtiness for strength and his gift as
dialectician for power of persuasion. Whatever the intentions of the
leading statesmen of both sides might have been, however, the wide
difference of the relations of the two great powers to the interests of
Germany as a whole forced them into continued strife with inexorable fate.

The two rocks on which the conferences foundered were the
question of the presidency of the confederate diet and the composition of the executive. Manteuffel, in the latter question, insisted on
either the formation of the supreme confederate organ on a dualistic
basis or a liberal participation of the lesser states. On the other hand,
Schwarzenberg was averse to seeing Germany divided into a northern and a southern part as fatally injurious to his plan for a united
empire of seventy millions. He, the Austrian statesman, proposed a
composition of the executive allowing him, by way of the votes of
the allied middle states, to wield the deciding influence in case of
conflict of opinion with Prussia. In the question of the presidency,
Manteuffel submitted a scheme for a monthly alternation of the
dignity; Schwarzenberg, though ready to whittle down the substance of the office to a phantom, remained adamant in claiming
the honor for the Emperor. The two problems became the foci of
all Austro-Prussian negotiations; they epitomized the old rivalry
between the two great powers in Germany. A solution could not
be found: "two stars keep not their motion in one sphere."

If Schwarzenberg's plans could not be achieved through nego-

[94] *Aus Drei Viertel-Jahrhunderten*, p. 138.

tiations in Dresden, could he force Prussia again into submission as
he had done at Olmütz? Prudence, however, counseled against a
repetition of the war threat of November, 1850. It was disagreeble
to be reserved, but dangerous not to be. In the fall of 1850 Schwarzenberg had England and France on his side on account of the
Danish affair; now they opposed him on account of his vigorously
resumed proposal for a mighty Central European empire.[95] Nor
would Russia have countenanced a war between Austria and Prussia for the establishment of Austria's hegemony in Germany. The
intimidation of Prussia, once so successfully undertaken, could
therefore not be renewed.

Schwarzenberg might have succeeded in carrying out his ideas if
he had appealed to the nation as a whole and dangled before the
eyes of the German people a popularly elected assembly as the confederate legislative organ. The Prussian king had been willing to
establish a system of popular representation for the Union; he was
ready, despite the revived six-point program of Warsaw (called a
"perfidy" by the Bavarian Pfordten), even to consider a people's
chamber for the wider Confederation. Suggestions made by Bavaria
and Saxony in this respect, strongly supported, surprisingly enough
for the Vienna statesmen, by the Prussian plenipotentiaries at Dresden, were not favorably entertained by the Emperor. Schwarzenberg was half-heartedly inclined to arrive at a compromise in the
matter, as shown by the conclusion of his first report to Francis Joseph on the Dresden Conferences, dated December 21,
1850:

Your Majesty, knowing my sentiments concerning popular representations,
is aware of the fact that I do not advocate them. But it cannot be denied
that the design of the Prussian plenipotentiaries will be materialized if the
well-calculated plan of the King is not nipped in the bud by the suggested
means.[96]

The Emperor's answer has not been preserved, but the first sentence
of Schwarzenberg's next report, "Your Majesty's renewed orders regarding the inadmissibility of a popular representation will be

[95] Napoleon, *Œuvres*, III, 256.
[96] Heller, *Mitteleuropas Vorkämpfer*, 133.

promptly followed," clearly reveals their contents.[97] The question
of popular representation was therefore ruled out from the beginning.

There was nothing else to be done but to return to the Frankfurt
ramshackle structure, the old confederate diet with its shadowy but
complacent existence in the Eschenheim palace. Thus, an Austrian
primacy was painfully restored. It was to a large extent a primacy
of honor, for the old Austro-Prussian diarchy ominously lurked
underneath. Prince Schwarzenberg had thwarted Prussia's ascendency over Germany and swept away Radowitz's Union; he had
brilliantly defended the stellar role of the Habsburg Monarchy in
the Germanies, especially in the summer of 1849, when, after the
reverses of the Austrian troops in Hungary, the sands seemed to
run low in Austria's glass of destiny and Germany's unification
under Prussian leadership appeared to be assured. But the creation
of a new organ assuring Austria's hegemony in Germany had proved
abortive.

On May 15, 1851, Schwarzenberg delivered the farewell address
to the congress. As he could not herald the birth of a new constitution to the German nation, he had to be content to refer to the
"valuable material" gathered at Dresden for further negotiations at
Frankfurt. This "valuable material" was just as "valueless" as the
oil painting depicting the Dresden Conferences in session. It is one
of the few canvases on which Prince Schwarzenberg is shown; unfortunately the best part of the figure is not his features or the pos-
ture (he converses with Baron Pfordten), but the white uniform of
an Austrian general. The Prince, too agile to endure the ordeal of
sittings and annoyed to be compelled to make an exception in this
case because a worthy professor of the Dresden Academy of Painting had told him (falsely) [98] that the king of Saxony desired to

---

[97] *Ibid.*

[98] The professor told the king that Schwarzenberg had suggested the painting. Old, he
was no longer a coryphaeus of his art, but evidently a good salesman of his merchandise.
Manteuffel sits at a table on the other end of the picture; Baron Beust leans over him, showing him a document. If Beust had straightened out, he would have come into collision with
the Mecklenburg representative who was selected for this ornate place on account of his
gorgeous red uniform. Professor Vogel had forgotten some of the rules laid down by Les-
sing in his *Laocoön.*

have the conferences immortalized by his brush, ironically remarked that he was needed for the picture as "Wouwerman's white horse."

Victory has its grandeur, but also its misery of disappointment. "We had hoped for better things," Schwarzenberg wrote Manteuffel on April 9, 1851,[99] "and have honestly striven for them. I confess that the malicious and inept allusions of the press which see in the restoration of the old Confederation a triumph of Austrian reactionary policy anger and nauseate me."

It was one of his political maxims not to mourn passively over the unattainable. "This is the course I intend to follow," he used to say; "if it is ineffective, I shall try something else." As his imposing plan of an empire of seventy millions had come to naught, he availed himself of an offer for an alliance made by Prussia. The two states concluded on May 16, 1851, one day after the closing of the Dresden Conferences, a secret agreement by virtue of which each of the contracting parties obligated itself, to the extent of all its power, to come to the assistance of the other if any one of the latter's possessions should be attacked inside or outside Germany. The treaty ran for three years and was renewed in 1854 for another three years. The safety of Austria's possessions in Italy and Hungary during these six years (1851–1857) was the positive gain brought home from the congress by the Prince.[100] Substantial as the substitute was, though temporary and therefore not altogether satisfactory from an Austrian standpoint, obviously, the treaty between two independent powers could not adequately take the place of Schwarzenberg's alluring and ambitious plans of Austria's one-sided dominion in Germany.

When the confederate diet assembled with its full number, Prussia and her German allies included, the hearts of the Viennese statesmen were filled with pride. Austria was secure in her position at Frankfurt because she could always rely on a safe majority in the diet. Her status as the presiding power covered the Danubian Monarchy with a bright luster that authoritatively pervaded the assembly. Like a star, the Austria of Schwarzenberg sparkled over the

[99] Heller, *Mitteleuropas Vorkämpfer*, p. 143.
[100] Srbik, *Deutsche Einheit*, II, 121.

German lands. Young German noblemen eagerly sought commissions in the Austrian army; leading German statesmen, among them the two brothers Gagern (Max von Gagern had zealously exerted himself for a Hohenzollern empire at Frankfurt) enlisted in the service of the Empire. Catholicism gained ground in Germany and fostered the idea of a great Germany and therewith the Austrian Monarchy's imperial pretenses. Schwarzenberg knew how to tap such sources of power.

There was one field in which he did not encounter the open or concealed rivalry of Prussia, namely, the suppression of democratic constitutions in Germany. On this point the two powers understood each other excellently. On August 23, 1851, the confederate diet adopted Austria's and Prussia's proposal for the institution of a committee ("the Reaction Committee," as its members called themselves with fine irony), with a view to summoning the German states to remodel their constitutions along conservative lines. Never before had the German central authority assumed so large an influence on the internal affairs of the individual states. The court of inquisition found no less than ten states guilty of having sinned against the principles of conservatism; the crusade against Hesse-Cassel was undertaken with particular fervor. As King Frederick William IV expressed it, "the foulness which had come upon the German constitutions in the year of shame [1848] was being wiped away." [101]

After the abolition of the Austrian constitution, Schwarzenberg would have welcomed the abrogation of the Prussian constitution also. Prompted by the well-known sentiments of Frederick William and animated by the desire to forestall a defeat of the European house of lords, as Talleyrand had wittily called the Austrian Empire, at the hands of the democratic Prussian commons, he sent a note to Berlin (September, 1851) in which he explained the advantages of co-ordinated action on the part of the two states in this matter. He boldly asserted that the reconstitution of the monarchical power in Austria, the victorious protest against revolutionary disintegration, was an indispensable prop for the Prussian Mon-

---

[101] Sybel, *The Founding of the German Empire by William I*, II, 117.

archy. For the King it was a great temptation to follow his suggestion, but even stanch royalists warned him that his subjects would never forgive a violation of the royal oath. The King, albeit reluctantly, kept his pledged word.

In July, 1851, only a few weeks after the convocation of the diet, Schwarzenberg took the first step toward narrowing the sphere of Prussia's influence. The proposal for a tariff union between Austria and the other German states, put on the agenda of the assembly upon his initiative, was to be the means of wresting from Prussia the leadership in the economic field in Germany. Prussia, her political reputation, but not her material well-being having been damaged, resisted coolly and effectively. The middle states, basking in the reflected glory that shone from Vienna, were inclined to enter into closer commercial relations with Austria, because, at worst, they might have to deal with two masters, one of whom could be played against the other in case of conflict. Negotiations between them were in flux at Bamberg and at Darmstadt with this end in view, when Schwarzenberg's premature death, on April 5, 1852, put an end to Austria's brilliant conduct of her diplomacy. Since August 29, 1851, Prussia had been represented at the diet by Otto von Bismarck-Schönhausen. He had come to Frankfurt "well disposed towards Austria." Gradually he realized, however, that "the Gordian knot of German circumstance was not to be untied by the gentle methods of dual policy, [but that it] could only be cut by the sword." [102] The removal of Schwarzenberg from this earth deprived the world of witnessing a titanic struggle for supremacy in Germany between Otto von Bismarck, Prussia's man of destiny, and Felix zu Schwarzenberg, Austria's last statesman of commanding stature.

A survey of the course pursued by Prince Schwarzenberg in his German policy leaves no doubt as to its aim: the establishment of a full-fledged Austrian hegemony in Germany. He did not engage in Prince Kaunitz's coalition policy of encirclement against Prussia. Nor was he following in Metternich's footsteps, although he had re-

[102] Bismarck, *The Man and the Statesman*, p. 319.

ceived his diplomatic training in the Metternich school. The creator
of the Acts of Confederation of 1815 recognized the equal status
of Austria and Prussia as great powers and operated the Austro-
Prussian dualism in Germany only under cover of an Austrian
primacy of honor. To this end he was content with erecting a loosely
articulated confederation of states in Germany. Along the same
pattern he set up an Italian confederation. These two confederations
were joined by a hyphen—the Danube Empire, which, on its part,
correspondingly granted far-reaching autonomy to its main component portions, the hereditary lands and Bohemia, the lands of the
Crown of St. Stephen, and the Lombardo-Venetian Kingdom. In
contrast thereto, Schwarzenberg created a unitary state by abolishing all political and economic differences within the Empire. The
new omnipotent superstructure of an empire of seventy million
people or of a Central European union, hierarchically constituted
and rigidly organized, should, by welding together its military and
economic forces, ultimately present an indissoluble whole to the
outside world. If these plans had materialized, Austria's numerical
and cultural superiority would have unquestionably secured for
her the undisputed leadership in Germany and a dominant position
as one of the great powers of this globe. Incidentally, Prussia's military expansion would have been successfully checked for the benefit
of the whole world.

The aim of Schwarzenberg's German policy and the means employed by him for its accomplishment found both panegyrists and
critics among his contemporaries. *Ne Jupiter quidem omnibus placet.* Some,[103] spell-bound by his intrepidity and vigorous will, admired his keen intellectual gifts and his ready grasp of things;
they gained the impression of a balanced, purposeful personality,
equipped with a strong feeling of his own uniqueness, resolute and
unswerving in his determination to reach a definite goal. Others,
chiefly those of the Metternich school, regretted "the empty striv-
ings against the principles of the Confederation as discussed by the
Austrian cabinet in the year 1815"; [104] besides the substance, they

[103] Especially the diplomatic corps in Vienna.
[104] Metternich, in a note of November 10, 1855, *Historische Zeitschrift*, LVIII, 384.

criticized the procedure because they thought it to be agitated, convulsive, impromptu, blunt, and forbidding. His most fervent encomiasts will readily concede that Prince Schwarzenberg's domain proper was diplomacy. Here he was an unexcelled master, knowing the stratagems, the finesse, and the etiquette of the game. By temperament and education he was less qualified to be the architect of new organic structures. Even if the remarkable force of his talent of boldly and adroitly exploiting the opportunities of the moment had not been all-consuming, the short span of his premiership, crowded with urgent business and a multitude of vexing problems, would not have permitted him to press the tendencies of his time into permanent molds. His epigoni, bungling imitators of an impressive force of will and intellect, injudiciously squandered the rich heritage which he had left them. One portion of that legacy was the primacy in German counsels.

❧ 4 ❧

BRITISH, FRENCH, &
RUSSIAN POLICY

T HE CLOSE RELATIONSHIP between the domestic policy
of all European states and their foreign policy prevailed at
all times. It was not restricted to the era of absolutism. The
creation of the rejuvenated absolutist Austrian state implied the
continuation of the dynastic will to keep the Empire's historic position of power through the hereditary possessions; furthermore, it
inferred the maintenance of the prestige of the Habsburgs in German and Italian lands, if necessary, with military force. The preceding pages have brought out the intimate interplay between foreign and domestic policy during Felix Schwarzenberg's stewardship.
Nothing, for instance, could be more clearly illustrative of this relationship than Bruck's economic imperialism, aiming, as it did, at the
commercial conquest of the Orient and the opening of maritime
routes.

Schwarzenberg played the game of diplomacy with skill and precision. It was his worldly education that gave him his intelligi-
bility. Even early in his diplomatic career the young attaché and
envoy distinguished himself through his reports so that Prince Metternich commented: "Le prince Félix a du talent, une grande connais-
sance de la situation et du nerf. . . . Un rapport aussi parfaitement
pensé que parfaitement rédigé" (marginal note of December 13,
1841).[1]

The criteria of Schwarzenberg's diplomacy were assurance, rapid-
ity, and *élan* in attack. His keen penetration of man and circum-

[1] Heller, *Mitteleuropas Vorkämpfer*, pp. 17, 195.

stances, however, readily allowed adjustment to an emergency. His adversaries—diplomatic foxes who hated the trap—like Count Bernstorff, complained of the deviousness and lack of candor in his relations with his fellow diplomats. But the main lines of Schwarzenberg's diplomacy were clearly marked off; it was not his fault if his illustrious counterplayers had difficulty in understanding him. "Distinguished merit will draw luster from reproach."

During Prince Schwarzenberg's incumbency Austria and England were usually at loggerheads. A great deal of acrimony was carried into the official relations between the two countries by the numerous indiscretions of England's foreign minister, Henry John Temple, Viscount Palmerston. In Schwarzenberg the Englishman found his equal in asperity. The Austrian, having "no false reptile prudence, the result not of caution but of fear," dexterously handed out the famous Palmerstonian "tit for tat." As a result, there were inky, acrid retorts from cuttlefish to cuttlefish—from the Ballhausplatz to Downing Street.

Palmerston had resumed the seals of office in July, 1846, in the ministry of Lord John Russell.

He was generally recognized on the Continent as the heir of the tradition of Canning; that is to say, as the adversary of the Holy Alliance, the patron of nascent nations struggling for independence, the opponent of intervention for the suppression of liberty, and the mainstay of the Balance of Power.[2]

As the protector and promoter of the right of the self-determination of peoples, Palmerston fulfilled a long-cherished ideal of British tradition.

The emergence of Schwarzenberg's unified Central Europe operating as a homogeneous economic entity would plainly have been in opposition to that policy, and therefore it aroused the antagonism of Great Britain, for the unity of Europe meant the exclusion of Britain from the continent. In line with this policy the French had been barred from unifying the European continent at

[2] Ward and Gooch, *The Cambridge History of British Foreign Policy,* II, 289.

the beginning of the nineteenth century, and the Germans are being thwarted in our days. Whatever the motives, in this respect British foreign policy has been consistent: *divide et impera*, the old
Austrian motto in internal affairs, has been Britain's maxim for centuries in dealing with the European continent. Austrian and German industry, commerce, and traffic, however, had been gradually
developed by 1850; oversea lines of communication had been established. Here, then, were two powers which could become dangerous
to England when united politically and economically. Still, Palmerston needed Austria as a counterweight against the Czar's dominions.
"Russia at this time was not only the greatest Empire in the world,
but the greatest Empire the world had ever seen. . . . And this
Empire, . . . so colossal and compact, was not merely great but
growing." [3] Thus, Palmerston declared in the House of Commons
during the debate on Russian intervention in Hungary, July 2,
1849:

Austria is a most important element in the balance of European power.
Austria stands in the center of Europe, a barrier against encroachment on
the one side, and against invasion on the other. The political independence
and liberties of Europe are bound up, in my opinion, with the maintenance
and integrity of Austria as a great European power; and therefore anything
that tends by direct, or even remote, contingency, to weaken and to cripple
Austria, but still more to reduce her from the position of a first-rate Power
to that of a secondary State, must be a great calamity to Europe, and one
which every Englishman ought to deprecate, and try to prevent. [4]

It is customary for diplomats to treat a friendly nation and an
"ally" with consideration. Palmerston was an exception to the rule.
The British Thersites, afflicted with "a protean tactlessness, tactlessness without parallel, sometimes even without point," [5] taunted and
reviled everyone. He called Emperor Ferdinand "the animal *implu-
mis bipes*, a perfect nullity, next thing to an idiot, a mere man of
straw, a Guy Faux." [6] Of Francis Joseph he spoke deprecatingly as

---

[3] Simpson, *Louis Napoleon and the Recovery of France, 1848–1856*, pp. 221–22.
[4] Hansard's *Parliamentary Debates*, CVII, col. 809.
[5] Cecil, *British Foreign Secretaries 1807–1916*, p. 191.
[6] Ward and Gooch, *The Cambridge History of British Foreign Policy*, p. 318.

of "the lad of sixteen or twenty." [7] In a letter to his horrified envoy at Vienna, Lord Ponsonby, dated September 9, 1849, he said: [8] "The Austrians are really the greatest brutes that ever called themselves by the undeserved name of civilised men."

Palmerston's "ill-considered, sometimes misleadingly impotent and often ineffectual interventions" [9] were of even graver concern to a foreign minister of another state than were his mud-pellets, his personal "uncovenanted asperities." And of this unconventional meddling in Austrian affairs there was a great deal. In November, 1847, believing that the Habsburg Empire was nearing disintegration, he sent the Earl of Minto, Lord Russell's father-in-law and a cabinet member, to Italy to encourage the Italian princes in their constitutional inclinations; he warned Austria at the same time that any interference with Italian reform would not be regarded with unconcern by Britain. By July 15, 1848—by this time "he had increased not in wisdom but stature" [10]—he had reached the conclusion, as revealed by a letter to the King of the Belgians, that Lombardy and Venetia were sources of weakness rather than of strength to the Habsburg Monarchy:

I cannot regret the expulsion of the Austrians from Italy. I do not believe, Sire, that it will diminish the real strength nor impair the real security of Austria as a European Power. Her rule was hateful to the Italians, and has long been maintained only by an expenditure of money and an exertion of military efforts which left Austria less able to maintain her interests elsewhere. Italy was to her the heel of Achilles, and not the shield of Ajax. The Alps are her natural barrier and her best defense. I should wish to see the whole of Northern Italy united into one kingdom. . . . Such an arrangement is now, in my opinion, Sire, inevitable; and the sooner the Austrian Government makes up its mind to the necessity, the better conditions it will be able to obtain.[11]

Palmerston was censured and ridiculed for this opinion by the Queen in her letters of July 25 and September 7, 1848.

---

[7] Sanders, *Life of Viscount Palmerston*, p. 126.
[8] Ashley, *The Life of Henry John Temple, Viscount Palmerston, 1846–1865*, I, 139.
[9] Cecil, *British Foreign Secretaries 1807–1916*, p. 177.
[10] *Ibid.*, p. 172.
[11] Ashley, *The Life of Henry John Temple, Viscount Palmerston, 1846–1865*, I, 98–99.

The Queen must tell Lord John [Russell] what she has repeatedly told Lord Palmerston, but without apparent effect, that the establishment of an *entente cordiale with the French Republic,* for the purpose of driving the Austrians out of *their dominions* in Italy would be a *disgrace* to this country . . . the notion of establishing a Venetian State under French guarantee is too absurd.[12]

What the Queen has long suspected and often warned against is . . . Lord Palmerston using the new *entente cordiale* for the purpose of wresting from Austria her Italian provinces by French arms. This would be a most iniquitous proceeding. It is another question whether it is good policy for Austria to try to retain Lombardy but that is for her and not for us to decide. Many people might think that we would be happier without Ireland or Canada.[13]

Enough has been said to show that no Austrian foreign minister with any stamina could have meekly bowed to these diplomatic irregularities. It was only natural that Felix Schwarzenberg's personal dignity and habitual self-respect rebelled against discourtesies and interferences à la Palmerston. He was no Anglophobe,[14] but Palmerston became his *bête noire.*[15] Almost from the moment he took office Schwarzenberg began to pitch into his British adversary, and from that time on the two ministers continued to exchange passes in their diplomatic duel. In order to teach Palmerston a lesson, he communicated Francis Joseph's accession to the throne through the regular diplomatic channels instead of despatching a special mission to London as he had done to all the other capitals of the great powers. The vexed Queen, "ashamed of his policy," wrote with verve:

The Queen has already, on Lord Palmerston's account, received two public affronts: the one by her Minister in Spain having been sent out of that country; the other now, by the new Emperor of Austria not announcing to her by special mission his accession to the Throne, which he did to all other

---

[12] *The Letters of Queen Victoria,* ed. by A. C. Benson and Viscount Esher, II, 221–22, by courtesy of the publishers, Messrs. Longmans, Green & Co., Inc.

[13] *Ibid.,* p. 230. Quotation by permission of the publishers, Messrs. Longmans, Green & Co., Inc.

[14] Bagger, *Francis Joseph,* pp. 196–97, condemns Felix Schwarzenberg for his Anglophobia without, however, adducing any evidence.

[15] Sproxton, *Palmerston and the Hungarian Revolution,* p. 131.

Sovereigns, avowedly, as it appears, to mark the indignation of Austria at the inimical proceedings of the British Foreign Secretary.[16]

After the defeat of Sardinia, Palmerston, in conjunction with the French government, continued his anti-Austrian policy by trying to obtain the best possible peace conditions for the vanquished country. The peace negotiations were conducted by Bruck on behalf of Austria. Peace was concluded on August 6, 1849, after Austria had scaled down her claim for a war indemnity from one hundred fifty to seventy-five million francs. Bruck, however, secured compensatory commercial advantages, especially navigation facilities on the Po. Sardinia's demand that Austria should declare an amnesty for her Italian subjects in the peace treaty was declined by Schwarzenberg, but he consented to a stipulation allowing Radetzky to grant pardons at his discretion.[17]

In Hungarian affairs, too, Palmerston was "innocent of the daintier diplomatic amenities." His despatches to the British envoy at Vienna were lectures on constitutional law. The self-appointed professor in *Weltpolitik* and tutor in international ethics criticized the Habsburg and Bourbon systems of government and showed that "the results of such false policy are that men like Metternich and Guizot meet in exile in London." [18] How little Palmerston really understood the Hungarian question in some of its broader aspects is revealed by the following remark.

I believe that the other races distinct from the Magyars have forgotten the former feuds that existed between them and the Magyar population, and that the greater portion of the people have engaged in what they consider a great national contest.[19]

But the fanatical hater of Russia, standing in haunting fear of her aggrandizement, would not extend any help to the Hungarian insurrectionists. When "liberal or humane considerations" clashed

---

[16] *The Letters of Queen Victoria*, II, 245–46; Palmerston remained unruffled. Ashley, *The Life of Henry John Temple, Viscount Palmerston, 1846–1865*, I, 113.

[17] Friedjung, *Österreich von 1848 bis 1860*, II, 138; see also Guichen, *Les Grandes Questions européennes et la diplomatie des puissances sous la Seconde République*.

[18] Ward and Gooch, *The Cambridge History of British Foreign Policy*, p. 319.

[19] Lorne, *Viscount Palmerston, K.G.*, p. 120.

with his doctrine of balance of power, the latter won out. He needed
the Austrian Empire as a rampart against Russia. Thus, he remarked
to Francis Pulszky, Kossuth's representative and propagandist in
England, "that, if Austria did not already exist, it would have to be
invented; that it was a European necessity and the natural ally of
England in the East: he therefore counselled us to reconcile ourselves with Austria, because in the frame of the European system it
would be impossible to replace Austria by small States." [20] Despite
his generally favorable attitude towards Austria in this respect,
Palmerston badgered Schwarzenberg with bluff admonition almost
to the day of the surrender of the Hungarians as to how he should
satisfy the national Hungarian feelings. On August 1, 1849, Lord
Ponsonby received two despatches from Palmerston, one in which
the latter pleaded the Hungarian cause and the other containing an
offer of mediation.[21] Schwarzenberg, however, refused to accept the
first document, on the ground that it interfered with the internal
affairs of his country, and was noncommittal on the offer of mediation.[22] Ponsonby, by order of his chief, left the document on
Schwarzenberg's table, and three weeks later Schwarzenberg had
still not read it.[23] In the course of events, on September 28, 1849,
Palmerston received a reply from Schwarzenberg which was an
inimitable masterpiece of Palmerstonian *brusquerie* and typical of
the acrimonious tone pervading the correspondence of the two
ministers.

Events have taken upon themselves to reply to these communications of
the Principal Secretary of State of her Britannic Majesty, better than I
could have done. There is no cause for surprise if the results to which the
Hungarian insurrection has led are different from those which Lord

---

[20] *Meine Zeit, mein Leben,* II, 322.

[21] For the text see Sproxton, *Palmerston and the Hungarian Revolution,* pp. 166–67.
The subject is treated in masterful fashion by the author.

[22] Ponsonby, Metternich's friend and furious at Palmerston, commented in a report to
his chief as follows: "I was well prepared for the reception that subject would meet with.
. . . I can see no good in continuing to urge on this Government things which it is determined not to do, for I see no means by which it can be forced to change its conduct."
—*Ibid.,* p. 108.

[23] Neumann, *The Diary of Philipp von Neumann,* II, 319.

Palmerston had anticipated, inasmuch as, destitute of the necessary elements on which he could form a competent opinion on this matter, he was reduced to information such as that promulgated in England by the agents of the Hungarian insurrection, whose interest it was to give the colouring of a generous and heroic impulse to an attempt which the English qualifies as high treason, and which it punishes without fail with death or transportation. The world is agitated by a spirit of general subversion. England herself is not exempt from the influence of this spirit; witness Canada, the Island of Cefalonia, and finally, unhappy Ireland. But wherever revolt breaks out within the vast limits of the British Empire, the English Government always knows how to maintain the authority of the law, were it even at the price of torrents of blood. It is not for us to blame her. Whatever may, moreover, be the opinion which we form as to the causes of these insurrectionary movements, as well as of the measures of repression employed by the British Government in order to stifle them, we consider it our duty to abstain from expressing that opinion, persuaded as we are that persons are apt to fall into gross errors, in making themselves judges of the often so complicated position of foreign countries. By this conduct we consider we have acquired the right to expect that Lord Palmerston will practice with respect to us a perfect reciprocity.[24]

A new Anglo-Austrian conflict arose after the Hungarian capitulation at Világos.[25] About 5,000 Hungarians and Poles had sought refuge in Turkish territory. On August 28, 1849, Austria, and a few days later Russia, confronted the Sultan with a peremptory demand for the surrender of Kossuth and his followers. Schwarzenberg based his demand of extradition on Article 18 of the Treaty of Belgrade (1739) and Article 14 of the Treaty of Passarowitz (1718); Nesselrode, the Russian foreign minister, based his on Article 2 of the Treaty of Kainardji (1774). The clauses in question applied to *sujets rebelles et mécontents* [26]—offenders in peacetime—but could it be argued that they also applied to a whole nation

[24] Sproxton, *Palmerston and the Hungarian Revolution*, p. 109. Reproduced here by the kind permission of the publishers, Cambridge University Press (England) and The Macmillan Company (New York).

[25] For a detailed description of this conflict see *ibid.*, pp. 113 *et sqq.*; Lane-Poole, *Life of the Right Honourable Stratford Canning*, Vol. II.

[26] "*Il sera désormais défendu de donner asyle et retraite aux méchants, aux sujets rebelles et mécontents.*" Noradounghian, *Recueil d'actes internationaux de l'Empire Ottoman*, pp. 245, 251.

in rebellion for its constitutional rights? Plainly, the critical issue would be decided, not by the ambiguous French of old treaties, but by the support the Sultan would receive from England and France. Palmerston, fearing the involvement of the Eastern question, and the British ambassador at Constantinople, Sir Stratford Canning, seeing the Russians another milestone on the road to Constantinople, promised the Turks "fullest moral and material assistance." [27] Against the advice of such outstanding statesmen as De Tocqueville, Thiers, and De Broglie, Louis Napoleon aligned himself ardently for a joint Anglo-French venture against Austria and Russia (October 10). The French fleet was ordered to steam towards Smyrna. Meanwhile, however, Fuad Effendi, one of Turkey's cleverest diplomats, had an interview with the Czar and, by appealing to his magnanimity, obtained the surrender of the claim of extradition (October 16). The clouds seemed to be disappearing from the international horizon, when a new complication set in: the British fleet had passed the Dardanelles. London received a formal protest note from the indomitable Prince Schwarzenberg, but Nesselrode, more tractable in this instance, expressed "entire satisfaction with the British foreign secretary's admission that a forced interpretation had been given to the Treaty of 1841 at Constantinople, and with his engagement that the obligation of that treaty should be more strictly observed in the future." [28] Schwarzenberg insisted on the confinement and surveillance of the Hungarian refugees at Kutaish in Asia Minor, under the control of an Austrian commissary. Diplomatic relations were severed between Austria and Turkey and were not renewed until April, 1850. Owing to Sir Stratford Canning's tireless efforts, the Sultan released the refugees in September, 1851. The affair of the refugees was to flare up again with much éclat in other parts of the word.

The next incident that troubled Anglo-Austrian diplomatic rela-

[27] Ward and Gooch, *The Cambridge History of British Foreign Policy*, p. 321.
[28] Sproxton, *Palmerston and the Hungarian Revolution*, p. 141. On the role which the French ambassador played at St. Petersburg as a mediator see the biography of Keller, *Le Général de la Moricière*, II, 149–50. Keller repeats the legend that a storm forced the British fleet to make its appearance in the Dardanelles.

tions was the Haynau affair.[29] In itself, the happening was trivial. Against Metternich's warning, the general incautiously went to England. When visiting the brewery of Barclay & Perkins on September 4, 1850, the draymen mobbed and assaulted him. Baron Koller, the Austrian chargé d'affaires, demanded an apology. Palmerston sent his regrets, but, instead of upholding the law, as he had done in the Don Pacifico case—on this occasion he made his celebrated *Civis Romanus sum* speech (June 25, 1850)—it suited his fancy to show that his sympathies were on the side of the ruffians. The Queen took occasion to advise her foreign minister in a letter of October 12, 1850:

> If Lord Palmerston could not reconcile it to his own feelings to express the regret of the Queen's Government at the brutal attack and wanton outrage committed by a ferocious mob on a distinguished foreigner of past seventy years of age . . . without adding *his censure of the want of propriety* evinced by General Haynau in coming to England, he might have done so in a private letter.[30]

She insisted on the redrafting of the despatch, but was informed that it had already been sent off. This high-handed procedure was most galling to Victoria, because she had shortly before lectured Palmerston, in the well-known memorandum of August 12, on constitutional amenities. In the exordium she stated exactly what she expected from her foreign minister; among her expectations was a distinct statement of his intentions in any case. Tamely Palmerston had agreed to respect the prerogative rights vested in his sovereign —and unblushingly he broke his promise almost at once. Again there happened what had happened so many times before: a strong representation by the Queen was followed by a mild rebuke by the prime minister to his foreign minister, and that censure was met with a blustering surrender. Palmerston was compelled to the humiliation of recalling the offensive despatch. To the Queen's open rejoicing,[31] a more gracious note was susbstituted. Schwarzenberg's note of soured friendship (November 27, 1850) momentarily closed

---

[29] Concerning General Haynau see *supra*, p. 56.
[30] *Letters of Queen Victoria*, II, 322.   [31] *Ibid.*, II, 324–25.

Palmerston's breach of diplomatic and constitutional etiquette. He wrote:

Because the government of Great Britain has not deemed it necessary officially to take steps against an attempted assassination that threatened the life of an Austrian citizen, we cannot but reserve to ourselves the right of eventually taking under advisement whether or not we consider it appropriate to take reciprocal measures against British subjects in Austria.[32]

In 1851 the withdrawal of the Austrian envoy was threatened when Kossuth landed in England on October 23. The Magyar rebel at once engaged in savage attacks on Austria and Russia. Palmerston was dissuaded only with some difficulty by court and cabinet pressure from seeing him at his private home. Although " 'the revolutionary firebrand who now presides at the Foreign Office in Downing Street' " ("as he lovingly christened himself in emulation of the 'Lord Feuerbrand' of the angry Viennese") [33] refrained from the forbidden fruit, he could not resist the temptation of receiving a deputation of Islington and Finsbury radicals who called the Emperors of Austria and Russia "odious and detestable assassins" and "merciless tyrants and despots." The impropriety of such language should have been reprehended by Palmerston, but his "stock of imprudence being as rich in recuperative power as the widow's cruse of oil," as Algernon Cecil puts it, he expressed himself as "extremely flattered and highly gratified" by the references to himself. He described to his delighted audience how he had foiled the Austrians and the Russians in the refugee affair and confessed in a figure of speech derived from the prize-fighter's arena (a spot not unfamiliar to the noble lord) and immortalized by Leed's cartoon in *Punch*, that "a good deal of judicious bottleholding was obliged to be brought into play." [34] Palmerston's dismissal was even seriously considered at this time. At the Queen's request the matter was brought before the cabinet. Palmerston defended himself by assert-

---

[32] *Wiener Zeitung,* December 19, 1850; Friedjung, *Österreich von 1848 bis 1860,* II, 141*n.*

[33] Guedalla, *Palmerston,* p. 297.

[34] Lorne, *Viscount Palmerston, K.G.,* pp. 118–19. For further details see Jennings, *Cabinet Government,* p. 158.

ing that he had not ascertained the terms of the address, and in view of his embarrassing popularity the cabinet declined to come to a formal decision. Yet Palmerston's dismissal from office (December 22) was at hand. By expressing approval of the *coup d'état* of Louis Napoleon (December 2, 1851) on his own account, he had disarranged the delicate mechanism of cabinet government. Vienna rejoiced at having no longer to deal with the "dangerous intriguer, a persistent intermeddler, and inveterate fomenter of discord," whom the Germans in an often repeated distich assigned to the family of Beelzebub.

> Hat der Teufel einen Sohn,
> So ist er sicher Palmerston.

In dealing with the German question, Prince Schwarzenberg had to consider two main aspects as far as Anglo-Austrian relations were concerned: the unification of Germany and the Schleswig-Holstein affair.[35] With regard to the second problem he found official Britain on his side, save the court. With regard to the former problem, Palmerston, while not being unfriendly to Germany,[36] in practice cared very little for German unity and combatted an extension of

---

[35] It has been shown in Chapter III that Schwarzenberg considered "the maintenance of the whole of the Danish Monarchy in its previous extension a necessity dictated by European conditions and not in conflict with the best interests of the confederation." Communication from the Vienna cabinet to Baron von Koller, Austrian envoy at London, July 25, 1850, cited by Precht, "Englands Stellung zur deutschen Einheit, 1848–1850," *Historische Zeitschrift*, Beiheft 3, 1925, p. 148. Palmerston was rather prejudiced and ignorant about North German politics. Sanders, *Life of Viscount Palmerston*, p. 130. Palmerston in later years remarked that "there were only three people in England who had ever understood the question thoroughly—the Prince Consort, who was dead; Mellish (a clerk in the foreign office) who had disappeared; and himself—who had forgotten it. Cecil, *British Foreign Secretaries 1807–1916*, p. 210. Steefel, *The Schleswig-Holstein Question*, p. 3n, reports Palmerston's *bon mot* somewhat differently.

[36] In the answer of September 16, 1847, in reply to the Prince Consort's memorandum of September 11, 1847, he wrote: "Both England and Germany are threatened by the same danger and from the same quarters. That danger is an attack from Russia or from France separately, or from Russia and from France united. . . . England and Germany, therefore, have mutually a direct interest in assisting each other to become rich, united and strong, and there ought not to be, in the mind of any enlightened man of either country, any feeling of jealousy as to the progress made by the other country in civilization and prosperity." Martin, *The Life of His Royal Highness the Prince Consort*, I, 447–48.

the *Zollverein* as an organization imposing prohibitive duties on British products; [37] the Tories were anti-Prussian; [38] the court favored a Prussian Union and an expansion of the German Customs Union.

It must not be forgotten that the Treaty of Vienna suspended the sword of Damocles over a new political order in Germany, in whatever form this new constellation might be set up. By no means did this control over German affairs exist only in theory. The conception of English statesmen, and of Palmerston particularly, is poignantly brought out in a speech made by him during the Dresden Conferences when the question of the incorporation of all Austrian and Prussian dominions into the Confederation arose:

It was therefore the opinion of Her Majesty's Government when they heard of this intention, that such could not be carried into effect consistently with the law of Europe, unless with the consent of all those Powers who had been parties to the Treaty of Vienna in 1815. And in accordance with that opinion, Her Majesty's Government did not . . . follow the example of France, but they anticipated France, and as early as the 3rd of December they made a remonstrance on that subject both here, and at Vienna, and at Berlin. . . . Knowing the great value which Austria and Prussia had always attached to the Treaty of Vienna . . . he could not entertain a doubt that that treaty would be observed.[39]

At first glance it seemed as if Schwarzenberg had to guard himself against British support of Prussia's Union policy in Germany. Palmerston regretted that Frederick William of Prussia did not accept the imperial crown offered to him by the German national parliament.

We should have had no objection to see Prussia take the first place: on the contrary, a German Union embracing all the smaller states, with Prussia at its head, and in alliance with Austria, would have been a very good European arrangement.[40]

[37] Sanders, *Life of Viscount Palmerston*, p. 130.
[38] See, for instance, Disraeli's speech of June 9, 1848, Hansard's *Parliamentary Debates*, XCIX, cols. 639 *et sqq.*
[39] Hansard's *Parliamentary Debates*, CXV, cols. 1355–56; speech of April 10, 1851.
[40] Ashley, *The Life of Henry John Temple, Viscount Palmerston, 1846–1865*, I, 242.

The Gagern plan [41] was favorably received in England.[42] Baron Stockmar,[43] the Prince Consort's confidant, wrote Heinrich von Gagern a letter from London on December 3, 1848, in which he wholeheartedly endorsed his plan and found British cabinet policy traditionally favoring a connection with Germany.

I . . . perceive, since I came here, ever more clearly than I did before, when in Germany, the impossibility of including Austria in the German Bund, now to be fomented anew.

The general political interests of Europe, the special necessities of Austria and Germany, evidently require that Austria, as she has long been, should continue as far as possible to form an independent whole. . . .

I can state that in the English Cabinet there existed a traditional desire to rest their own policy on Germany, on the supposition that Germany, strengthened by greater union, would prove a better ally for the preservation of the peace of the world, than any other Power which England could find in the North and West.

Schwarzenberg knew, however, that Palmerstonian idealism and liberalism would fade away before hard economic and political facts. While he had to figure on England's resistance to his empire of seventy millions, he could safely count on British resistance (just as French or Russian resistance) to a well-knit German empire under Hohenzollern leadership. As the Prince Consort keenly observes in his Memorandum on German Affairs, September 11, 1847,

There was another side of the question, which had an obviously preponderating influence on the mind of the British Minister—The Zollverein, or Customs' Union. . . . All consideration of the gain to Germany, to Europe, or to England, from a strong and united Germany, in intimate alliance with England, drops out of view, and Lord Palmerston sums up his argument by the conclusion, "That any British Ministry would be thought to have much neglected its duty, and to have sacrificed the commercial interests of the country if it did not make every proper effort to persuade the States of Northern Germany who have not joined the Zollverein to continue to refrain from doing so." [44]

[41] See *supra*, p. 113.
[42] Precht, "Englands Stellung zur deutschen Einheit, 1848–1850," *Historische Zeitschrift*, Beiheft 3, pp. 77, 120.
[43] Stockmar, *Memoirs*, ed. by F. Max Müller, II, 327, 336.
[44] Martin, *The Life of His Royal Highness the Prince Consort*, I, 448.

The English envoys at the German courts were distinctly pro-Austrian in sentiment. Foremost among the champions of the Austrian cause was Mr. Forbes at Dresden. To the annoyance and surprise of the Queen, this ultra-royalist miraculously thought that the League of the Three Kingdoms infringed upon the dynastic rights of his sovereign. Victoria complained to Lord Palmerston about her representatives abroad. In a letter of November 18, 1850, she wrote:

The Queen is afraid . . . that all our Ministers abroad,—at Berlin, Dresden, Munich, Stuttgart, Hanover, etc. (with the exception of Lord Cowley at Frankfort)—are warm partisans of the *despotic* league against Prussia and a German Constitution, and *for* the maintenance of the old Diet under Austrian and Russian influence. Ought not Lord Palmerston to make his agents understand that their sentiments are at variance with those of the English Government? [45]

In his answer to the Queen's letter, dated November 18, 1850, Lord Palmerston correctly submits "that the conflict between Austria and Prussia can scarcely be said to have turned upon principles of Government so much as upon a struggle for political ascendency in Germany." [46] Undisturbed by the Queen's remonstrance, the great autocrat at the foreign office let his subordinates abroad continue their pro-Austrian activities. Could Prince Schwarzenberg expect more?

An excellent insight into Palmerston's true attitude towards Prussia is given in the letter to Lord Cowley of November 22, 1850,[47] already referred to. In it Prussia is showered with invectives. Evidently Lord Palmerston was peeved, for Prussia had twice refused his mediation offer in the Schleswig-Holstein question and had declined to sign the London Protocol of August 2, 1850. Palmerston's endorsement of Prussia's Union and his gestures on behalf of the Gagern plan were mere flourishes. When Prussia undertook some-

---

[45] *Letters of Queen Victoria,* II, 328. Reproduced here by permission of the publishers, Messrs. Longmans, Green & Co., Inc.
[46] *Ibid.,* p. 330.
[47] Ashley, *The Life of Henry John Temple, Viscount Palmerston, 1846–1865,* I, 242–44.

thing tangible, he accused her of stealth and ill-will. He did not object to a union, but he rejected a union as designed by Prussia. He desired a union parliament, but not the Erfurt parliament. What Prussia was to do in order to please him he did not indicate with precision. Such protean beings as crochety Palmerston wanted to make out of Prussia exist in the realm of fable only.

During the Austro-Prussian crisis in 1850 the cause of Austria found more sympathy at the hands of Palmerston than that of Prussia. Nevertheless, the British foreign minister declined to acquiesce in Vienna's repeated requests for recognition of the Frankfurt Confederation, but he tempered his refusal by adding that in his opinion recognition was not absolutely necessary for the validity of the Confederation's resolutions, in fact, might be better dispensed with for the Confederation's prestige in Germany.[48] The policy of the Whig cabinet was therefore not much different from that of the Tories. All English political leaders were, of course, anxious to see a war avoided between Austria and Prussia. As Palmerston remarked to Baron Koller, such a conflict would be a great calamity for Germany and a triumph for Russia and France.[49]

Palmerston was favorably impressed by the spirit of moderation shown by Schwarzenberg at Olmütz.[50] Only Queen Victoria, pouring out her heart to her uncle, the King of the Belgians, in a letter of December 3, 1850, bemoaned Prussia's weakness.

The State of Germany is indeed a very anxious one. It is a mistake to think the *supremacy of Prussia is what we wished for.* General Radowitz who was in England on a special mission from the King of Prussia himself says that what is necessary for Germany is that she should take the lead, and should redeem the pledges given in '48. . . . Prussia is the *only large* and powerful really *German* Power there is, and therefore she must take the lead. . . . Unfortunately, *Lord Palmerston* has contrived to make us *so hated* by all

[48] Baron Koller to Prince Schwarzenberg, October 25, 1850, *Haus-, Hof- und Staatsarchiv*, cited by Precht, "Englands Stellung zur deutschen Einheit, 1848–1850," *Historische Zeitschrift*, Beiheft 3, p. 176.
[49] *Ibid.*
[50] Baron Koller to Prince Schwarzenberg, December 17, 1850, *Haus-, Hof- und Staatsarchiv*, cited by Precht, *ibid.*, p. 177.

parties abroad, that we have lost our position and our influence, which, considering the flourishing and satisfactory state of this country, *ought* to have been *immense*. . . . What a noble position we *might* have had, and how wantonly has it been thrown away! [51]

Prince Schwarzenberg was enchanted at seeing England isolated in international relations at the end of 1851, the time of Palmerston's dismissal. Lord Palmerston had conducted his office in such a manner that a member of Parliament returning from the continent reported "that an Englishman could hardly show himself without becoming aware of the hatred they were held in; the only chance one had to avoid being insulted was to say *Civis Romanus non sum*." [52] All the resentment that had accumulated in Schwarzenberg's heart against England manifested itself in a language more deficient in the graces than Palmerston's. Even Queen Victoria, aggrieved as she was over the permanent tension between her country and Austria, believed that Schwarzenberg had overreached himself in haughtiness. In a letter of March 9, 1852, to the King of the Belgians, she wrote: "All the admirers of Austria consider Prince Schwarzenberg a madman, and the Emperor Nicholas said that he was 'Lord Palmerston in a white uniform.' " [53] The King of the Belgians answered on March 12, 1852: "I must say that in Austria, at least Schwartzenberg [sic], they were very much intoxicated. I hope they will grow sober again soon." [54] Although the Queen's censure was undoubtedly overlaid with feminine exaggeration, it was understandable because she disapproved any disturbance in the amicable relations between states. She enlisted the good offices of Prince Metternich, who had returned to Vienna a couple of months before to urge his successor in office to moderation. Schwarzenberg consented, since he did not want to drive the quarrel with England to the breaking point. And in the few days of life still granted to him, the Queen no longer said about Prince Schwar-

---

[51] *Letters of Queen Victoria*, II, 333. Reproduced here by courtesy of the publishers, Messrs. Longmans, Green & Co., Inc.

[52] Memorandum by Prince Albert, in *Letters of Queen Victoria*, II, 423.

[53] *Letters of Queen Victoria*, II, 458. A white coat was the dress uniform of an Austrian general.   [54] *Ibid.*, p. 459.

zenberg the worst that could be said of anybody as far as she was concerned—"Lord Palmerston in a white uniform."

A few days after Prince Schwarzenberg became prime minister of Austria, Louis Napoleon was elected president of the French Republic (December 10, 1848). Schwarzenberg appraised the event serenely: as long as a foreign government allowed his country to pull its weight in Europe, it did not matter to him whether it was "legitimate" or "revolutionary." Austria's conservatives were shocked to see the heir of the revolution return to power and could not understand why the Vienna cabinet sought his handshake. When Windisch-Graetz reproached his brother-in-law for assuming too complacent an attitude towards a Napoleon, he answered him on January 5, 1849:

Our relations with France must be conceived realistically and should not be adjusted to the principle of legitimacy or that of the *juste milieu*. . . . The little nephew of the great uncle gives us no reason to sulk, least of all out of regard for the Elder and Younger Bourbons who have always been hostile towards us.[55]

With Napoleon's advent to power, French foreign policy no longer practiced abstention in the conflict of sovereigns and nationalities as the Second Republic had done at first. Now, by exulting speeches, revenge for the humiliation of 1815 was avowed; by glorious actions, the revision of the treaties of Vienna was to be undertaken. The language and the tendencies of French nationalism—pacific if possible, bellicose if the occasion so demanded—were revived. Dynamic power politics were directed towards the Rhine and Italy—the ideal of those in whom the glory of Louis XIV lingered as well as of those who cherished the memory of the revolution with its struggle against the rest of Europe.

In Italian affairs Schwarzenberg played a dilatory game with the western powers when they urged mediation upon him. The English envoy at Vienna threatened that if he did not send a delegate to a conference at Brussels the responsibility for an eventual war with

[55] Müller, *Feldmarschall Fürst Windischgrätz*, p. 164.

France would rest upon Austria.[56] But Schwarzenberg remained unperturbed. He had faith in the ancient splendor of the Habsburg Empire and Marshal Radetzky's abilities as a general—and won his ends. Piedmont's provocative denunciation of the armistice with Austria (March 12, 1849) put him in an excellent diplomatic position towards France and England. Radetzky's victories made Austria's military position in the Apennine peninsula seemingly impregnable. Napoleon had repeated to King Charles Albert the declaration of General Cavaignac that France was unable to come to his assistance, but after the battle of Novara (March 23, 1849) he impatiently longed for armed interference by France. He excitedly declared to Thiers: [57] "You see the result of your pacific policy! I cannot endure this Austrian aggrandisement. We must immediately send an army across the Alps." Impetuosity was checked by prudence. Thiers, taking a synoptic view of the European political alignment, warned that a war with Austria meant a war with Russia and suggested negotiations through the Austrian envoy at Paris. Baron Hübner voiced Schwarzenberg's policy when he stated in conversation with Thiers: "We do not propose to crush Piedmont; we only require her to pay the expenses to which she has put us by her treacherous aggression." In accordance with the guarantees given by Schwarzenberg, Piedmont was suffered to retain her territories intact; the war indemnity owing to French and English pressure was reduced to seventy-five million francs.[58] Schwarzenberg had shown dauntless courage in resisting the joint exertions of the western powers, but master of the diplomatic art that he was, he knew when to yield.

The silver cord of good understanding between Austria and France, loosed during the Piedmont negotiations, was not retied during the peace arrangements with Venice. De Tocqueville suggested to Schwarzenberg through his envoy at Vienna that he pursue a prudent and generous policy with an eye to the future. This

[56] Guichen, Les Grandes Questions européennes et la diplomatie des puissances sous la Seconde République, I, 294.

[57] Senior, Conversations with M. Thiers, M. Guizot, ed. by M. C. M. Simpson, I, 48.

[58] Supra, p. 179.

policy, he asserted, was in the interest of general tranquillity and would serve Austria's interests best. Schwarzenberg received these unsolicited counsels with displeasure [59]—and concluded peace with rebellious Venice on his terms.

With Piedmont beaten, the danger for France was that Austria would occupy Rome. Such a strategic position would have spelled Austria's absolute supremacy over the entire Apennine peninsula. Thus fortified, "with Russia behind her and all Italy under her," [60] Austria's might would have been formidable. Schwarzenberg suggested, *inter alia,* to convoke a congress composed of Catholic states to discuss ways of bringing the Pope back to Rome and of dealing with the Roman insurgents. Since he would have dominated the congress, his proposal was rejected by France.

The French anticipated further Austrian military operations in Italy by ordering an expeditionary corps to occupy Rome. This move was not unwelcome to Schwarzenberg; in fact, it had been discussed in advance between the two governments. Since French public opinion, hostile to Austria, had to be placated, Foreign Minister Drouyn de Lhuys [61] played a patriotic act in the assembly in order to obtain the necessary credits for the undertaking—after having told Baron Hübner how he would time his dramatic scenes.[62] Accordingly, Schwarzenberg wrote on April 30, 1849: "France does by herself nothing else but what the powers assembled at Gaëta would have done for the benefit of the Pope and his Catholic subjects." [63] He could sit back in Metternich's chair well satisfied. The Romans did not care to be liberated by the French; the Pope would have preferred restoration of his domains through Austria. Louis

[59] De la Cour to Tocqueville, August 24, 1849; Guichen, *Les Grandes Questions européennes,* I, 397.

[60] Simpson, *Louis Napoleon and the Recovery of France,* p. 66.

[61] The French foreign ministers during Schwarzenberg's premiership were: Jules Bastide (May 10, 1848–December 10, 1848); Drouyn de Lhuys (December 19, 1848–June 2, 1849); Alexis de Tocqueville (June 2, 1849–November 16, 1849); Vicomte de la Hitte (November 16, 1849–January 9, 1851); Drouyn de Lhuys (January 9, 1851–January 24, 1851); Baron Anatole Brenier (January 24, 1851–April 10, 1851); Jules Baroche (April 10, 1851–October 26, 1851); Louis Marquis de Turgot (October 26, 1851–July 28, 1852).

[62] Engel-Janosi, *Der Freiherr von Hübner, 1811–1892,* pp. 84–85.

[63] Bourgeois, *Manuel historique de politique étrangère,* III, 341.

Napoleon had permitted himself to be drawn into an adventure that eventually led to Sedan.[64]

It has been mentioned in the preceding pages [65] that during the Austro-Prussian conflict the Prince-President stretched out feelers in Berlin with a view to selling his military assistance at a price. As early as the end of 1848 and the beginning of 1849 he intimated to Prussia that she could satisfy her ambition in German lands provided he received a free hand in Italy. Radetzky's victory at Novara put an end to these unscrupulous machinations.[66] During the height of the Austro-Prussian crisis French assistance was once again offered to Prussia. On June 15, 1850, Napoleon made it clear to Berlin, however, that he expected compensation for his help at the expense of Bavaria's Rhenish province.[67] Radowitz later resumed negotiations, but they came to naught. While the bellicose Prince-President was incessantly scheming how to improve his fortune, the assembly was pacific. On November 30, 1850, the chamber, by a sizable majority, passed a resolution of neutrality in German affairs, although secretly it favored Austria rather than Prussia.[68]

The Parisian government had reacted calmly to the offer of the imperial crown to Frederick William IV. Frankfurt was alternately described as a metaphysical institution, fit to be showered with derision, and then again it was pictured in Paris as a bugbear of German expansionist policy. France might have acquiesced in the absorption of small states north of the River Main line by Prussia, but, naturally, she opposed the diminution of the powers of the middle states or the erection of a strong German empire.

Likewise, France blocked Schwarzenberg's attempts at incorporating all Austrian lands into the Germanic Confederation. Not only

[64] Simpson, *Louis Napoleon and the Recovery of France*, p. 89.

[65] *Supra*, p. 138.

[66] "France, [Napoleon] said, would not now be jealous of our gaining more power in Egypt, and France and England could remodel everything. This means to me to hint at an idea that France would take part with Prussia, and if that Power gained territory in Germany, France would advance her frontier and allow England compensation in the Levant." Malmesbury, *Memoirs of an Ex-minister*, p. 244 (entry under date of March 30, 1849).

[67] See on the subject Lange, *Frankreichs Preussenpolitik in den Jahren 1849 und 1850*, pp. 34 *et sqq.*

[68] Bourgeois, *Manuel historique de politique étrangère*, p. 354.

did Napoleon protest during the Dresden Conferences to Vienna, but the Vienna despatch of February 23, 1851, was communicated to all the representatives of the German governments at Dresden. Even stronger light was thrown on the meaning of the despatch by the closing words of a letter simultaneously addressed to the French envoy at Dresden: "The President's policy of watchful waiting must be replaced by an active policy." [69] Some of the German princes—Schwarzenberg called them Judases—remembering the creator of the Confederation of the Rhine, were inclined to bow to his nephew; other Germans, like the Bavarian minister, von der Pfordten, vigorously defended Austria's cause. It must have been gratifying to Schwarzenberg that the German delegates at Dresden countered a renewed Franco-British disapproval of his plan with a protest against foreign interference in German affairs. The move was a gesture, but as a symbol of national pride and endorsement of Schwarzenberg's policy it had its value.

In general, it was Schwarzenberg's policy to bar French or any other intervention in German matters. "I want to render Germany capable of repelling any attack so that her component parts will be masters in their own houses," he remarked sharply, for instance, to the British envoy in December, 1850. And he added with self-confidence: "I assure you I shall succeed in that." [70] In January, 1852, Napoleon proposed to take action against Switzerland in conjunction with Austria but exclusive of Prussia. Although Prussia had just obstructed the customs conference convoked at Vienna and had assumed an unfriendly attitude towards Austria in Frankfurt, Schwarzenberg declined to pass over Prussia, on the ground, as he wrote Baron Hübner,[71] that "it cannot be our wish to see the French government conduct isolated negotiations with one or the other German cabinet which concern the foreign security of the Confederation." On February 25, reverting to the subject, he stressed the fact that any discord between Austria and Prussia was only a domestic affair, carefully to be concealed from foreign powers and

---

[69] Heller, *Mitteleuropas Vorkämpfer*, p. 138.
[70] Guichen, *Les Grandes Questions européenes*, II, 52.
[71] Heller, *Mitteleuropas Vorkämpfer*, p. 165.

certainly not to be regarded by them as a convenient opportunity to play the role of arbitrator between his country and the Hohenzollern kingdom. Incidentally, these statements repudiate the rumors, afloat at that time, that Schwarzenberg schemed to defeat Prussia with France's help.[72]

In Hungarian affairs De Tocqueville, then French foreign minister, spared Schwarzenberg the annoyance caused him so often by the British Foreign Minister Palmerston. A communication to his envoy at St. Petersburg reveals his attitude.

I need not tell you with what keen and melancholy interest we follow events in Hungary. Unfortunately, for the present, we can only take a passive part in this question. The letter and spirit of the treaties open out to us no right of intervention. Besides, our distance from the seat of war must impose upon us, in the present state of affairs and of those of Europe, a certain reserve. Since we are not able to speak or act to good purpose, it is due to our dignity not to display, in respect to this question, any sterile excitement or impotent good feeling. Our duty with respect to Hungarian events is to limit ourselves to carefully observing what happens, and seeking to discover what is likely to take place.[73]

When addressing Schwarzenberg through the French envoy at Vienna, De La Cour, De Tocqueville did not roar with Palmerston's Olympian thunder. On April 22, 1849, he had a despatch read which was more in the nature of a friendly advice than of "interference in internal matters." There were no ruffled feelings.

The energetic resistance of the Hungarians has evoked warm sympathies in Europe, even outside revolutionary circles. It would be an unenlightened policy to treat Hungary with severity. Otherwise two things will happen: first, Austria will arouse against herself the moral strength of public opinion which nowadays can no longer be overlooked; secondly, the germ of discontent will be planted in Hungary that will force the imperial cabinet to keep Hungary subdued with all its forces and leave it anywhere else severally powerless. It could no longer exercise in European affairs the influence to which it is entitled as a first-class power. We are anxious to see

[72] See also Lange, *Frankreichs Preussenpolitik in den Jahren 1849 und 1850*, p. 40n.
[73] Sproxton, *Palmerston and the Hungarian Revolution*, p. 101.—Quoted here by courtesy of the publishers, Cambridge University Press (England) and The Macmillan Company (New York).

Austria coming into her own again, to see her no longer exhausting herself in sterile struggles, to see her retaking in the direction of European affairs the place to which she is justly entitled.[74]

In the Hungarian refugee question all the chiefs of the majority of the French chamber, Molé, Thiers, Broglie, held that it would be a mistake to engage in war for the refugees.[75] But Napoleon was eager for the adventure, despite the warnings of his foreign minister. His stand "was owing to the influence of Lord Normanby the English envoy at Paris over the President," as De Tocqueville narrated later.[76] "It was a fine *succès de tribune*," he continued. "It gave the English Government and ours an occasion to boast of their courage and of their generosity, but a more dangerous experiment was never made." Not without good reason did the Czar ironically remark that France was taken in tow by England.[77]

Schwarzenberg was confronted with a weighty problem when on December 2, 1851, Louis Napoleon, supported by the army, dissolved the national assembly and the council of state. The Vienna aristocracy was disappointed because it had hoped for the return of the Bourbons, but Schwarzenberg mocked at them. When he was asked how he could sympathize with a Napoleon, he replied curtly that he preferred anything to a government of "imbeciles," that is, the liberal chamber majority. The republican government had antagonized him when it obstructed his plan to hold Switzerland to account for sheltering Austrian political refugees. Here was a chance to come to an understanding with Napoleon on a conservative basis and wean him away from England.

The success of the *coup d'état* had assured the stability of the regime in power. At the same time, it had opened a wide gap between Napoleon and radicals in all countries. Naturally, it was greeted with rejoicing by the conservative states that in consequence of the changed French governmental system tension be-

[74] Guichen, *Les Grandes Questions européennes,* I, 390–91.

[75] Sproxton, *Palmerston and the Hungarian Revolution,* p. 131.

[76] Tocqueville, *Correspondence and Conversations with Nassau William Senior,* ed. by M. C. M. Simpson, II, 14.

[77] Guichen, *Les Grandes Questions européennes,* I, 455.

tween France and England arose. The possibility of a regrouping of
the great powers seemed to be given. But the advantages of the international situation were counteracted by a danger. Louis Napoleon, the three-pointed oriflamme of order, nationality, and glory,
might overstress glory. Evidently he was embarking on the path of
his great uncle. It was to be expected that he would not stop before
he had attained his supreme aim—to put the imperial crown on his
head.

On December 5, 1851, Schwarzenberg sent a despatch to the
Austrian envoy at Paris in which he declared as his policy that Austria would never interfere in the domestic affairs of France. He was
desirous, so he stated, of maintaining friendly relations with the
French government in order to hold the fabric of society together
and to insure peace everywhere. One condition he attached to his
wish for co-operation: he expected France to honor the treaties she
had concluded.[78] The despatch of December 5 was elaborated by
Schwarzenberg's two despatches of December 18 in reply to Hübner's inquiry as to what Austria's position would be in case Napoleon should assume the imperial title. Through his first despatch,
evidently drafted for official use, Schwarzenberg assured France
that no new coalition would be formed against France, provided she
did not aim at territorial changes. In the second despatch, framed in
terms of private instructions, he expressed agreement with his envoy that Napoleon's action would lead to an estrangement between
France and England so that the "revolutionary complicity," as he
expressed it,[79] between the two powers could be severed. A private
letter to Hübner summarized Schwarzenberg's general attitude regarding the cardinal political issue of the time: "A France regulating her domestic affairs will have our sympathy and support; an
expansionist France, whether empire or republic, will arouse our
enmity. Every attack by France on any part of Austria or Prussia
will be considered a cause for war by both countries. In this respect

[78] Heller, *Mitteleuropas Vorkämpfer*, p. 162.
[79] *Ibid.*, p. 163.

there are definite understandings with Prussia, behind which stands Russia." [80]

In the memorandum of December 29, 1851,[81] memorable for his common-sense arguments and gliding urbanity of style, Schwarzenberg took up the question of Napoleon's assumption of the imperial title with the cabinets of St. Petersburg and Berlin. The significance of the subject matter dealt with deserves a brief analysis; besides, the document reveals Schwarzenberg's keen feeling for language, a characteristic of a great man of the world. After the Foreign Minister had outlined the propitious circumstances that might induce Napoleon to take the fatal step, he stressed the importance of concerted action between the conservative powers in order to warn Napoleon and to impress the German and Italian courts. The question is examined whether in view of Article II of the treaty of November 20, 1815, it would be permissible and advisable to recognize Napoleon as emperor of the French. The document comes to the conclusion that the powers, without committing themselves on the legal issue, could accept an accomplished fact. The reason was advanced that Napoleon's government was preferable to the doubtful restoration of the Bourbons and their parliament, because then the social order would be preserved. With an unerring eye for the main point Schwarzenberg referred to the facts that the cabinets had already recognized Napoleon's *coup d'état* of December 2, 1851, and therefore had to all intents and purposes permitted his ascent to the imperial dignity; consequently, only a question of title was involved, he argued, and that alone would never condone a rupture with France.

Schwarzenberg, however, wanted to play safe, and therefore he wanted to exact a positive assurance from Napoleon that he would respect treaties and would not embark upon the expansionist policy of his uncle. The three powers should declare that every attempt at

[80] *Ibid.*, p. 164.

[81] The document is reprinted in General Zaïonchkovskiï's *Eastern War 1855–1856* (in Russian), pp. 196–97.

a change of the territorial *status quo* in Europe by France would find their concerted hostility. Thus, Napoleon was to enter into a definite understanding, but, on the other hand, the powers, too, were to underwrite a positive obligation.

A precedent for Schwarzenberg's proposal can be found in Metternich's plan in 1830 on the occasion of the question of acknowledging Louis Philippe. When Friedjung contends [82] that the document is permeated with a spirit of naked power politics, disregarding treaties and principles, it may be persuasively replied, as Heller did,[83] that Schwarzenberg did not seek to attain an extension of power but only to safeguard the *status quo*. Can the accusation be maintained that Schwarzenberg established a record of craft worthy of Caesar Borgia? He cared no more and no less for treaties and principles than Metternich and Nesselrode had done in 1830. In a word, Schwarzenberg was a realist.

Schwarzenberg saw his main enemy in England; he did not care to have two enemies, England and France. Consequently, he endeavored to be on the best terms with the new empire, and, as a matter of fact, when he stood on the pinnacle of fame's temple, after his success at Olmütz, the relations between France and Austria were excellent. The conflicts of 1849, leading almost to war, had been forgotten. Significant are Schwarzenberg's references to England in the document of December 29; they are illustrative of his suspicion of her policies and of his desire to isolate her. He wrote:

> England, one of the contracting parties, will surely not declare herself bound to the treaty of November 20, 1815; therefore, the validity of the Act will be breached, and the other Powers, Austria, Russia, and Prussia may *ipso jure* regard themselves as freed from the engagement undertaken vis-à-vis Napoleon.

> The similarity of the institutions existing between France and England has been the cement of their alliance. For this reason England will look at the changes in France with malevolence, and this is a much stronger reason for the Allied Cabinets to isolate England by placating Louis Napoleon. If we follow another policy, the British government would quickly

---

[82] *Österreich von 1848 bis 1860*, II, 146.
[83] *Mitteleuropas Vorkämpfer*, p. 166.

recognize the new empire and attach it to England by friendship and the necessity imposed by France to find herself an ally in a conflict which sooner or later might break out between her and the continental powers. This eventuality would be contrary to the interests of Austria, Russia, and Prussia, because it would retard again the old political regime in Europe, in which France, quiet at home, and under monarchical institutions, formed the strongest bulwark against England's transgressions and preponderance.

Thus, Schwarzenberg considered France's solid and tranquil consolidation necessary for the welfare of Europe, or as he expressed it, "when France catches a cold, Europe sneezes."

After Schwarzenberg's death a protocol was signed between Austria and Russia on May 13, 1852, adhered to by Prussia on May 22, in which definite arrangements were made. It was stipulated that Napoleon's proclamation as Emperor of the French should not be considered a *casus belli,* but that he should be recognized only after he had given guarantees for his love of peace. A *fait accompli* should not be considered a *chose jugée,* and consequently the legality of the treaties of 1815 was upheld. The question of the dynastic succession was held in abeyance. The main principles of this important understanding between the conservative powers were therefore conceived in accordance with the deceased statesman's memorandum.

Mindful of the cavalier promise he had given the Emperor Francis of Austria at Münchengrätz in 1833 to be a friend and protector of his mentally sick son Ferdinand, Nicholas I of Russia, carrying his pledge over to the Schwarzenberg era, treated Austria with great sympathy. He entertained truly paternal feelings toward the young monarch Francis Joseph. Illustrative of his genial sentiments is a letter which he addressed to "his young friend in Vienna," dated April 7/19, 1852.

If Thou will permit it, I shall visit Thee this time in Vienna. The hope of embracing Thee again gives me new life, and I feel more than ever the need of telling Thee how I love and prize Thee and how greatly I rejoice to see Thee daily more admired and honored, as Thou deservest, as I have perceived from the first moment that brought us together.[84]

[84] Redlich, *Emperor Francis Joseph of Austria,* pp. 125–26.

The July revolution and the establishment of the French Republic unpleasantly reminded Nicholas of the Dekabrist rising, that revolt of noble officers of the guard who, imbued with Western ideas, disputed the omnipotence of the autocrat. When the Poles, seized by the revolutionary wave surging up from Paris, revolted against Russia's dominance, the Czar's prime governmental principle was directed toward Russia's hermetic seclusion from the West. Any contact with France, even a war with the hotbed of all revolutionary disorders, should be avoided. Thus Nicholas became the self-appointed guardian of legitimacy, fired on by a blind faith in his own ability and the truth of his beliefs. The brutal simplicity of his methods gave him force and drive; it made him a powerful figure in European politics that bears little resemblance to Chadschi Murat, the shallow pretender Leo Tolstoi makes out of him.

Central Europe was designed to play an important role in the Czar's scheme. It was to form the dyke stemming any revolutionary flood from the West, and, at the same time, it was to cover his rear for Russia's oriental policy. It should therefore be strong enough to relieve Russia of waging war against France, yet it should not be too strong so that it could become unfettered of his help and endanger his aims in the East.

Felix Schwarzenberg accurately appraised Nicholas and his system as thoroughly Russian. According to the Czar's design—and this was the Austrian Foreign Minister's correct interpretation—the welfare of the European society of nations, so often conjured up by the Russian Czar, was in the last analysis to be founded on the greatness and solidity of the Russian empire. Who else would have profited more by the security of throne and altar than the Czar whose worldly authority was surrounded by a sacerdotal halo? When Schwarzenberg took office it was his opinion that Austria had referred and deferred too much to Russia. While he made an alliance with the Muscovite empire the pillar of his foreign policy, nevertheless he wanted to steer the Austrian ship alongside the Russian Leviathan by compass rather than by star. Vis-à-vis Russia, too, the rejuvenated Monarchy was to assume an independent, planned

course, commensurate with Austria's interests and dignity. He instructed Count Buol, made envoy to St. Petersburg shortly after his
own appointment, to conduct negotiations with Russia in this
spirit.[85] His audacious, domineering manners did not make Schwarzenberg popular at St. Petersburg, but, despite the fact that he attempted to unshackle Austrian policies from Russian dictates, he
was skillful enough to keep on the whole on cordial terms with his
Russian colleague Count Nesselrode.

Emperor Nicholas was a determined enemy of national movements. Pan-Slavic ideas did not find favor with him. The South
Slavs, endangering Austria's integrity, were not encouraged by him
in their national aspirations. If summoned, the Czar stood ready to
defend Austria's possessions in Galicia and Hungary, and that sum-
mons came, as has been described.[86] By appealing for Russia's help
against the Hungarian revolutionists and thus risking Austria's
prestige, Prince Schwarzenberg strengthened the Czar's inclination
to support him in his struggle against Prussia. The Czar's primitive
legitimistic ideology, combined with cold calculations for the grandeur of his empire, offered the surest guarantee against the creation
of a German empire, under Prussian supremacy. Russian, as well as
French egotism, needed a divided Germany. To Russian imperialism, to Russian autocracy, German liberty and unity, an imperial
dignity conferred upon a Prussian king, the Frankfurt parliament
("the insane asylum"), and the division of Denmark were repugnant. The tortuous Austro-Prussian relationship with Russia, the
ebb and flow of receiving and being denied favors from the Czar,
and Schwarzenberg's final triumph in the Austro-Prussian quarrel
have been dealt with in the preceding chapter.

No foreign minister could have wished for more handsome support of his policy. But "gratitude is a burden upon our imperfect
nature." It is understandable that the acceptance of benefits from
Russia severely wounded Schwarzenberg's pride. He has been credited with the utterance that "Austria would astonish the world by

[85] Heller, *Mitteleuropas Vorkämpfer*, p. 41.
[86] See *supra*, p. 53.

the magnitude of her ingratitude." This callous remark was current
during his lifetime among his Prussian antagonists and has often
been quoted since. Frederick William's aide-de-camp, General von
Gerlach, for instance, made an entry to this effect in his diary on
November 14, 1851. Bismarck, in his memoirs, wrote [87] that "flagrant ingratitude, such as Prince Schwarzenberg proclaimed, is not
only unlovely but unwise in politics as in private life." The "unlovely and unwise" remark, loosely carried over by many historians,
is, however, a legend. It has been exposed as a *canard* by Thouvenel,
the son of the French foreign minister (1860–1862), who writes:
"This saying, just as many other historical sayings, does not bear
the stamp of authenticity. The inquiry into its truth conducted by
me results in finding that the words have never been pronounced by
Prince Schwarzenberg." [88]

Gratitude, at least in diplomacy, has also been defined as "the
expectation of favors yet to come." But the excessive attentions of
the devouring polar bear, to which Eduard von Bauernfeld compared the Russian Empire in *The Republic of Animals,* could become unpleasantly obtrusive and dangerous. Nesselrode's exhorta-
tion of November 13, 1850, to a "cool-headed and circumspect"
statesman to deal moderately with a retreating enemy was vexa-
tious.[89] The Russian envoy's two visits a day during the Olmütz
crisis were importunate.[90] When the thick vapors of international
conflicts had dispersed and the sky had grown lighter, Schwarzenberg looked for freedom of action, not for further favors from
Russia. In accordance with these ideas, the instructions of April 19,
1852, to the new Austrian envoy at St. Petersburg, Count Mensdorf-
Pouilly, Buol's successor, were drawn up after Schwarzenberg's
death. They breathe his spirit as if they had been penned by his
own hand. Russia, it was said at the beginning, would always remain
Austria's most intimate ally. The joint war against the revolutionary

[87] Bismarck, *The Man and the Statesman* (tr. from the German under the supervision
of A. J. Butler), I, 302. See also, *ibid.,* II, 279.
[88] Thouvenel, *Nicholas Ier et Napoléon* III, p. 311*n.*
[89] Nesselrode, *Lettres et papiers,* IX, 323.
[90] Meyendorff, *Ein russischer Diplomat an den Höfen von Berlin und Wien,* II, 336.

forces and the restraining influence on Prussia exercised by the Emperor Nicholas were given as the main reasons for knitting this
alliance closely together. An intimate compact between Austria and
Russia was, however, made subject to clarifying understandings on
certain questions. The first concerned German affairs. At no time
should Russia be allowed to mix in them or to play the role of arbiter.
Therewith the principle set by Schwarzenberg with regard to Napoleon was extended to the Muscovite empire. The second restric-
tion dealt with the question of the Orient. It was pointed out that
in 1849 Schwarzenberg had assumed a temperate attitude in the
matter of the Hungarian refugees, just as he had done in 1851 with
respect to their release from confinement because of Austria's other
international engagements, but these acts of pliant behavior did not
spell Austria's willingness to renounce her interests in the East.
"Austria desires to maintain the complete independence of Turkey
and to prevent her surrender to England," the document read, "but
neither was Austria, supported by the Münchengrätz agreement,
willing to let Russia regulate the destiny of the Turkish empire
single-handed." [91] The third issue raised was that of the thanks due
to Russia for her help in 1849. The debt of gratitude was not
denied, but the envoy was instructed to emphasize at every opportunity that Russia had, after all, defended her own cause in Hungary. This conception of the matter had already been expressed by
Schwarzenberg in the autumn of 1849. Summarized, it may be said
that a hyphen joined the instructions to Count Mensdorf with those
given to Count Buol: maintenance of best relations with Russia,
but without sacrificing Austria's dignity and interests.

Russia, indeed, was a power to be taken into account. Around
the middle of the last century, the people of Central Europe felt the
cold wind blowing over their lands from the steppes. The shadow of
the "polar bear" was looming large in the background. What Grillparzer, the poetic recorder of political events, predicted—the coming rule of the Slavs, so long the "servants" but now the "masters"
over Latins and Teutons, not through primary but through deriva-

[91] Heller, *Mitteleuropas Vorkämpfer*, p. 171.

tive force—did not come true in his time. But are the words spoken in *Libussa* destined to become a reality in our days?

> Dann kommt's an euch, an euch und eure Brüder,
> Der letzte Aufschwung ist's der matten Welt.
> Die lang gedient, sie werden endlich herrschen,
> Zwar breit und weit, allein nicht hoch, noch tief;
> Die Kraft, entfernt von ihrem ersten Ursprung,
> Wird schwächer, ist nur noch erborgte Kraft.
> Doch werdet herrschen ihr und euren Namen
> Als Siegel drücken auf dis künftige Zeit.

5

CONCLUSION

A PRIL 5, 1852, was a day Felix Schwarzenberg thought he would pass in a routine manner. He had spent the early part of the preceding night bent over state papers, as had become his custom, and only toward morning did he try to find some rest. Since he had been given the opportunity of showing his talents, the former reveler had become an ascetic, an incessant, energetic and autocratic worker. He rose at half-past eight; at ten o'clock he called in his staff to listen to reports on current affairs; at one o'clock he was at the Hofburg to be present when the Swedish envoy handed his credentials to the Emperor; afterwards he received envoys, and granted audiences. The Russian envoy, Baron Meyendorff, called the Prince's attention to the fine weather on that day and suggested an outing. But Schwarzenberg did not allow himself any respite. He attended a cabinet meeting, during which Hungary's organization was discussed. Before the sitting closed, he excused himself, because he intended to go to a ball where he expected to meet the wife of an Austrian officer, Baroness Octavie Löwenthal, a native Pole, with whom he was carrying on a flirtation.[1] In the morning he had jokingly replied to an inquiry on the part of his sister-in-law, Princess Eleanore Schwarzenberg, whether she could count on his presence at the ball: "Most certainly—unless I am dead." [2] In the sense of the second part of the sad alternative he kept his word. A few minutes before five he hastened to his private

[1] Przibram, *Erinnerungen eines alten Österreichers*, pp. 205–6. Baron Löwenthal was later military attaché in Paris. The daughter of the couple married the Duc de Décazes, MacMahon's foreign minister.

[2] Berger, *Felix Fürst zu Schwarzenberg*, p. 490.

apartment to change his dress for the festive occasion. His valet had left the room for a moment, when he heard the dull sound of a fall. His sister and Dr. Bach, hastily summoned, found the Prince unconscious, prostrated by a stroke. It was 5:45 P.M. Medical aid proved unsuccessful. Priests administered the last rites of the church. Count Grünne, the Emperor's aide-de-camp, appeared shortly afterwards, followed a few minutes later by the Emperor himself. Francis Joseph, kneeling at the deathbed, wept bitterly and said a prayer for the soul of the savior of his dynasty. Before leaving, the Emperor recovered, ordered Prince Schwarzenberg's office to be locked, and took the office key with him.

Schwarzenberg's prostration did not come entirely unexpectedly. During the winter of 1851–1852 his nervousness had increased; he had been subject to attacks of vertigo and had shown symptoms indicative of cardiac thrombosis. His vision began to fail; for instance, when functioning as minister of the imperial household, he had difficulty in reading the marriage certificates of the Archduchess Maria Anne and Archduke Rainer on February 21, 1852. The Prince feared complete blindness and discussed a plan of staying in the sanitarium of the ophthalmologist Dr. Schmalz, at Pirna in Saxony, with the Saxon diplomat Vitzthum-Eckstädt.[3] His physicians, however, reassured him, but warned him of the possibility of apoplexy. "That manner of death meets with my full approval," remarked the Prince dryly. A vacation to Italy was then contemplated, but pressure of business postponed it, with fatal results.

The death of the Prince evoked general popular sorrow. On April 7 the burial services, as resplendent as they were mournful, took place. The funeral cortège proceeded from the chancery to the court chapel of St. Michael, where, in the presence of the Emperor and the highest dignitaries of the state, his body was blessed. A huge crowd stood in reverent silence along the route of the somber procession that transported Felix Schwarzenberg's mortal remains to his native land. He was buried in the family cemetery at Třeboň (Wittingau) with all the honors a great state can shower on its de-

[3] Vitzthum von Eckstädt, *Berlin und Wien in den Jahren 1845–1852*, p. 325.

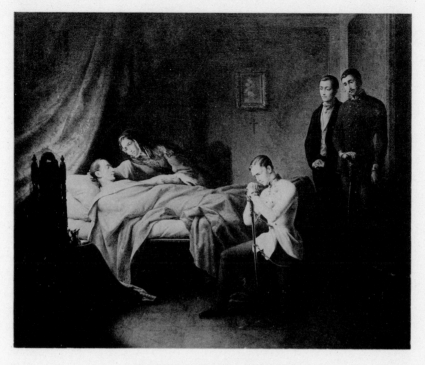

EMPEROR FRANCIS JOSEPH
AT THE DEATHBED OF FELIX ZU SCHWARZENBERG

ceased top-ranking servant,[4] on April 12, 1852, an Easter Monday
that seemed to proclaim: "He will rise again in the resurrection."
Grillparzer, who as a patriot and a centralist admired in the Prince
the creator of Austria's reborn grandeur and unity, wrote this
epitaph:

> Ein Mann der Einsicht und der Tat.
> Der Tod, der ihn auf dem Schlachtfelde verschonte,
> Erreichte ihn am Ratstische.
> Hier wie dort—ein Held
> Fuer seinen Kaiser, fuer sein Vaterland.
> Seine Feinde mussten ihn loben,
> Alle Guten haben ihn beweint,
> Oesterreich wird ihn nie vergessen.

Felix Prince zu Schwarzenberg was Austria's last prime minister
of truly first-class rank. Without exaggeration it may be said that
none of his successors attained his stature. This Bohemian aristocrat,
the scion of a mediatized sovereign family hailing from Franconia,
grown early to maturity of mind and talent, was an Austrian
through and through. Unlike the old Chancellor Metternich, he did
not believe in an ideological structure of a European society of nations superimposed upon the Austrian Empire or in a balance of
power, or in a system of conservative universalism.[5] He rejected
the doctrine of legitimacy as a universally valid order. For Felix
Schwarzenberg's cold reasoning there existed only an Austrian interest pointing to Austria's position as a great power and, connected
therewith, to Central European foundations. He did not recognize
a German nationalistic will. Although he was respectful of the co-
hesive strength of German culture and economic forces, the German people could not expect him to equate nation and state.
Schwarzenberg represented the Austrian dynastic idea in the fullest sense.

[4] The prime minister and foreign minister was a lieutenant field marshal, honorary colonel of the Infantry Regiment No. 21, and a privy councillor. He held the highest Austrian
orders with the exception of the Golden Fleece; of foreign orders, he held, for instance,
the Alexander Nevsky Order in diamonds and the Prussian Order of the Black Eagle. The
Emperor had a warship called "Fürst Felix Schwarzenberg."

[5] Taylor, *The Habsburg Monarchy 1815–1918*, pp. 80, 93, 95.

Salus rei publicae suprema lex esto was the motto with which
Schwarzenberg governed this Austrian state. His conception of the
state was Hegelian; it was Roman, not Germanic. For him the state
represented an absolute value; it was master over all spheres of societal life. The state's omnipotence should not be diminished through
privileges and immunities of individuals, classes or nationalities. On
the other hand, this state should be obligated to secure justice to its
subjects; it was responsible for their cultural progress and material
welfare. In this pattern there was no room for personal liberty.
Schwarzenberg denied the people, whatever their status and birth,
the faculty and the right of determining their lives.

Guided by Roman imperialistic ideas, this rationalist, rejecting
any historical relativism, openly confessed that "in decisive moments
a less rigid interpretation of the law and a flexible application of
legal principles become demands of self-preservation; only deeds,
not legal provisions could control certain situations." [6] With his
advent to power the time of theorizing had come to an end.

Maintenance of Austria's predominant position among the German states, the establishment of a Central European-Austrian empire of seventy million people, and the creation of the Austrian
unitary state, these were the three pivots around which Schwarzenberg's policy turned. This policy was motivated by the nature and
the structure of the Austrian Empire, and in opposition thereto, by
Prussia's powerful position and rivalry in German affairs. Guided
by these considerations, Schwarzenberg had conceived his own idea
of a Central European empire. Only a firm Austrian core, placed in
the larger and looser whole of such an empire, could guarantee Austria's dominating position therein.

Austria could not find a stronger champion than Schwarzenberg
to defend her dominating position in German lands. It is a fallacy,
however, to attribute to him the intention of Prussia's "mediatization." He adhered to his scheme that Prussia should remain the
second power after Austria and that she should not be crushed either
as a great power or as an influential power in the Germanic Con-

[6] Srbik, *Deutsche Einheit*, I, 386; see also Bossi-Fedrigotti, *Österreichs Blutweg*, p. 236.

federation. The higher flights of the Prussian Eagle were to be checked; overweening ambition was to be curbed, but Schwarzenberg did not want "to run his head through the wall in order to ruin Prussia," as the Prince of Prussia expressed it.[7]

For the smaller German states Schwarzenberg had only contempt. He used the middle states as pawns in his game against Prussia to prevent her from gaining parity with Austria and winning supremacy over a lesser Germany. First he allied himself to the middle states, then dropped them as auxiliaries when co-operation with Prussia seemed possible, and finally returned to his first policy when Prussia was unwilling to renounce her Union. His German policy has been criticized for the instability and militaristic ruthlessness of its execution. Inasmuch as he refrained, or was compelled to refrain through imperial influence and the recognition of Prussia's value as a counterrevolutionary element, from bringing on the ultimate decision by force of arms, he, according to these critics, only poisoned the relations between his country and the Hohenzollern kingdom, without finding a final solution for the German problem. But would he have gained his victory at Olmütz by means of paper protests in Metternich's style, instead of resorting to an ultimatum and preparation for war? And is changing one's methods to suit the occasion not good strategy akin to a general's conduct on the battlefield? Dresden proved that he was not a superman who could produce diplomatic victories with almost mathematical certainty; still, vanquished as he was at Dresden because his Central Europe scheme was wrecked on the rocks of dualism, he remained victorious by terminating the Prusso-Austrian duel with an alliance. When he died, he had regained for Austria the first position in the Germanic Confederation. Was the restoration of the ancient splendor of the Habsburg dynasty in German lands not a rich legacy to be left to his heirs? On this heritage they could have built further, but already his immediate successor, Karl Ferdinand Graf von Buol-Schauenstein, an unskillful imitator of a despotic nature, began to

[7] Brandenberg, ed., *Briefe Kaiser Wilhelms I*, p. 96, quoted by Srbik, *Deutsche Einheit*, II, 138.

spend it unwisely. It is safe to assume that if Schwarzenberg had lived longer he, with his dauntless courage and unshakable energy, would have resumed his plan for the creation of a Central European empire.

With regard to France, Schwarzenberg pursued a policy of non-intervention in her internal affairs, believing that a strong republic would be more beneficial for Europe's social tranquillity than a weak Bourbon kingdom. Napoleon's advent to power was not unwelcome to him because it led to an estrangement between France and England and to England's temporary isolation. France was to be restrained from exciting revolutionary movements on the continent or from becoming an aggressor in Europe. To this end he wanted to shift her attention from the continent to the sea, where French and British colonial aspirations might collide. Every French attack upon the Germanic Confederation was to be thwarted; if necessary, with the aid of Russia as Austria's faithful ally. Nor did he tolerate France's intervention in the Prusso-Austrian quarrel. No French troops were to stand on German soil, even against his country's rival, Prussia, just as he did not want to see Prussian troops march into the southern German states. Towards Russia he maintained a position of dignity and independence, despite Austria's obligation towards the Muscovite empire on account of the help rendered by Czar Nicholas against Hungary and Prussia. At his death he left Austria in close alliance with Russia and on excellent terms with France. Those who seek to take the measure of his art in international affairs will agree that his diplomacy was of the highest technical construction.

Schwarzenberg's internal policy has found less favor than his foreign policy. It is not disputed that he was eminently serviceable to his country in re-establishing the Emperor's sway over Hungary and northern Italy. Nor is it denied that he drew order and design out of chaos and revolution. But it is erroneous to portray Schwarzenberg in internal affairs as a statesman without constructive ideas and to picture him merely as a bold and skillful foreign minister, the representative of the Austrian power state pursuing his aims

with militaristic pitilessness. What is true is that he knew less about
the details of the internal administration and was less interested in
them than he was in the conduct of foreign policy. Recognizing his
shortcomings, he surrounded himself with able collaborators such
as Bach and Bruck. Their reforms fulfilled to a large extent the
economic expectations of the liberal middle classes.

Some of Felix Schwarzenberg's critics regard as ill-advised his
destruction of the Kremsier constitution, because its democratic-
federalistic features, if allowed to become operative, would have
been the Rosetta stone, they assert, for transforming a nationality-
torn state into one certain of future security.[8] Others, conceding him
rich gifts and political imagination, regret that he underestimated
the force of national drives. Among his contemporaries, two powerful classes opposed his policies. One was the aristocratic-conservative
class, led by Prince Windisch-Graetz, which desired to reorganize
Austria along feudal-agrarian lines—an archaic postulate obviously
impossible of fulfillment in 1850. The other class was the high bureaucracy, headed by men like Kübeck and Hübner, who preferred
the Metternich system with its semi-patriarchal absolutism—as if
the clock could simply have been turned back again to pre-March
days. The judgments of unfriendly historians who are dissatisfied
with this phase or that phase of his policy are of necessity influenced
by later events. The victory of the idea of a lesser Germany, the
ascent of the German Empire, the triumph of parliamentary democracy, the quarrels among the nationalities in Austria, the optimistic
confidence placed in a federal system after World War I, and the
creation of the League of Nations, all these factors have conditioned
these opinions. But it is not uncommon for theoreticians to hurl
criticisms at a man of action.

Neither the Emperor nor Schwarzenberg thought that Austria in
1849 was ripe to receive a parliament representing all the peoples.
Whereas, however, Schwarzenberg was willing to play with "that
drollery, a representative government," as long as Austria's internal

[8] Schlitter, *Versäumte Gelegenheiten*, p. 74, believes that even Serbia and Rumania would
have joined such a confederation of states—a rather far-fetched conception.

weakness and his plans concerning a Central European empire required it, Francis Joseph declined any sort of constitution. It is doubtful, indeed, whether a Reich parliament would have been capable of holding together the Austrian Monarchy still heaving with the after-swell of the revolutionary tempest. Furthermore, a period of disintegration, as the *annus mirabilis* of the nineteenth century and its aftermath unquestionably constituted, was followed by a reaction in the opposite direction, a reaction expressing itself in a centralistic, rigid regime. But it is also an irrefutable fact that Felix Schwarzenberg was by education and temperament violently opposed to "Western democracy." He used the March constitution to combat Prussia's rivalry and to win the people of the Germanic Confederation over to his idea of a Central European empire. The statement is also correct that the constitution was only a means to an end for him, not an end in itself, and that he was willing, even anxious, to amend or abolish it as soon as practicable. There was a certain grandeur in the good faith he kept with himself. Schwarzenberg was less interested in the structure of the Austrian state than in its welfare. It was his firm belief, however, that only a monarchical constitution, with the Habsburg dynasty forming the keystone of the constitutional arch, would make the Empire "great, powerful and happy." And with unswerving fidelity he served the Habsburgs without a break.

Whether federalism would have been able to guarantee a powerful Austrian state, composed as it was of various nationalities, is a question that must be answered in the negative. Doctrinaire federalism, like liberalism, is a child of an optimistic philosophy and stems from the hopeful belief that far-reaching liberty of the component parts of a federation will assure the harmony of the whole. Now, as events have shown in Hungary and Galicia, decentralization did not bring forth the hoped-for accord. The scenes of national struggles were shifted from the center to the decentralized regions. The equality of nationalities could only have been secured, and the problem of minorities solved, by a strong central power. The Emperor's hereditary lands gave such strength to the Holy Roman Empire.

Some such center bearing a national character would have been needed to hold the Monarchy together, but should that national character have been German or Slavic? Would not Austria have been drawn into a struggle between Germans and Slavs regardless of whether Austria was a federation or a unitary state? Furthermore, it must be borne in mind that Schwarzenberg planned to form a Central European empire. This empire may have been an illusion, but granting the premise, any other construction of the Austrian Monarchy than a unitary state would have been an impossibility.[9]

Schwarzenberg's reconstruction of Austria as a unitary state was intended as a farewell message to the revolution, but by no means as a return to prerevolutionary conditions. Of his reforms, with their accidental stamp of liberalism, the greatest was the liberation of the peasants from the payment of feudal dues. Imitating Napoleon in his absolutist ideology, he did not desire any individual strata to arise between the monarch and his subjects. At least with regard to legal status, he rejected all class privileges, especially those of the nobility, because he saw in them only impediments blocking a comprehensive unison of all societal forces of the state. There was to be equality of all citizens before the law. His was a revolutionary doctrine, a doctrine somewhat incompatible with the traditions of hereditary monarchies, as his Tory enemies correctly pointed out. Equality before the law also embraced the confessions. "Had not every government since the days of the Pharaohs fared badly that had persecuted the Jews?" he asked.[10] But he subordinated the interests even of his own church to those of the state. He did not hesitate to bring to justice ecclesiastics found guilty of revolutionary activities.

After the crushing of the revolution he did not envisage a national and cultural unification of the Austrian peoples as Joseph II

[9] Similarly, Heller, *Mitteleuropas Vorkämpfer*, especially pp. 214–16.

[10] Friedjung, *Österreich von 1848 bis 1860*, II, 285; on the status of the Jews in this period see Wertheimer, *Die Stellung der Juden in Österreich*. Equality before the law for Jews was not incorporated in the law of December 31, 1851, upon imperial order. *Supra*, p. 109.

had done. He rejected Stadion's proposals aiming at the abolition of the historic regions and the creation of administrative districts on the French model. Special privileges of the historic regions should, however, be set aside, but not the historic territories themselves. Even in Hungary it had not been his original idea to abolish the traditional institutions; only revolutionary events pushed him farther than he had planned at the beginning. Personal embitterment over the success of the Hungarian revolution and over the endangering of his projects disturbed his cool consideration. In the last analysis, the state's will had to predominate. No doubt it would have been wiser to show mercy to the Hungarians after victory had been won.

Felix Schwarzenberg rolled back the advancing tide of democracy and the flow of events in German and Italian lands with tremendous consequences for the next decades. He rescued Austria from the storm of the revolution and re-established her position as a great power. If Austria had disintegrated in his time, Central Europe, unable to withstand the pressure from the East and the West, would have been dragged along into the abyss. World War I permitted the survival of a modified political Central Europe; World War II gives the question again poignancy and immediate interest —whether for weal or for woe. The fact that Schwarzenberg saved Austria [11] and maintained for almost a century a Central Europe indicates the high importance of his activities, an importance which will assign him forever a niche in the pantheon of history.

[11] Sir J. A. R. Marriott, shortly before his death, wrote: "Had it [the Habsburg Empire] not existed, it might, as Palacky, the great Czech historian and statesman declared . . . 'have been necessary to invent it.' Yet 'invented' we may be certain it never would have been. Built up by astute dynastic statesmanship and rewarded by a series of happy accidents, the Habsburg Empire owed its survival in 1849 partly to individuals—to the high statesmanship of Prince Felix Schwarzenberg, to the firmness and tact of Prince Windischgrätz, and to the military genius of Marshal Radetzky—partly to circumstances. . . ." "The Problem of Central Europe," *The Fortnightly*, 1945, p. 238. In my opinion, even today at least a strong economic asssociation of the Danubian countries is a command of necessity. Conceivably Vienna might not be its political focus as it was in Felix Schwarzenberg's times. Its center should be reserved to that country which, by virtue of its geographical position and its economic importance, best serves as the connecting link between the East and the West.

Dignity and affability were the first impressions which the bearing of the Bohemian noble conveyed. His was an organism in which ambition, conscientiousness, and hard work were matched by a penetrating intellect and a powerful mind. He had contempt for average humanity; still, he did not always size up men correctly. He was both cold and passionate. Outwardly a glacier, of impassive gravity bordering on boredom, inwardly "his life beat was that of short, sharp waves" in a tarn, "fretting under the squall against the rocky shore." He could treat people who served a lost cause with ostentatious disdain, but virile opposition did not fail to impress him. Scornful rejection of responsible co-operation on the part of the citizens, a certain brusqueness in public life in sharp contrast to his superb courtesy in private life, and a corroding sarcasm were the defective sides of his character.

His cousin Frederick Prince zu Schwarzenberg, the son of the field marshal, the colorful *Landsknecht*,[12] asserted that Felix Schwarzenberg demanded of his subordinates only intelligent obedience and did not care whether they represented moral values. He upbraided Felix for looking at all things with the eyes of a martinet. Although Frederick credited Felix with high intelligence and indefatigable energy and acknowledged Felix's ability to bring order out of chaos, he held that the Prime Minister's lack of an ethical philosophy barred him from becoming a true statesman.[13] But even the Czech writer Zdeněk Tobolka finds more kindly words for Felix Schwarzenberg. They are quoted in rebuttal: "Schwarzenberg was completely devoted to the Monarchy, he was not without humor, he was a clear thinker who spoke openly . . . and who in the most critical moments was able to keep calm." [14]

Frederick Schwarzenberg's evaluation of his cousin was that of a

[12] On Friedrich Schwarzenberg see Bettelheim-Gabillon, "Der Landsknecht," *Österreichische Rundschau*, Vol. XXII (Jan.–March, 1910); Paoli, *Gesammelte Aufsätze*. Some of his own writings were: *Aus dem Wanderbuche eines verabschiedeten Lanzknechtes; Aus den Papieren eines verabschiedeten Lanzknechtes; Karl Fürst Schwarzenberg.*

[13] Meyer, *Erlebnisse*, p. 337.

[14] *Politické dějiny československého národa od r. 1848 až do dnešní doby*, Part I, pp. 129–30.

highly gifted but somewhat erratic personality; yet it is illustrative of the fact that not all members of Felix's own family were enthusiastic followers of his equalitarian program. Cardinal Schwarzenberg, archbishop first of Salzburg and then of Prague,[15] was reconciled to his brother's centralistic regime of a German tinge as long as Austria was also governed by the clergy; in later years, however, like many representatives of the high nobility, he became a federalist and attempted to secure Slavic support for the Roman Catholic Church. Felix Schwarzenberg's stern subordination of the individual to the state, his dynamic belief in the might of the community, his irresistible energy and driving power, all these were characteristics alien to the plastic Austrian ethos which prefers the role of a mediator of culture to that of master. A rule by the army and the civil service, the selection of bourgeois, irrespective of their political past, ready to execute his will, and the agrarian reforms were factors setting him apart from his compeers.

From the beginning Felix Schwarzenberg won Emperor Francis Joseph's confidence. His diplomatic and military successes, as well as dynastic patriotism, inspired in Francis Joseph complete reliance on his prime minister's practical statesmanship. There was a certain affinity between their characters: they both lacked pathos and sentimentality. Fundamentally, they both took a pessimistic view of the world and of man. On April 6, 1852, the Emperor wrote to his mother:

A heavy blow has struck me, has struck us all; it is not easy to conceive a severer loss, and more difficult to replace, than the one which we so suddenly suffered yesterday. The man has gone who had since the beginning of my activity stood by my side with self-sacrificing loyalty and blind affection, with iron consequence and indefatigable energy. Such a man will never come back again.[16]

Archduchess Sophia, the Emperor's mother, who saw in Schwarzenberg "a knight sent by the grace of heaven" to save the throne for

[15] See *supra*, p. 93.
[16] Schnürer, *Briefe Kaiser Franz Joseph I. an seine Mutter 1838–1872*, p. 176.

her son, made the following entries in her diary under dates of
April 5 and 8:

. . . la plus affreuse des nouvelles télégraphiques, la mort de notre cher,
brave Félix Schwarzenberg, ce soir à 6 h. d'un coup d'appopléxie . . .
perte irréparable, affreuse qui me bouleverse et me fait verser bien des larmes
et m'agit extrêmement pour mon pauvre fils.

. . . [une lettre] de mon enfant bien aimé qui sent si profondément et
douleureusement tout ce qu'il a perdu dans l'ami le plus devoué, le plus fidèle
qu'il ait jamais eu.[17]

What the Emperor had expressed, overwhelmed by the pain of separation, he, decades later, repeated with the words that Felix Schwarzenberg was beyond all comparison the greatest of his ministers.[18]
Thereby he renewed, almost at the end of a long and eventful reign,
his confession to the ideas and political faith of his first counsellor.
These facts, better than words, show Schwarzenberg's importance
for Austrian history and, beyond that, for European history in
general.

[17] Reinöhl, "Aus dem Tagebuch der Erzherzogin Sophie," *Historische Blätter*, Heft 4,
p. 136.
[18] Redlich, *Emperor Francis Joseph of Austria*, pp. 98–99.

BIBLIOGRAPHY

Allgemeine Deutsch Biographie. Leipzig.
   Vol. III "Karl Ludwig von Bruck," by von Sommaruga.
   Vol. XXXIII "Schwarzenberg," by Sch., and "Felix Fürst Schwarzen-
         berg," by von Zeissberg.
   Vol. XXXVIII "Graf Leo Thun-Hohenstein," by Frankfurter.
   Vol. XLVI "Alexander Freiherr von Bach," by Ilwolf.
Amante, A., Di Ferdinando II, re delle due Sicilie. Turin, 1925.
Anders, Erwin, Schwarzenbergs Disposition für den 14. Oktober 1813.
   Berlin, 1908. Diss.
Andlaw, Franz, Freiherr von, Mein Tagebuch. Frankfurt a/M., 1862.
Andrian, V., Freiherr von, Denkschrift über die Verfassung und Ver-
   waltung in Österreich. Vienna, 1859.
——— Zentralisation und Dezentralisation in Österreich. Vienna, 1850.
Angyal, D., "Der Hochverratsprozess des Grafen Ludwig Batthyany," in
   Jahrbuch des Instituts für ungarische Geschichtsforschung, Vienna,
   1933.
Arneth, Alfred, Ritter von, Aus meinem Leben. Stuttgart, 1893.
Ashley, Evelyn, The Life of Henry John Temple, Viscount Palmerston,
   1846–1865. London, 1876.
Ayala, M. d', Vita del re di Napoli. Naples, 1860.
Babarczy, Major von, Licht- und Schattenseiten aus dem Soldatenleben und
   aus der Gesellschaft. Prague, 1876.
Bagehot, The Works. Ed. by Forest Morgan. Hartford, Conn., 1899. Vol.
   III.
Bagger, Eugene, Francis Joseph. New York and London, 1927.
Balfanz, Martin, Beiträge zur staatsmännischen Wirksamkeit des Freiherrn
   Johann von Schwarzenberg. Greifswald, 1900.
Balzac, Honoré de, Le Lys dans la Vallée. Paris, 1836.
Barbiera, R., La Principessa Belgioioso. Milan, 1903.
Beer, Adolf, Die Finanzen Österreichs im XIX. Jahrhundert. Prague, 1877.
——— "Fürst Schwarzenbergs deutsche Politik bis zu den Dresdener Kon-
   ferenzen," in Historisches Taschenbuch, Leipzig, 1891.
——— Die österreichische Handelspolitik im neunzehnten Jahrhundert.
   Vienna, 1891.
Beidtel, Ignaz, Geschichte der österreichischen Staatsverwaltung 1740–
   1848. 2 vols. Innsbruck, 1896–98.

Beirão, Caetano, El-Rey Dom Miguel I. e a sua descendência. Lisbon, Portugal, 1943.

Berger, A. F., "Das Fürstenhaus Schwarzenberg," *Österreichische Revue*, Heft 11 (1866).

—— Felix Fürst zu Schwarzenberg. Leipzig, 1853.

—— "Zum Ehrengedächtnisse des k.k. Feldmarschalls Karl Fürsten zu Schwarzenberg," *Wiener Zeitung*, 1867.

Bernatzik, Eduard, comp., Die österreichischen Verfassungsgesetze. 2d ed. Vienna, 1911.

Bernstorff, Albrecht, Count von, The Bernstorff Papers; the Life of Count Albrecht von Bernstorff, by Karl Ringhoffer; tr. by Mrs. Charles Edward Barrett-Lennard and M. W. Hoper. New York, 1908. Vol. I.

Bettelheim-Gabillon, Helene, "Der Landsknecht," *Österreichische Rundschau*, Vol. XXII (January–March, 1910).

Beust, Friedrich Ferdinand, Graf von, Aus Drei Viertel-Jahrhunderten. Stuttgart, 1887.

Bibl, Victor, Der Zerfall Österreichs. Vienna, 1824. Vol. II.

Bismarck, Fürst Otto von, Fürst Bismarck's Briefe an seine Braut und Gattin. Stuttgart, 1900.

—— Bismarck, the Man and the Statesman; being the reflections and reminiscences of Otto, Prince von Bismarck, written and dictated by himself after his retirement from office, tr. from the German under the supervision of A. J. Butler. New York and London, 1899.

Bossi-Fedrigotti, Anton, Graf, Österreichs Blutweg; ein Vierteljahrtausend Kampf um Grossdeutschland. Berlin, 1939.

Bourgeois, Eugène, Manuel historique de politique étrangère. Paris, 1919. Vol. III.

British and Foreign State Papers, Vol. XLI. London, 1864.

Canitz, Carl Ernst Wilhelm, Freiherr von, Denkschriften des Freiherrn von Canitz. Berlin, 1888. Vol. II.

Canning, George, The Speeches of the Right Honourable George Canning; comp. by R. Therry. London, 1828. Vol. V.

Capelletti, L., Storia di Carlo Alberto e del suo regno. Rome, 1891.

Carutti, D., Bibliografia Carlo-Albertina. Turin, 1899.

Carvalho, Freire de, Ensaio politico as causas que preparão a usurpação do infante Dom Miguel. Lisbon, 1842.

Castro, José de, Portugal em Roma. Lisbon, 1939.

Cecil, Algernon, British Foreign Secretaries 1807–1916. London, 1927.

—— Metternich, 1773–1859; a study of his period and personality. New York, 1933.

Charmatz, Richard, Deutsch-österreichische Politik. Leipzig, 1907.

———— Minister Freiherr von Bruck; der Vorkämpfer Mitteleuropas. Leipzig, 1916.

———— Österreichs innere Geschichte von 1848 bis 1895. 2 vols. Leipzig, 1918.

Corti, Egon Caesar, Conte, König Ludwig I. von Bayern. Munich, 1937.

Coxe, William, History of the House of Austria. London, 1895. Vol. IV.

Croce, Benedetto, Storia del regno di Napoli. Bari, 1931.

Czoernig von Czernhausen, Karl, Freiherr, Österreichs Neugestaltung, 1848–1858. Stuttgart, 1858.

Delbrück, Rudolf von, Lebenserinnerungen 1817–67. 2 vols. Leipzig, 1905.

Ebersberg, "Das Fest des österreichischen Botschafters am 1. Juli 1810 in Paris," in Feierstunden, Nos. 50–52, Vienna, 1833.

Eisenmann, Louis, Le compromis Austro-Hongrois de 1867. Paris, 1904.

Engel-Janosi, Friedrich, Der Freiherr von Hübner, 1811–1892. Innsbruck, 1933.

Eötvos, Joseph, Baron, Die Gleichberechtigung der Nationalitäten in Österreich. 2d ed. Vienna, 1851.

"Feuersbrunst in Paris, Eine," Temesvarer Zeitung, 1860, No. 127.

Frankfurter, S. "Graf Leo Thun-Hohenstein, Franz Exner und Hermann Bonitz," in Beiträge zur Geschichte der österreichischen Unterrichtsreform, Vienna, 1893.

Friedjung, Heinrich, "Fürst Felix Schwarzenberg und Graf Albrecht Bernstorff," Historische Zeitschrift, September, 1911.

———— Österreich von 1848 bis 1860. 2 vols. Stuttgart and Berlin, 1908 and 1912.

"Fürstenhaus Schwarzenberg, Das," Transylvania (Beiblatt zum Siebenbürger Boten), No. 3, 1856.

Gaertner, Alfred, Zollverhandlungen zwischen Österreich und Preussen von 1849 bis Olmütz. Salzburg, 1908.

Gerlach, Leopold von, Denkwürdigkeiten aus dem Leben Leopold von Gerlachs. Berlin, 1891. Vols. I and II.

Geschichte der Eisenbahnen der österreichisch-ungarischen Monarchie. Vienna, 1898. Vol. I.

Girardin, Stanislas de, Mémoires. Paris, 1828.

Götz, Wilhelm, Frankenland. Bielefeld and Leipzig, 1909. Monographien zur Erdkunde.

Grillparzer, Sämtliche Werke; ed. by August Sauer. Stuttgart, 1893.

Grünberg, Karl, Die Bauernbefreiung und die Auflösung des gutsherrlich-bäuerlichen Verhältnisses in Böhmen, Mähren und Schlesien. Leipzig, 1894.

Grünberg, Karl, "Bauernbefreiung," in Handwörterbuch der Staatswissenschaften, 3d ed., Jena, 1909.

────── "Die Grundentlastung," in Geschichte der österreichischen Land-
und Forstwirtschaft und ihrer Industrien 1848–1898, Vienna, 1899.

Guedalla, Philip, Palmerston. London, 1926.

Guichen, Eugène Vicomte de, Les Grandes Questions européennes et la
diplomatie des puissances sous la Seconde République. Paris, 1925. Vol. I.

Haimb, Schwartzenberga gloriosa sive epitome historica. Ratisbon, 1708.

Hansard's Parliamentary Debates. Vols. XXIII, XCIX, CVII, CXV.

Hartig, Franz, Graf, Zwei brennende Fragen in Österreich. Vienna, 1852.

Hauer, Julius, Ritter von, Über Österreichs Staatsausgaben und Verwaltung. Vienna, 1849.

Helfert, Alexander, Freiherr von, Geschichte Österreichs vom Ausgange
des Wiener October–Aufstandes 1848. Prague, 1872 and 1876/87.
Vols. III, IV.

────── Geschichte der österreichischen Revolution im Zusammenhange
mit der mitteleuropäischen Bewegung der Jahre 1848–1849. 2 vols.
Freiburg i/Br. and Vienna, 1907, 1909.

Heller, Eduard, Mitteleuropas Vorkämpfer: Fürst Felix Schwarzenberg.
Vienna, 1933.

Herchen, Arthur, Dom Miguel I., König von Portugal; sein Leben und
seine Regierung. Luxembourg, 1908.

Hermes, Karl Heinrich, Geschichte der letzten fünfundzwanzig Jahre.
Braunschweig, 1845.

Herrmann, Emil, Johann Freiherr zu Schwarzenberg; ein Beitrag zur Geschichte des Criminalrechts und der Gründung der protestantischen
Kirche. Leipzig, 1841.

Hirsch, Rudolph, Franz Graf Stadion. Vienna, 1861.

Historische Zeitschrift. Vol. LVIII, November 10, 1855.

Hock, Karl Ferdinand, Freiherr von, Die Finanzen und die Finanzgeschichte
der Vereinigten Staaten. Stuttgart, 1867.

Hrnčíř, František, Dějepis národa československého. Nymburk (Nim-
burg), 1919.

Hübner, Johann, Genealogische Tabellen. Leipzig, 1728.

Hübner, Josef Alexander, Graf von, Ein Jahr meines Lebens, 1848–49.
Leipzig, 1891.

────── Neun Jahre der Erinnerungen eines österreichischen Botschafters
in Paris unter dem zweiten Kaiserreich 1851–1859. Berlin, 1904.

Illustrierte Zeitung, No. 1040. Leipzig, 1863.

Jászi, Oscar, The Dissolution of the Habsburg Monarchy. Chicago, 1929.

Jennings, W. Ivor, Cabinet Government. New York, 1936.

Karas, J. F., Stručná kronika československá. Moravian Ostrau, 1919.

Keller, E., Le Général de la Moricière. Paris, 1874.

Kempen von Fichtenstamm, Johann Franz, Das Tagebuch des Polizei-ministers Kempen von Fichtenstamm von 1848 bis 1859. Vienna and Leipzig, 1931.

Kerchnawe, Hugo, "Feldmarschall Alfred Windisch-Graetz und die Russenhilfe 1849," *Mitteilungen des österreichischen Instituts für Geschichtsforschung*, Vol. XLIII (1929).

Kerchnawe and Veltzé, Fürst Karl zu Schwarzenberg, der Führer der Verbündeten in den Befreiungskriegen. Vienna, 1913.

Kotrč, Josef, and Josef Kotalík, Stručné dějiny československé literatury. Prague, 1934.

Kriegsbegebenheiten bei der kaiserlich österreichischen Armee in Italien. Vienna, 1848.

Krofta, Kamil, Malé dějiny československé. Prague, 1938.

Kübeck von Kübau, Karl Friedrich, Freiherr von, Metternich und Kübeck; ed. by his son, Max von Kübeck. Vienna, 1910.

———— Tagebücher; ed. by his son, Max von Kübeck. Vienna, 1909.

Lamarmora, A., Alcuni episodi della guerra nel Veneto. Turin, 1857.

Lane-Poole, Stanley, Life of the Right Honourable Stratford Canning. New York and London, 1888. Vol. II.

Lang, Ludwig, Hundert Jahre Zollpolitik. Vienna, 1906.

Lange, E. G., Frankreichs Preussenpolitik in den Jahren 1849 und 1850. Berlin, 1930. Diss.

Lebey, André, Louis Napoléon Bonaparte et le ministère Odilon Barrot. Paris, 1912.

Lima, Oliveira, Dom Pedro e Dom Miguel; a querela da successão. São Paulo and Rio, 1925.

Lorne, Marquis of, Viscount Palmerston, K.G. New York, 1892.

Malbank, Julius Friedrich, Geschichte der peinlichen Halsgerichtsordnung Kaiser Karl V. von ihrer Entstehung und ihren weiteren Schicksalen bis auf unsere Zeit. Nuremberg, 1783.

Malmesbury, Earl of, Memoirs of an Ex-minister. London, 1884.

Manteuffel, Otto, Freiherr von, Unter Friedrich Wilhelm IV.; ed. by Heinrich von Poschinger. Berlin, 1901.

Mareš, F., "Nové příspěvky k pam. roku 1848," in Česky Časopis Historický. Prague, 1848. The gazette published by the Bohemian Muesum.

Margarita, see Solaro della Marghuerita.

Margherita, see Solaro della Marghuerita.

Marriott, Sir. J. A. R., "The Problem of Central Europe," *The Fortnightly*, April, 1945.

Martin, Theodore, The Life of His Royal Highness the Prince Consort. London, 1875. Vol. I.

Matlekovits, Alexander, Die Zollpolitik der österreichisch-ungarischen Monarchie von 1850 bis zur Gegenwart. Budapest, 1877.

Memoir of the Operations of the Allied Armies under Prince Schwarzenberg and Marchal [sic] Blücher during the Latter End of 1813 and the Year 1814, by the author of "The Duke of Wellington in Portugal and Spain." London, 1822.

Menzel, Wolfgang, Geschichte der Deutschen bis auf die neuesten Tage. Stuttgart and Augsburg, 1855.

Metternich-Winneburg, Clemens Lothar Wenzel, Fürst von, Memoirs of Prince Metternich, 1773–1829; ed. by Prince Richard Metternich; tr. by Mrs. Alexander Napier. 4 vols. New York, 1880–1881.

Meyendorff, Peter von, Ein russischer Diplomat an den Höfen von Berlin und Wien; ed. by Otto Hoetsch. Berlin and Leipzig, 1923.

Meyer, Bernhard, Ritter von, Erlebnisse. Pressburg, 1879.

Militär Schematismus. Vienna, 1863.

Mörath, A., Das Schloss Schwarzenberg in Franken. Krummau, 1902.

——— "Friedrich Kardinal Schwarzenberg," Zeitschrift des Bergischen Geschichtsvereins. Vols. XII, XVI. 1877, 1881.

Molisch, Paul, Briefe zur deutschen Politik Österreichs von 1848 bis 1918. Vienna and Leipzig, 1934.

Müller, Paul, Feldmarschall Fürst Windischgrätz. Vienna and Leipzig, 1934.

Napoléon III, Œuvres. Paris, 1857. Vol. III.

Neumann, Philipp, Freiherr von, The Diary of Philipp von Neumann; tr. by E. Beresford Chancellor. 2 vols. London, 1928.

Nesselrode, Karl Robert, Graf von, Lettres et papiers du chancelier Comte de Nesselrode 1760–1856. Paris, 1911. Vol. IX.

Nisco, N., Ferdinando II e il suo regno. Naples, 1884.

Noradounghian, Gabriel Effendi, Recueil d'actes internationaux de l'Empire Ottoman. Paris, 1897.

Oddie, E. M., Portrait of Ianthe. London, 1935.

Österreichische militärische Zeitschrift; ed. by Streffleur. 1863.

Ostaszewski-Barański, K., Rok Złudzeń. Złoczów, 1899.

Paoli, Betty, Gesammelte Aufsätze; ed. by Helene Bettelheim-Gabillon. Vienna, 1908. Schriften des Literarischen Vereins in Wien.

Pillersdorf, F. von, Die österreichischen Finanzen. Vienna, 1851.

Plaček, Franz, Die österreichische Grundentlastungsoperation. Prague, 1853.

Poschinger, H., Ritter von, Preussen im Bundestag. Leipzig, 1884.

Precht, Hans, "Englands Stellung zur deutschen Einheit 1848–1850," *Historische Zeitschrift*, Beiheft 3, 1925.

Prokesch von Osten, Anton, Graf, Denkwürdigkeiten aus dem Leben des Feldmarschalls Fürsten K. von Schwarzenberg. Vienna, 1872.

———— Aus den Briefen des Grafen Prokesch von Osten (1849–1855). Vienna, 1896.

Przibram, L., Ritter von, Erinnerungen eines alten Österreichers. Stuttgart, 1910.

Pulszky, Franz, Meine Zeit, mein Leben. Pressburg and Leipzig, 1881.

Redlich, Joseph, Emperor Francis Joseph of Austria. New York, 1929.

———— Das österreichische Staats- und Reichsproblem. Leipzig, 1920.

Reichsgesetzblatt, Vienna, 1850. Reports of Count Thun to the Emperor, April 7, 13, 1850.

Reinöhl, Fritz, "Aus dem Tagebuch der Erzherzogin Sophie," *Historische Blätter*, 1931.

Remm-Whitehouse, H., Une Princesse Révolutionnaire. Lausanne, 1907.

Renner, Karl, see Springer, Rudolf.

Rogge, Walter, Österreich von Világos bis zur Gegenwart. Leipzig and Vienna, 1872. Vol. I.

Rothan, G., "Souvenirs diplomatiques," *Revue des Deux Mondes*, May 1 and 15, 1889.

———— Souvenirs diplomatiques; l'Europe et l'avènement du Second Empire. Paris, 1892.

Sanders, Lloyd C., Life of Viscount Palmerston. London, 1888.

Schäffle, Albert E. F., Aus meinem Leben. Berlin, 1905.

Schiemann, Theodor, Geschichte Russlands unter Kaiser Nikolaus I. 4 vols. Berlin, 1904–1919.

Schlitter, Hanns, Versäumte Gelegenheiten; die oktroyierte Verfassung vom 4. März, 1849. Vienna, 1920.

Schmidt, A. A., Das Kaiserthum Österreich. Stuttgart, 1843.

Schnürer, F., Briefe Kaiser Franz Joseph I. an seine Mutter 1838–1872. Munich, 1930.

Schönfeld, I., Ritter von, Adels-Schematismus des österreichischen Kaiserstaates. Vienna, 1824–25.

Schüssler, Wilhelm "Die nationale Politik der österreichischen Abgeordneten im Frankfurter Parlament," in Abhandlungen zur mittleren und neueren Geschichte, Berlin and Leipzig, 1913.

Schwäbischer Kurier, No. 48, Feb. 24, 1850.

Schwarzenberg, Friedrich, Fürst von, Karl Fürst Schwarzenberg. Vienna, 1860.

Schwarzenberg, Friedrich, Fürst von, Aus den Papieren eines verabschiedeten Lanzknechtes. Vienna, 1848.
—— Aus dem Wanderbuche eines verabschiedeten Lanzknechtes. Vienna, 1844/45.
Schwarzenberg, Johann, Freiherr von, Trostspruch um abgestorbene Freunde (Kummertrost); ed. by Willy Scheel. Halle an der Saale, 1907.
"Schwarzenberge, Die," Neue Freie Presse, No. 2742, April 13, 1872.
Sedláček, August, Sbírka pověstí historických lidu českého v Čechách, na Moravě a ve Slezsku. Prague, n.d.
Senior, N. W., Conversations with M. Thiers, M. Guizot; ed. by M. C. M. Simpson. London, 1878. Vol. I.
Siebertz, Paul, Freimaurer im Kampf um die Macht. Hamburg, 1938.
Sieghart, Rudolf, Zolltrennung und Zolleinheit; die Geschichte der österreichisch-ungarischen Zwischenzoll-Linie. Vienna, 1915.
Simpson, F. A., Louis Napoleon and the Recovery of France, 1848–1856. New York and London, 1923.
Solaro della Marghuerita (or Margarita or la Margarita), Conte, Memorandum storico-politico. Turin, 1852–1853.
Springer, Rudolf (Karl Renner), Der Kampf der österreichischen Nationen um den Staat. Leipzig and Vienna, 1902.
—— Grundlagen und Entwicklungszeiten der österreichisch-ungarischen Monarchie. Vienna and Leipzig, 1906.
Sproxton, Charles, Palmerston and the Hungarian Revolution. Cambridge, 1919.
Srbik, Heinrich, Ritter von, Deutsche Einheit. 2 vols. Munich, 1935.
Steefel, Lawrence D., The Schleswig-Holstein Question. Cambridge, 1932.
Stockmar, Christian Friedrich, Freiherr von, Memoirs of Baron Stockmar; ed. by F. Max Müller. London, 1873. Vol. II.
Sybel, Heinrich von, The Founding of the German Empire by William I; tr. by Marshall Livingston Perrin. New York, 1890–1891. Vols. I and II.
Taylor, A. J. P., The Habsburg Monarchy 1815–1918. London, 1941.
Telle, R. C., Das österreichische Problem im Frankfurter Parlament im Sommer und Herbst 1848. Marburg, 1933. Diss.
Thouvenel, L., Nicholas Ier et Napoléon III; les préliminaires de la guerre de Crimée 1852–1854; d'après les papiers inédits de M. Édouard Antoine Thouvenel. Paris, 1891.
Tobolka, Zdeněk, Politické dějiny československého národa od r. 1848 až do dnešní doby. Prague, 1932.
Tocqueville, Alexis de, Correspondence and Conversations with Nassau Wilhelm Senior; ed. by M. C. M. Simpson. London, 1872. Vol. II.

Tomaschek, J. A., Die Rechte und Freiheiten der Stadt Wien. Vienna, 1877.

Traub, H., Naše politické dějiny v 19. století. Prague, 1926.

Valentin, Veit, Geschichte der deutschen Revolution von 1848–49. Berlin, 1931. Vol. II.

Victoria, Queen of Great Britain, The Letters of Queen Victoria; ed. by A. C. Benson and Viscount Esher. New York, 1907. Vol. II.

Vidal, C., Charles Albert et le Risorgimento italien. Paris, 1927.

Vitzthum von Eckstädt, Carl Friedrich, Graf, Berlin und Wien in den Jahren 1845–1852. Stuttgart, 1896.

Wagner, Adolf, Die Ordnung des österreichischen Staatshaushaltes. Vienna, 1863.

Waliszewski, K., La Russie il y a cent ans, le règne d'Alexandre Ier. Paris, 1925.

Ward, Sir A. W., and G. P. Gooch, The Cambridge History of British Foreign Policy. Cambridge, 1923. Vol. II.

Wertheimer, Joseph, Die Stellung der Juden in Österreich. Vienna, 1853.

Wien 1848–1888; Denkschrift zum 2. Dezember 1888. Vienna, 1888.

Wirkner, Ludwig von, Meine Erlebnisse. Pressburg, 1879.

Wolfsgruber, Coelestin, Friedrich Kardinal Schwarzenberg. 3 vols. Vienna, 1906, 1917.

———— Joseph Othmar Cardinal Rauscher, Fürsterzbischof von Wien; sein Leben und Wirken, Freiburg i/Br., 1888.

Wurzbach, Constant von, "Felix Schwarzenberg," in Biographisches Lexicon des Kaiserthums Österreich. Vienna, 1877.

Zaïonchkovskiï, Andreï Medardovich, Eastern War 1855–1856 [in Russian]. St. Petersburg, 1908.

Zimmermann, Alfred, Geschichte der preussisch-deutschen Handelspolitik. Oldenburg, 1892.

Zugschwerdt, J. B., Das Bankwesen und die privilegierte österreichische Nationalbank. Vienna, 1855.

INDEX

Bernstorff, Albrecht von, Count, 74, 116,
119, 128, 133, 135, 139, 142, 143, 155,
162, 175; quoted, 130
Beust, Friedrich Ferdinand, Baron, 163, 166,
168*n*
Beyer, Karl, 91
Biedermeier epoch, 23
Biegeleben, Ludwig Maximilian, Baron,
112*n*, 128
Bill of rights abolished, 109
Bishops, conference of 1849–50 and its results, 93-98; powers granted to, by imperial decrees: demands fulfilled by concordat of 1855 with Holy See, 96
Bismarck-Schönhausen, Otto von, 36, 74,
88, 125, 157, 165, 171; quoted, 55*n*,
165*n*, 204
Bohemia, 172; "Schwarzenberg Kingdom,"
3, 87; other estates, 4; factions among
nobles, 31*n*
Bonitz, Hermann, 98
Bourgeoisie, civil servants, 58, 60, 83, 102;
improvements in position of, 90; crusade
against constitution and, 100
Brandenburg, Friedrich Wilhelm, Count,
119, 125, 129, 130, 148, 150; parents:
death, 151
Brandenberg, Georg Wilhelm, Elector of, 3
Bregenz, Treaty of, 78
Bregenz League, 154
"Brescia, The Hyena of," 55
Bretzenheim, Ferdinand, Prince, 6
Broglie, Achille, Duc de, 182, 197
Bronzell, episode of "The White Horse of,"
152; evacuation, 153
Bruck, Karl Ludwig, 39, 41, 60, 90, 123,
179, 213; background: qualifications, 29,
68 f., 76; ministries: of commerce, 29,
69; of finance, 30; commercial policies
and reforms, 69-81; collaborators, 81;
resignation: successor, 103; aim of his
economic imperialism, 174
Brühl, Count, 113, 116, 117, 119
Brunetti, Count, 15
Budgetary deficit, 66
Bülow, Hans, Count, 116, 119, 145
Buol-Schauenstein, Johann Rudolf, Count,
65, 69, 165, 166, 203, 204, 205, 211
Bureaucracy, civil servants in Bach's administration, 58 ff., 83, 102; became one

of motive powers of state, 84; gainers by
reforms of 1848, 90; conflict between
aristocrats and bourgeois liberals, 102;
type who opposed Schwarzenberg's policies, 213

Cabinet, the Schwarzenberg, personnel and
portfolios, 28-30; constitutional monarchy pledged, 31; confidence in, expressed, 32; resignation of liberal ministers refused, 39; its dictated constitution
of March 4, 1849, 41, 45-49; reform program, 63-98 (*see under* Reform); war
ministers, 64; position of ministers enhanced, 82; hostility of military and
court protagonists concentrated on bourgeois members, 100; viewpoint of Reichsrat, 102; conflict with its president,
102 ff.; subservience to Reichsrat, 104 ff.;
ministerial responsibility, 105-11
Canitz, General von, 125
Canning, George, quoted, 12*n*
Canning, Sir Stratford, 182
Carl, theater director, 99
Cassel, *see* Hesse-Cassel
Cassel Conference, 78
Cavaignac, General, 192
Central Europe, role in scheme of Russia,
202; her shadow over, 205; maintained
for almost a century: question of postwar
survival, 216
Central European customs union, *see* Cus-
toms union
Central European empire, Bruck's place in
struggle for, 72; Schwarzenberg's plans,
and aim, for, 121, 130, 152, 162, 210,
215; grandeur of conception, 123; why
opposed by France, 164, 167; by England,
164, 167, 175, 185; plan for, came to
naught, 169, 211
Chambers of commerce, 71*n*
Charles X, King of France, 13
Charles, Prince, of Prussia, 113
Charles, Field Marshal, Archduke, 17
Charles Albert, King of Sardinia, 15, 21, 25,
53, 192
Christian of Sondersburg-Glücksburg, 143
Church, *see* Ecclesiastical matters; Roman
Catholic church

Windisch-Graetz, Alfred, Field Marshal
Prince, 26, 36, 40, 45, 97, 101, 191, 216;
wife, 6; characteristics: reputation:
career, 8; relations with Schwarzenberg,
9, 21 f., 52; capacity, will, 21; influence
in cabinet formation, 22, 28, 29; political
philosophy, 33, 37, 39, 40; privilege of
sanctioning constitution, 38; expedition
into Hungary, 50 f.; dismissed by Emperor, 52; spokesman of nobility's grievances, 89; leader of aristocratic-conservative class opposed to policies of
Schwarzenberg, 213
Wirkner, Ludwig von, 59

Wohlgemuth, General, 51, 56
Wolkenstein, Count, 89
Workers, regarded as rebels and held in
restraint, 91
World War I, II, 216
Wratislaw, General Count, 147
Wurmbrand, Count, 89
Würth, Josef von, 92, 121
Württemberg, 121, 127, 131, 134, 146 f.

Zichy, Edmund, Count, 55n
Zichy, Eugene, Count, 56
Zollverein, see Tariff Union
Zuchi, General, 19